6

# Christ Our Life

## God Calls a People

**AUTHORS**

Sisters of Notre Dame of Chardon, Ohio

Sister Mary Joan Agresta, S.N.D.
Sister Mary Theresa Betz, S.N.D.
Sister Mary Kathleen Glavich, S.N.D.
Sister Mary Patricia Lab, S.N.D.
Sister Mary Andrew Miller, S.N.D.

**THEOLOGICAL ADVISOR**

Sister Agnes Cunningham, S.S.C.M.


**CONSULTANTS**

Reverend Edward E. Mehok
Most Revered Robert F. Morneau


**GENERAL EDITOR**

Sister Mary Kathleen Glavich

**LOYOLAPRESS.**

CHICAGO

**Nihil Obstat:** The Reverend Thomas H. Weber, S.T.L., S.S.L., Censor Deputatus
**Imprimatur:** The Most Reverend Anthony M. Pilla, D.D., M.A., Bishop of Cleveland
Given at Cleveland, Ohio, on 5 March 1996.

The *Nihil Obstat* and *Imprimatur* are official declarations that a book or pamphlet is free of doctrinal or moral error. No implication is contained therein that those who have granted the *Nihil Obstat* and *Imprimatur* agree with the contents, opinions, or statements expressed.

*Christ Our Life* found to be in conformity

The Ad Hoc Committee to Oversee the Use of the Catechism, National Conference of Catholic Bishops, has found this catechetical series, copyright 1997 and 2002, to be in conformity with the *Catechism of the Catholic Church.*

*Dedicated to St. Julie Billiart, foundress of the Sisters of Notre Dame, in gratitude for her inspiration and example*

## Acknowledgments

This present revision of the Christ Our Life series is the work of countless people. In particular, we acknowledge and thank the following:

- The Sisters of Notre Dame who supported the production of the Christ Our Life series, especially Sister Mary Joell Overman, S.N.D., Sister Mary Frances Murray, S.N.D., and Sister Mary Margaret Hess, S.N.D.
- The Sisters of Notre Dame and others who over the past twenty years have shaped, written, and edited editions of the Christ Our Life series, in particular Sister Mary de Angelis Bothwell, S.N.D., the former editor
- Those who worked on different stages involved in producing this edition, especially Sister Mary Julie Boehnlein, S.N.D., Sister Linda Marie Gecewicz, S.N.D., Sister Mary Beth Gray, S.N.D., Sister Joanmarie Harks, S.N.D., Sister Mary Andrew Miller, S.N.D., Sister Mary Catherine Rennecker, S.N.D., and Sister Mary St. Jude Weisensell, S.N.D.
- Those catechists, directors of religious education, priests, parents, students, and others who responded to surveys, returned evaluation forms, wrote letters, or participated in interviews to help improve the series

Scripture selections are taken from the New American Bible, copyright © 1991, 1986, 1970 by the Confraternity of Christian Doctrine, Washington, D.C., and are used by license of copyright owner. All rights reserved.

Excerpts from THE JERUSALEM BIBLE, copyright © 1966 by Darton, Longman & Todd, Ltd. and Doubleday, a division of Random House, Inc. Reprinted by permission.

Excerpts from *Sharing the Light of Faith*, National Catechetical Directory for Catholics of the United States © 1979 by the United States Catholic Conference, Washington, D.C., are used with permission. All rights reserved.

Excerpts from the English translation of *Rite of Penance* © 1974, International Committee on English in the Liturgy, Inc. (ICEL); excerpts from the English translation of *A Book of Prayers* © 1982, ICEL; excerpts from the English translation of *Book of Blessings* © 1988, ICEL. All rights reserved.

English translation of Canticle of Zechariah and Canticle of Mary by the International Consultation on English Texts.

Grail translation of Psalms 28 and 100 taken from *The Psalms: A New Translation* © 1963 by Wm. Collins Sons & Co. Ltd. and published by HarperCollins Ltd. Used by permission of A. P. Watt Ltd., London, on behalf of The Grail, England.

Excerpt from ANNE FRANK: THE DIARY OF A YOUNG GIRL by Anne Frank, copyright 1952 by Otto H. Frank. Used by permission of Doubleday, a division of Random House, Inc.

All attempts possible have been made to contact publisher for cited works in this book.

## Photographs

© **Archivo Iconografico, S.A./CORBIS** (p. 122C); © **Bettman/CORBIS** (pp. 120, 157 bottom); © **Dirck Bouts/The Bridgeman Art Library International, Ltd.** (p. 155); © **Cleo Freelance Photography** (pp. 30, 66 bottom left, 109); © **Corbis Corp.** (pp. vi, 49, 91 top right, 166, 193, 198 middle, 233 bottom); © **Scott Dalton/AP/Wide World Photos** (p. 201); © **Digital Stock Corp.** (pp. 40A, 66 top right, 83); © **Bill Ellzay** (p. 18); © **Ercole de Roberti/The Bridgeman Art Library International, Ltd.** (p. 93); © **Ric Ergenbright/CORBIS** (p. 71); © **ET Archive, London/SuperStock, Inc.** (p. 123); © **EyeWire** (pp. 13, 23 top, 28, 74); © **Myrleen Ferguson/PhotoEdit** (p. 90); © **Galleria Borghese, Rome/Canali Photo Bank, Milan/ SuperStock, Inc.** (p. 132); © **Jeff Greenberg/PhotoEdit** (p. 169); © **George Hall/CORBIS** (p. 29 top right); © **Historical Picture Archive/CORBIS** (p. 111); © **R. Hutchings/PhotoEdit** (p. 122A); © **ikonographics** (p. 29 top left); © **Jewish Museum, New York/SuperStock, Inc.** (p. 161); © **Earl Kogler** (pp. 99, 107); © **Bob Krist/CORBIS** (p. 152 top); © **Library of Congress, Washington, D.C./SuperStock, Inc.** (p. 177); © **Karen Moskowitz/ Tony Stone Images** (p. 188A); © **Museum of the History of Religion, St. Petersburg/ SuperStock, Inc.** (p. 151); © **Newberry Library, Chicago/ SuperStock, Inc.** (p. 205); © **PhotoDisc, Inc.** (pp. 7, 23 middle and bottom, 26 bottom, 27, 31, 41, 66 middle right, 70A, 82, 98, 150A, 152 bottom, 157 top, 172, 194, 196 right, 198 bottom, 209, 233 top); © **Eugene D. Plaisted, O.S.C./Crosiers** (pp. i, 134 top, 178–179, 200, 203); © **Carl Purcell/CORBIS** (p. 81); © **Rijksmuseum Vincent Van Gogh, Amsterdam, Netherlands/SuperStock, Inc.** (p. 168); © **Rev. Raymond Schoder/ SuperStock, Inc.** (p. 140); © **Sistine Chapel, Vatican, Rome/SuperStock, Inc.** (p. 24); © **Skjold Photographs** (pp. 26 top, 29 bottom, 33–34, 51, 54, 66 bottom right, 86, 100, 124, 156, 164); © **Ted Spiegel/CORBIS** (p. 76); © **SuperStock, Inc.** (p. 25); © **W. P. Wittman Limited** (pp. 19, 21, 56, 66 top right, 77, 91 left and bottom right, 104, 106, 115, 134 middle and bottom, 189, 196 left, 198 top, 231); © **David Young-Wolff/PhotoEdit** (p. 190).

Reprints from **Reuven Rubin's** *The Prophets Collection* (pp. 184 middle, 185, 215 top right and bottom left and bottom right) courtesy of **Transworld Art;** *Zund's* *La Strada per Emmaus* (p. 10) courtesy of **John Brandi Co., Inc.;** *Our Lady of Guadalupe* (p. 195) courtesy of **Queen of the Americas Guild;** *Mother of Perpetual Help* (p. 204) courtesy of **Ligouri Publications;** photo of **Sister Thea Bowman** (p. 135) courtesy of **Gerard Pottebaum, Treehaus Communications;** photo of **Trevor Farrell** (p. 160) courtesy of **Trevor's Campaign.**

## Artwork

**Ray App** (pp. 72, 73, 76, 81, 96, 103, 105 top, 112, 162 bottom, 170, 171, 175, 176); **William Gorman** (pp. 8, 9 top and bottom, 16, 20 bottom, 30, 32 top, 36, 44, 46, 47, 52, 59, 60, 65, 214 top left and top right); **Lydia Halverson** (p. 131); **Robert Korta** (pp. 138, 139, 141, 214 bottom left); **Robert Masheris** (pp. 55, 106); **Michael Muir** (pp. 75, 82, 84, 89, 90, 97, 108, 113, 121, 126 middle and bottom, 127, 128, 132, 136, 142 bottom, 143, 145 bottom, 153, 163, 207 right top, 208, 214 bottom right, 215 top left); **Kevin Peschke** (p. 70C); **Proof Positive/Farrowlyne Assoc., Inc.** (pp. 45, 53, 55, 61, 62, 67 color type, 69, 75 color type, 93, 106, 125, 126 top, 137, 142, 148, 164 color type, 165, 176 color type, 184, 199 bottom, 227, 228, 229, 230, 231 top, 232, 233, 234, 235, 236, 237, 239, 240); **Robert Voigts** (pp. 9 middle, 11, 12, 13, 15, 17, 18, 20 top, 22, 24, 25, 32 bottom, 35, 36 color type, 37, 38, 40, 42–43, 45 top, 48, 50, 53, 58, 63, 64, 69, 78, 80, 85, 87, 88 right, 92, 95, 102, 105 bottom, 110, 114, 117, 118–119, 122D, 130, 133, 137, 145 top, 146, 147, 148 bottom, 149, 154, 159, 162 top, 167, 173, 180, 181, 182, 184 bottom, 186, 191, 192, 195 top, 199 top, 202, 204 left, 206, 207 left and right bottom, 214–215 scroll and color type, 225, 226, 231 bottom); **Justin Wager** (pp. 210–211, 212–213).

Cover design by Donald Kye.
Cover art © Eugene D. Plaisted, O.S.C./Crosiers.
03 04 05 06 DBH 6 5 4

**LOYOLA PRESS.**

3441 N. ASHLAND AVENUE
CHICAGO, ILLINOIS 60657
(800) 621-1008

# CONTENTS

## 6

# Things Every Catholic Should Know

## The Ten Commandments

1. I, the Lord, am your God. You shall not have other gods besides me.
2. You shall not take the name of the Lord, your God, in vain.
3. Remember to keep holy the Sabbath day.
4. Honor your father and your mother.
5. You shall not kill.
6. You shall not commit adultery.
7. You shall not steal.
8. You shall not bear false witness against your neighbor.
9. You shall not covet your neighbor's wife.
10. You shall not covet anything that belongs to your neighbor.

## Duties of a Catholic Christian
(Precepts of the Church)

1. To keep holy the day of the Lord's resurrection (Sunday). To worship God by participating in Mass for every Sunday and holy day of obligation. To avoid those activities (such as needless work) that would hinder worship, joy, or relaxation.
2. To lead a sacramental life. To receive Holy Communion frequently and the Sacrament of Reconciliation regularly.
3. To study Catholic teachings in preparation for the Sacrament of Confirmation, to be confirmed, and then to continue to study and advance the cause of Christ.
4. To observe the marriage laws of the Church. To give religious training, by word and example, to one's children. To use parish schools and catechetical programs.
5. To strengthen and support the Church— one's own parish community and parish priests, the worldwide Church, and the pope.
6. To do penance, including abstaining from meat and fasting from food on the appointed days.
7. To join in the missionary spirit and apostolate of the Church.

## Holy Days of Obligation in the United States

*Solemnity of Mary, Mother of God: January 1*
We honor Mary, Mother of God.

*Ascension: Fortieth Day after Easter*
Jesus ascended into heaven.

*Assumption: August 15*
Mary was taken into heaven, body and soul.

*All Saints' Day: November 1*
We honor all the saints in heaven.

*Immaculate Conception: December 8*
Mary was free from sin from the first moment of her life.

*Christmas: December 25*
We celebrate the birth of Jesus.

## The Seven Sacraments
Baptism, Confirmation, Eucharist, Reconciliation (Penance), Anointing of the Sick, Matrimony, Holy Orders

## Corporal Works of Mercy
Feed the hungry.
Give drink to the thirsty.
Clothe the naked.
Visit the sick.
Shelter the homeless.
Visit the imprisoned.
Bury the dead.

## Spiritual Works of Mercy
Warn the sinner.
Instruct the ignorant.
Counsel the doubtful.
Comfort the sorrowing.
Bear wrongs patiently.
Forgive all injuries.
Pray for the living and the dead.

## The Theological Virtues
Faith, Hope, Love (Charity)

## The Cardinal Virtues

Prudence, Temperance, Justice, Fortitude

## The Beatitudes (Matthew 5:3–10)

Blessed are the poor in spirit,
    for theirs is the kingdom of heaven.
Blessed are they who mourn,
    for they will be comforted.
Blessed are the meek,
    for they will inherit the land.
Blessed are they who hunger and thirst for
    righteousness, for they shall be satisfied.
Blessed are the merciful,
    for they will be shown mercy.
Blessed are the clean of heart,
    for they will see God.
Blessed are the peacemakers,
    for they will be called children of God.
Blessed are they who are persecuted for the
    sake of righteousness, for theirs is the
    kingdom of heaven.

## The Way of the Cross

I. Jesus is condemned to death on the cross.
II. Jesus accepts his cross.
III. Jesus falls the first time.
IV. Jesus meets his sorrowful mother.
V. Simon of Cyrene helps Jesus carry his cross.
VI. Veronica wipes the face of Jesus.
VII. Jesus falls the second time.
VIII. Jesus meets and speaks to the women of Jerusalem.
IX. Jesus falls the third time.
X. Jesus is stripped of his garments.
XI. Jesus is nailed to the cross.
XII. Jesus dies on the cross.
XIII. Jesus is taken down from the cross and laid in his mother's arms.
XIV. Jesus is placed in the tomb.
V. Jesus rises from the dead.

## The Mysteries of the Rosary

*Joyful Mysteries*

The Annunciation
The Visitation
The Nativity
The Presentation in the Temple
The Finding of Jesus in the Temple

*Sorrowful Mysteries*

The Agony in the Garden
The Scourging at the Pillar
The Crowning with Thorns
The Carrying of the Cross
The Crucifixion and Death of Jesus

*Glorious Mysteries*

The Resurrection
The Ascension
The Descent of the Holy Spirit
The Assumption of Mary
The Crowning of Mary as Queen of Heaven and Earth

## The Divine Praises

Blessed be God.
Blessed be his holy name.
Blessed be Jesus Christ, true God
    and true man.
Blessed be the name of Jesus.
Blessed be his most Sacred Heart.
Blessed be his most Precious Blood.
Blessed be Jesus in the most Holy
    Sacrament of the Altar.
Blessed be the Holy Spirit, the Paraclete.
Blessed be the great Mother of God,
    Mary most holy.
Blessed be her holy and Immaculate
    Conception.
Blessed be her glorious Assumption.
Blessed be the name of Mary,
    Virgin and Mother.
Blessed be St. Joseph, her most chaste
    spouse.
Blessed be God in his angels and in his
    saints.

## Goals of This Year's Program

This year your child will study the Old Testament and its meaning for us. God revealed himself to the people he bound to himself in covenant love: the Israelites. God calls each person into a similar relationship. The study of the Old Testament leads your child to see in Jesus the fulfillment of all the Father has promised as well as the perfect response to his love. He or she is encouraged to respond to God's call to enter into a love relationship with God and with the Church. This response manifests itself in love and care for all people.

As your child becomes familiar with salvation history, he or she is encouraged to read the Bible and to use it for prayer.

## A Family Program

Mindful that your faith makes a profound impact on your child, the Christ Our Life series provides family features for each unit. These give you an opportunity to share the faith experience as a family and help you and your child understand the message of each unit.

### Parent Pages

At the beginning of each unit you may receive a parent page. It informs you about the scriptural concepts your child is studying, allows you to ponder the Word of God in your own life, and offers suggestions for family prayer and activities related to the topic of the unit.

### Family Celebrations

At the end of each unit you may receive a family celebration, which combines knowledge, good works, and prayer. It may be carried out as part of a family night or before dessert at a family meal. The celebration gives your child a chance to take a leadership role and to share what he or she has learned.

### Other Means for Family Involvement

In the student book at the end of each chapter is a section called Things to Do at Home. At the end of each unit there is a Family Feature section that includes stories and activities for your family members to read and do together to enrich your faith-life.

You can also help your child memorize Things Every Catholic Should Know found in the front of this book. Your child should also master the contents under the We Remember section at the end of each chapter.

# God Reveals a Plan of Love

## Invited by God

How do you feel when you are invited to a party or to a friend's house? Every time you receive an invitation, you are chosen to take part in something. You must decide how you will respond. If you say yes, you can enjoy all that has been planned. You can deepen your friendship with the person who invited you and with all the other guests.

Name two places you would like to be invited.

*A party and a friend's place.*

This year God invites you to go on a journey with his chosen people through a study of the **Old Testament,** sometimes called the Hebrew Scriptures. As you journey, you will see how much God loves his people. You will learn how God's people responded to that love. You will see that their journey is much like your own journey to God's kingdom.

Who is this God who invites you? God is the all-powerful, all-knowing, all-loving one who is perfect in every way. God always was and always will be. God is so great and so far beyond our understanding that we can never completely grasp who God is. Fortunately, God helps us know him. God reveals himself to us.

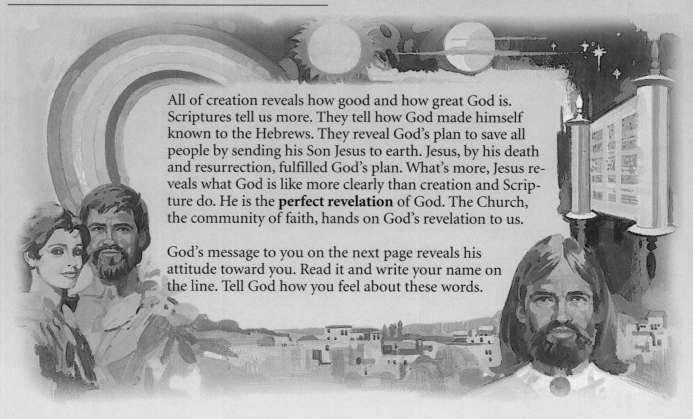

All of creation reveals how good and how great God is. Scriptures tell us more. They tell how God made himself known to the Hebrews. They reveal God's plan to save all people by sending his Son Jesus to earth. Jesus, by his death and resurrection, fulfilled God's plan. What's more, Jesus reveals what God is like more clearly than creation and Scripture do. He is the **perfect revelation** of God. The Church, the community of faith, hands on God's revelation to us.

God's message to you on the next page reveals his attitude toward you. Read it and write your name on the line. Tell God how you feel about these words.

Fear not, _Sidesh Sachithananthan_,
for I have redeemed you;
I have called you
by name:
you are mine.

Isaiah 43:1

## Why Study the Old Testament?

Here are seven good reasons to study the Old Testament. Check the three that are most convincing to you.

- ❏ The history of the Jewish people is our history too.
- ❏ Jesus read, studied, and prayed the Hebrew Scriptures.
- ☑ The Old Testament is God's Word.
- ❏ Educated people are expected to know Bible stories.
- ☑ The Old Testament helps us to understand Jesus.
- ☑ God speaks to us personally in the Bible.
- ❏ Reading the Old Testament helps us to understand our Jewish brothers and sisters.

A story in Luke's gospel tells how Jesus used Scripture to teach about himself. On Easter Sunday, Cleopas and a companion, disciples of Jesus, were on their way from Jerusalem to Emmaus. As they walked, they talked about Jesus' death and the rumors of his resurrection. The risen Jesus joined them on the road, but they did not recognize him. When Jesus asked what they were discussing, the disciples told him how disappointed and confused they were. They had hoped that Jesus was their Messiah, the Savior. Jesus listened to their story. Then he explained how the Hebrew Scriptures foretold the events in Jerusalem. He pointed out how passages about the Messiah referred to Jesus. The disciples were filled with joy as their fellow traveler spoke.

By evening they were near Emmaus. The two disciples invited Jesus to stay with them. While they were eating supper, Jesus took bread and said the blessing. Then he broke the bread and gave it to them. With that, Cleopas and his friend recognized Jesus. Then Jesus disappeared. The disciples said to each other, "Weren't our hearts burning within us as he spoke to us and opened the Scriptures to us?" Excitedly they returned to Jerusalem. There they spread the news that Jesus was risen. They told others what he had taught them.

Jesus helps us, too, to know him and understand his teachings through Scripture. The persons and events in the Bible reveal to us the greatness of God's love.

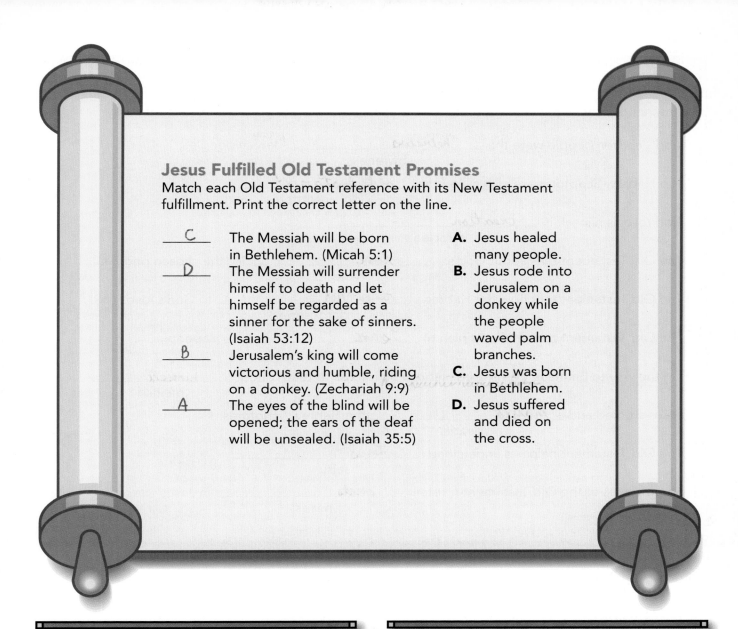

### Jesus Fulfilled Old Testament Promises

Match each Old Testament reference with its New Testament fulfillment. Print the correct letter on the line.

___C___ The Messiah will be born in Bethlehem. (Micah 5:1)

___D___ The Messiah will surrender himself to death and let himself be regarded as a sinner for the sake of sinners. (Isaiah 53:12)

___B___ Jerusalem's king will come victorious and humble, riding on a donkey. (Zechariah 9:9)

___A___ The eyes of the blind will be opened; the ears of the deaf will be unsealed. (Isaiah 35:5)

**A.** Jesus healed many people.

**B.** Jesus rode into Jerusalem on a donkey while the people waved palm branches.

**C.** Jesus was born in Bethlehem.

**D.** Jesus suffered and died on the cross.

## Things to Do at Home

1. Ask five people why they think it's important to read the Bible. Report their answers to your class.
2. Read Psalm 91 and write a prayer telling God how you feel about his promises to protect you.
3. Find Jeremiah 7:23. What does God tell us we must do to enjoy life with him?
4. Every night for a week, read a short passage from the Bible before you go to bed.
5. What do this Sunday's readings tell you about God? Discuss this with a family member or friend.

## We Remember

**How does God reveal himself to us?**
God reveals himself to us through creation, through Scripture, and through Jesus.

### Words to Know
Hebrew Scriptures

## We Respond

The promises of the LORD I will sing forever, proclaim your loyalty through all ages.
Psalm 89:2

## We Review

Unscramble the words in these sentences as you count down to your Old Testament study.

God's chosen people were the ___hebrews___, Jewish people.
sbwrehe

The Hebrew Scriptures are also called the ___old testament___.
dol ansetttem

God reveals himself in ___creation___.
ntrociea

The Old Testament tells about God's ___love___ for the chosen people.
vole

The Old Testament tells how the Hebrews ___responded___ to God's love.
dnrdosepe

The Old Testament reveals God's plan to ___save___ all people.
vsea

On the way to Emmaus, Jesus used Hebrew Scriptures to teach about ___himself___.
meihslf

Jesus studied and ___prayed___ the Hebrew Scriptures.
ypeadr

The Old Testament helps us understand ___Jesus___.
sejsu

Some verses of the Old Testament foretell ___events___ in Jesus' life.
nevest

**A Book Drenched in Love**   Complete this ad for the Bible.

# ★ ★ Take and Read ★ ★

Journey with the chosen people by studying the ___Bible___.

Come to know about God's great ___love___.

Find out about God's plan to ___salvage___ you.

Learn more about your journey to God's _____.

Discover how to meet God and speak with God through his Word in the

___scripture or Old Testament___.

___Jesus___, the Son of God, will help you.

12

# Scripture Is God's Saving Word

**2**

## What a Revelation!

Ms. Jones sat down to read the first writing assignment she had received from her students. She had asked them to write three sentences telling about one of their parents. Here are several of the papers.

Sarah wrote this about her dad:

> My dad died last year, but I remember how he took care of me when I was hurt in a car accident. He lay down on the road beside me so that I wouldn't be afraid. Mom and I miss Dad.

Tom told about his mother:

> My mom is great! Even though she works every day, she still has time to come to soccer games with Jim and me. She makes us feel good even if we lose.

Louis wrote about his dad:

> My dad is a very important lawyer. He graduated from Harvard Law School. He likes to play golf.

Karen told about her mother:

> My mom has an important job as a bank president. She wears expensive clothes and likes to go shopping for new ones. She is tall, blond, and pretty.

I share this about someone:

_____

Ms. Jones found there were two kinds of papers. Some students told facts about their parents. Put a (✓) beside those paragraphs. Some children told about the love of their parents. Put an X beside those paragraphs.

We can describe God in these two ways, too. We can list the facts we know about him or we can tell about the love between God and us. Tell one fact about God.

_____

Write one sentence about the love between God and you.

_____

Hebrew people often spoke of God's love for them and their response to God. That was the way God revealed himself to them.

_____

## Bible Facts Self-Taught

The following frames contain information about the Bible. Teach yourself using the frames and a sheet of paper. Cover the page with the paper and reveal one frame at a time to read and study. Most frames end with a question. Answer the question silently without looking back. When you move the paper down to reveal the next frame, you will see the answer to the previous question on the right. When you finish this activity, you will be a Bible expert!

We call all that God has taught about himself and his will for his people **revelation.** Revelation is contained in Tradition and Scripture, which form a single deposit of God's word.

**Tradition** is a group of beliefs that have been passed down by word of mouth and made a part of the Church's teaching. Tradition is found in the prayers and practices of God's people.

*What do we call all God has taught about himself and his will for his people?*

**revelation**

God showed his love and power by working wonderful deeds for his people. They told stories of his loving kindness over and over.

*What are the beliefs passed down by word of mouth and made a part of the Church's teaching?*

**Tradition**

Sometimes different people told the stories and the details were changed. But God himself guarded the stories so that they revealed the message he wanted his people to have. He **inspired** those who told these stories. This means God guided their thoughts and their desires to tell others of his love and care.

*Where is revelation found besides Tradition?*

**Scripture**

After these stories had been repeated for hundreds of years, they were written down. God inspired the writers to write what he wanted his people to know. But he left the writers free to express the message in their own way. God also inspired the editors who gathered the writings together. Through inspiration God is the **primary author** of the Bible.

The collection of writings through which God revealed himself to the Hebrew people was completed about one hundred years before Jesus was born. Jewish and Christian people consider these **Hebrew Scriptures** sacred.

*Why are the Hebrew Scriptures the Word of God?*

**God is the primary author.**

Christians believe that God revealed more about himself through his Son Jesus. After Jesus' death and resurrection, God inspired certain people to write about Jesus. Their writings are called the New Testament, or **Christian Scriptures.** In it the Gospels are central. The last of the Christian Scriptures was written about A.D. 100.

*What does* inspired *mean?*

**guided by God**

Together the Old Testament and New Testament make up the Bible, or Sacred Scripture. It took almost a thousand years to write and collect the entire Bible.

*What are other names for the Old and New Testaments?*

**Hebrew Scriptures (Old), Christian Scriptures (New)**

God speaks to us in the Scriptures, and the Holy Spirit helps us to understand God's Word. The Church, too, teaches us the meaning of the Bible.

*Who is the primary author of the Bible?*

**God**

How else does God speak to us?

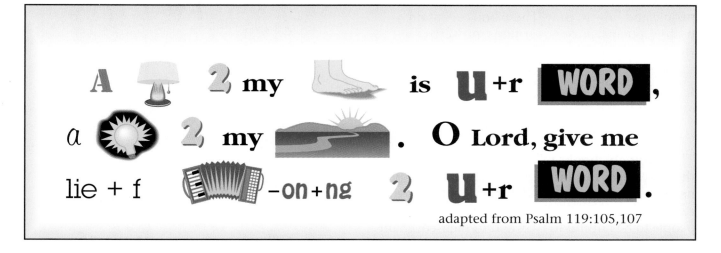

adapted from Psalm 119:105,107

## A Sacred Library

The word *Bible* comes from the Greek word for book, *biblios.* But the Bible is really a collection of books, a minilibrary. The writers of the Bible wrote God's message in different kinds of books. They wrote in a way that people of their time would understand.

The **Law** is the first five books of the Bible. It is usually called the **Pentateuch,** which means "five scrolls." These were not the first books written, but they tell stories about the beginnings of God's people. They tell the story of the creation and the covenant. They also tell how God cared for his people on their journey to the Promised Land and called them to live by his Law. These books are also called the **Torah.**

The **historical books** tell how God cared for his people during their history. These books show God is the Lord of history. They are not always complete or scientifically and historically accurate. Their purpose is to remind the Hebrew people that God was with them during all the events of their lives.

The **wisdom books** tell people how to live wisely. They showed the Israelites how to act as God's people and how to pray. These books contain psalms, poems, prayers, sermons, proverbs, riddles, and parables.

The **prophetic books** tell about the prophets and their messages to God's people. When the people had turned away from God, the prophets reminded them of God's love. They called the people to be faithful to God and to their covenant with him. The prophets also told the people to be just to one another.

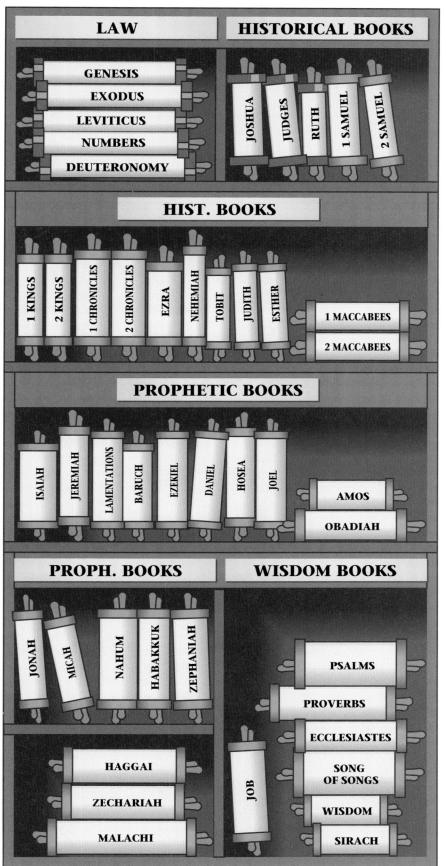

**Taking Inventory**

Count the books in each section of the Old Testament. List your answers below.

| | |
|---|---|
| The Law | 5 |
| The Historical Books | 16 |
| The Wisdom Books | 18 |
| The Prophetic Books | 7 |
| Total Books in the Old Testament | 46 |
| Total Books in the New Testament | 27 |
| Total books in the Bible | 73 |

To what category do each of the following books belong? Use *L* for Law, *H* for historical books, *W* for wisdom books, *P* for prophetic books.

L  **1.** Genesis

H  **2.** Judith

W  **3.** Psalms

P  **4.** Jonah

W  **5.** Wisdom

H  **6.** Ruth

L  **7.** Exodus

P  **8.** Isaiah

W  **9.** Job

P  **10.** Ezekiel

## Locating Scripture Passages

Each book of the Bible is divided into chapters. Each chapter is divided into verses. Biblical references list first the book, then the chapter, and finally the verse or verses.

Find the Emmaus story in Luke 24:13–35. Be sure to look for verses after the chapter number on the page and not before it.

### A Lucky Throw

In 1947 a shepherd boy in Judea looking for his lost goat tossed a stone into a cave. It turned out that the cave held a treasure: an ancient library. Excavators found ten more caves. The caves held about six hundred manuscripts called the Dead Sea Scrolls. These scrolls had been wrapped in linen and preserved in jars. They included almost every book of the Hebrew Scriptures. Experts are still trying to piece together the thousands of manuscript fragments. Until the boy's discovery, the oldest copies of Scripture dated from A.D. 9. Some of the Dead Sea Scrolls were from about 100 B.C.

The Hebrew language is written from right to left. The word *shalom*, which means peace, looks like this:

om      l      sha

**Praying the Bible**

God speaks to us at every Mass as his Word is proclaimed. He speaks to us whenever we read the Bible. It is a good practice to read the Bible every day. Begin with a prayer asking the Holy Spirit to help you understand the message. As you read, think about what God is saying to you. What do you say in return?

## Things to Do at Home

1. The original Sacred Scriptures were written in Hebrew or Greek. There are many English translations of the Bible done by different groups. Each group gives its version a name. Two translations used in the Catholic Church are the Jerusalem Bible and the New American Bible. See which Bible you have at home. If you do not have a family Bible, talk to your family about getting one. Your teacher or parish priest can help you.

2. Look in your Bible for a table of contents, an index, a list of abbreviations, and a Bible dictionary. Does it have a list of the Bible readings used at Mass each Sunday and a prayer to the Holy Spirit? How many maps are in your Bible? What is the copyright date of your Bible? Family Bibles are often very old because they are passed on from generation to generation.

3. Plan to keep the Bible where you can read from it and honor it as the Word of God.

4. Find an inspiring verse or two in the Bible. Print it backwards, and give it to a classmate to interpret. He or she might have to use a mirror.

## We Remember

**What is revelation?**

Revelation is all that God has taught us about himself and his will for his people.

**What is inspiration?**

Inspiration is God's action in guiding the human authors of the Bible. God guided their thoughts and desires to pass on truths that he wanted to teach, but left the authors free to express the truths in their own ways.

### Words to Know

| | |
|---|---|
| revelation | Tradition |
| inspiration | Law |
| historical books | Pentateuch |
| prophetic books | Torah |
| wisdom books | Dead Sea Scrolls |

### Words to Memorize
books in the Pentateuch

## We Respond

Read Psalm 136:1–7. Write two things God has done for you. After each one write, "God's mercy endures forever."

_____

_____

_____

_____

_____

_____

_____

**Translate This!** Decode the following message that tells us how God's revelation became our Sacred Scripture.

S H A R I N G    T H E
12 5 1 11 6 8 4    13 5 3

R E V E L A T I O N:
11 3 14 3 7 1 13 6 9 8

G O D    I N S P I R E D
4 9 2    6 8 12 10 6 11 3 2

P E O P L E    T O    T E L L
10 3 9 10 7 3    13 9    13 3 7 7

I T,    W R I T E    I T,
6 13    15 11 6 13 3    6 13

G A T H E R    I T.
4 1 13 5 3 11    6 13

| A | D | E | G | H | I | L | N | O | P | R | S | T | V | W | Y |
|---|---|---|---|---|---|---|---|---|---|---|---|---|---|---|---|
| 1 | 2 | 3 | 4 | 5 | 6 | 7 | 8 | 9 | 10 | 11 | 12 | 13 | 14 | 15 | 16 |

**Words about the Word**   Match each term with its definition.

A. revelation

B. Pentateuch

C. Dead Sea Scrolls

D. inspiration

E. 100 B.C.

F. A.D. 100

G. Tradition

H. Holy Spirit

I. primary author

J. Christian Scriptures

K. Bible

L. editor

M. Hebrew Scriptures

___D___ **1.** God guiding the thoughts of biblical authors and editors

___M___ **2.** Sacred writings from the time before Jesus that tell about God

___B___ **3.** First five books of the Bible, Torah

___A___ **4.** All that God has taught about himself and his love for his people

___F___ **5.** When the Bible was completed

___G___ **6.** Beliefs passed down by word of mouth and made a part of the Church's teaching

___C___ **7.** Early Scripture manuscripts found in 1947

___K___ **8.** Word that means "book"

___H___ **9.** Person who helps us understand the Bible

___I___ **10.** Title given to God because he inspired the Bible

**Categories**   Name the type of biblical books described.

**1.** Books that call the people to be faithful to God and to be just.

_Prophetic Books_

**2.** The first five books of the Bible that tell about the beginnings of God's people.

_Books of Law_

**3.** Books that tell how to live wisely.

_Wisdom Books_

**4.** Books that tell how God cared for his people in the events of history.

_Historical Books_

# Everything God Created Is Good

## A Sign of God's Power and Love

**C** reator of heaven and earth,

**R** evealing yourself in your work,

**E** ver continuing the glorious

**A** ct of creation!

**T** hank you for created beauty, for my

**I** mmortal soul, my wonderful body, for

**O** ther gifts of your love!

**N** ever will I forget your goodness.

What is the most beautiful sight you have ever seen? Describe it here.

_____

The world is full of marvelous things. You yourself are a fantastic being. How did the world and all its wonders begin? From the earliest times, people told stories of how the earth was formed and how people came to live on the earth. In these stories there were many gods, both good and evil. The universe was always created from something that already existed. For example, in one story the god Marduk killed a sea monster who was also a goddess. He then made the heavens and earth out of her body.

The Israelites did not believe the story. They knew from experience that the one true God was loving and caring. They were inspired by God to write their own creation stories. These are found in the book of **Genesis.** Through creation our minds can see that God exists.

Creation is a sign of God's wisdom and power. It is most of all a sign of God's love. Think of all the love in the world, all the people who love us, and all the love we have for others. All of this love combined is not even a drop compared to the ocean of God's love. Through God's creation we learn that God loves us and wants to be loved in return. Although we speak of the Father as Creator, the Son and the Spirit are united with him as one creating God.

The biblical story of creation is based on theories of the world at the time Genesis was composed. For instance, the Hebrews thought that the earth was flat and held up by columns. The sky was like a dome over the earth. There was water below and around the earth, and water above the dome. When gates in the dome were opened, it rained or snowed.

The story of creation sounds like a poem. The rhythm of its words makes it enjoyable to hear, even in an English translation. Here is part of the story to read aloud.

**Solo 1:** In the beginning,

**All:** when God created the heavens and the earth,

**Solo 1:** the earth was a formless wasteland,

**Solo 2:** and darkness covered the abyss,

**All:** while a mighty wind swept over the waters.

**Solo 1:** Then God said,

**All:** "Let there be light,"

**Solo 1:** and there was light.
God saw how good the light was.
God then separated the light from the darkness.

**Solo 2:** God called the light "day,"
and the darkness he called "night."

**All:** Thus evening came, and morning followed—the first day.

**Solo 2:** Then God said, "Let there be a dome in the middle of the waters, to separate one body of water from the other."

**All:** And so it happened:

**Solo 1:** God made the dome, and it separated the water above the dome from the water below it.

**Solo 2:** God called the dome "the sky."

**All:** Evening came, and morning followed—the second day.

Genesis 1:1–8

There are two stories in the Bible about the creation of the first man and woman. Read Genesis 1:26–30 and then Genesis 2:7, 18–23. How do these stories show that people are important creations of God?

Did God create the universe as we know it in just six days or over millions of years? Did God make the first people from earth or through a series of changes in different life-forms (evolution)? No one really knows. The creation stories are not scientific reports. Rather, they are stories meant to teach religious truths. Some of these truths are given here.

- There is only one God.
- God created all things, so these things are not gods.
- God is good, wise, powerful, orderly, and loving.
- Everything and everyone depends upon God.
- God created human beings in his image.
- Men and women have equal dignity.
- God made people masters and stewards of creation.
- Things of creation were made to help all people and to bring them joy.

## The Ladder of Creation

Under each heading write a kind of creature that belongs to that category. The first one is done for you.

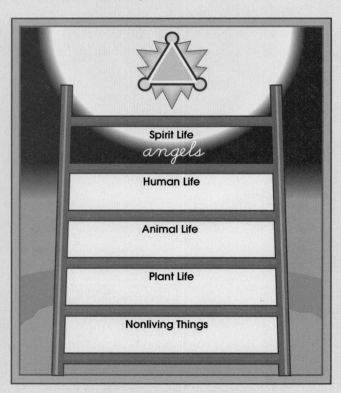

Spirit Life
*angels*

Human Life

Animal Life

Plant Life

Nonliving Things

The ladder of creation lists the things God created from the lowest to the highest. The higher on the ladder the creatures are, the more powers they have to know and love. The angels are types of spirit life. They are **pure spirits,** which means that they, like God, have no bodies. The triangle at the top of the ladder is a symbol of God, the Trinity. God is the **uncreated Spirit** who always was and always will be.

God created all things in heaven and on earth out of nothing. He also continues to bring forth new beings and to keep all things in existence. Without God, everything would turn back to nothingness! But as long as God keeps things in existence, whatever he created might change forms but will not go back into nothingness.

In the story of creation this line was repeated five times: "God saw how good it was." Everything God made is good. However, his gifts can be used for good or evil. Medical technology, for instance, can be used to benefit or harm humankind.

Name another of God's gifts.

_____

How can it be used for good?

_____

How can it be used for evil?

_____

### God's First Gift

Our first gift from God was our human life. God made each one of us special and unique, loving and lovable. God gave us wonderful gifts of body and soul.

Like plants and animals, we grow, eat food, and reproduce. Like animals, we feel, sense, and move from place to place. But unlike any other creatures on earth, we have a **soul** that enables us to think, judge, choose, love, and live forever! It is through the special gifts of **intellect** and **free will** that we are like God, made to God's image and likeness. God shares with us his knowledge, freedom, and power. God gives us freedom and the right to exercise it. Best of all, by love, God gives himself to us and dwells within us.

The gift of human life is more precious than we can imagine. The variety and differences in persons make life more beautiful and enjoyable. No wonder the psalmist could pray,

I thank you for the wonder of my being, wonderful are all your works!
adapted from Psalm 139:14

What does the quotation on the plaque say about

you? _____

How can we show God we are grateful to him for creating us and that we respect the gift of life in ourselves and others?

_____

_____

"GOD DOES NOT MAKE JUNK!"

## Doing God's Work

God wants to share another gift with us—his creative work. That is why God calls us to be **stewards** of the earth. We must first care for human life and protect it. We must also care for and protect the gifts of the earth, such as water, air, minerals, trees, and land. Caring for creation means replacing what we've taken from the earth, repairing any damages, and disposing of wastes properly. If we care for creation, we also avoid using products that harm the earth.

God wants us to find new, creative ways of using his gifts through art, science, and labor. The earth belongs to everyone. God wants us to share the gifts and their products with others in the world. In this way we also promote peace and justice among all peoples and nations.

Name an occupation: _____

How do people in this line of work act as stewards

of the world? _____

_____

All work has dignity because it is participation in God's work of creation.

## How Can You Help?

Environmental organizations help to keep our earth-home beautiful and safe. Members work to protect our environment. You can do your part in the following ways. Color the box green before the sentences that describe you.

I care . . .

❑ I do not litter.
❑ I pick up papers from lawns, rooms, and halls.
❑ I keep my room clean.
❑ I take care of my things.
❑ I do not waste water.
❑ I do not waste food.
❑ I help clean our house.
❑ I take care of my clothes.
❑ I donate time, money, or possessions to help the poor.
❑ I do not vandalize buildings or objects.
❑ I recycle cans, glass, and plastic bottles.
❑ I do not waste paper.
❑ I am kind to animals.

## Things to Do at Home

1. With your family, read about creation in Psalm 104. Add anything you think was skipped.
2. Make a creation poster based on a poem like the one on page 22.
3. Take a walk and name all the things you see that God created. List ways you can use these items properly or help to protect and save them.
4. Exchange ideas with family members on what you can do to be good caretakers of the earth. Recycle or conserve one item this evening or clean an area at home that needs attention.
5. Visit a zoo, an aquarium, or a planetarium in order to marvel at the wonderful things God has made. Write a prayer about one thing that impressed you.

## We Remember

**What did God create?**
God created us and gave us gifts of body and soul. God created the earth and all its gifts to help us and give us joy.

### Words to Know

| | |
|---|---|
| Genesis | free will |
| pure spirits | evolution |
| uncreated Spirit | stewards |
| intellect | |

## We Respond

Complete this prayer of adoration by filling in the names of creatures that reflect God's qualities.

I praise and thank you, God, for

your wisdom that I see in

_____,

your power that I see in

_____,

your gentleness that I see in

_____,

and your love that I see in

_____.

## We Review

**Beginnings**   Identify what is described.

**1.** The first book of the Bible: _Genesis_

**2.** What God created everything out of: _nothing_

**3.** What God created on the first day: _earth and the heavens ; on the same day, light_

**4.** Creatures that are above us on the ladder of creation: _pure spirits or spirit life_

**5.** What we have in addition to a body: _soul_

**6.** The stewards of the earth: _us, humankind_

**7.** Two gifts that make us like God: _intellect and free will_

**The Master at Work**   Check (✓) the sentences that are true descriptions of God's work of creation.

✓   **1.** Everything God created is good.

✓   **2.** God keeps everything in existence.

_____   **3.** God created evil things.

✓   **4.** God created some creatures that were like himself.

✓   **5.** God created to show his love.

✓   **6.** God created the world for all people to share.

_____   **7.** The description of creation in the Bible is scientifically correct.

✓   **8.** God expects us to care for his creation.

**Levels of Being**   Number these creatures from the lowest (1) to the highest (5):

_3_   animals

_2_   plants

_1_   nonliving things

_5_   angels

_4_   human beings

"It's really a wonder that I haven't dropped all my ideals because they seem so absurd and impossible to carry out. Yet, I keep them, because in spite of everything I still believe that people are really good at heart."

*Anne Frank: The Diary of a Young Girl*

## The Problem of Evil

Today we see suffering and destruction, war and conflict, poverty and pain all around us. Evil seems to be everywhere. Yet there is still reason to hope, still reason to believe in the deep goodness of life.

Where did evil come from? How did sin enter our world? And with so much suffering around us, how are we still able to hope and trust?

People of all ages and places have tried to answer these questions. The book of Genesis, under God's inspiration, addresses some of these mysteries. The writers of Genesis used stories to tell us about sin and God's faithful love and mercy. One story they told was about the first man and woman.

## The Fall

God created all things good. The Adam and Eve story explains how sin came into the world. God created Adam and Eve to live close to him. He created them in his own image, gifting them with intellect and free will. They could freely find happiness in life and remain united with him.

God knew what could make people happy and at peace with themselves, others, and the world. He asked Adam and Eve to obey. By trusting God's plan for them, they would know true happiness.

But by their own free choice, Adam and Eve disobeyed God. They were proud and refused to depend on God and his plan for them. They broke faith with God. They brought sin into the world and lost God's life in them: the gift of **sanctifying grace.** They became divided from God and from each other. Love unites, but sin divides.

This first sin, the original sin, changed everything. Because of it, human beings are born without grace and with a tendency to sin. This condition is called **original sin.** It is through baptism that grace is restored, and we again become children of God. After the sin of the first man and woman, sin spread throughout the world, repeating its story of pain and separation.

## The Story of Adam and Eve

Adam and Eve lived in the garden of Eden, paradise. God had given them only one rule. They were not to eat the fruit from the tree of knowledge of good and evil. If they did, they would die.

One day a serpent came to Eve and asked her why she didn't eat the fruit from this tree. The serpent said to her that she and Adam would not die if they ate the fruit, but they would have great knowledge and be like gods.

Eve ate the fruit and gave some to Adam who also ate it. At that moment Adam and Eve had knowledge of their sin. When they heard God calling them, they tried to hide from him.

But God knew they had disobeyed. When God questioned them, Adam blamed Eve, and Eve blamed the serpent. God then told how each would be punished. The serpent would have to crawl on the ground and be an outcast from all other animals. Eve would bear children with pain. Adam would work for food with much difficulty. Then God made clothes for Adam and Eve and sent them from the garden. They left with God's promise that he would send someone to overcome sin and restore life. God had said to the serpent,

"I will put enmity between you and the woman,
and between your offspring and hers;
He will strike at your head,
while you strike at his heel."

Genesis 3:15

The savior would be Jesus, the new Adam who would bring about the new creation. Mary, the mother of Jesus, would be the new Eve, the new

mother of all the living. She would be the sinless one who always listened to God. Through her Son, Satan would be conquered forever.

## Triumph of Love and Mercy

God created us because he wanted to share his life and love with us. He wants us to be happy. When we sin, we turn away from God's love and look for happiness in the wrong places. We direct our power to love to ourselves, rather than to God and others.

When this happens, sin spreads and divides. Soon everyone is affected. Many problems in the world today come from the evil of sin.

The effects of sin are **separation from God, unhappiness, destruction, conflict, suffering,** and **death.** These evils are with us, but God's love and mercy are also with us.

God's response again and again has been one of love and mercy. The message of Genesis is not only that people sin. It is also the message that God's love is faithful and total.

Nothing could prevent God from calling us to union with him. When Adam and Eve sinned, God promised to send a savior who would redeem us and unite us with God!

No matter how much evil we may find in the world, nor how hard things may become for us, we still hope, we still believe, we still love.

How are we able to do this? Read 1 Peter 1:3–7. Spend a few moments thinking about God's word to you. Respond to God's message by writing your thoughts or your own prayer.

## Relationships in Conflict

The writer of the book of Genesis tells of the spread of sin in the world. The following three stories illustrate how sin weakens and destroys relationships with God and with others. They also show us God's merciful love.

### The Story of Two Brothers

The first son of Adam and Eve, Cain, was a farmer. The second son, Abel, was a herder. Each of them brought offerings to God from their labors. Cain brought the fruit of the land he tilled. Abel brought one of the best animals in his flock. God accepted Abel's offering, but he did not accept Cain's. Cain was hurt and jealous.

God reminded Cain that his heart and attitude were more important than any offering. If Cain did not have love and gratitude in his heart, his offering was not acceptable. But Cain refused to change his way of life. Instead, he invited Abel to go out into the field with him. There Cain killed Abel. God called to Cain, "Where is your brother Abel?"

In Genesis 4:9 you can find Cain's reply. Write it here.

_____

God punished Cain by sending him away from his land to wander about the world as an outcast. Even so, God showed mercy. God loves sinners, too. He continually tries to save them. He protected Cain in a special way.

Read Genesis 4:15. Write what God did for Cain.

_____

Later Adam and Eve had another son, named Seth.

### The Story of the Flood

Like many people of long ago, the Hebrews had a flood story they passed on from generation to generation. Their story told how common sin had become. God was displeased with the wickedness of the people and regretted making them.

He told Noah, who had remained faithful to him, to build a special boat called an ark. He directed Noah to take with him on the ark his family and one pair of every kind of animal.

When Noah had done this, the rains began. Soon the whole earth was covered with water. Every living creature except those in the ark was destroyed. For many days and nights the rain continued. When it stopped and the dry land appeared, God called Noah from the ark. Noah offered sacrifices to God. Then God made a covenant between himself and Noah and every living creature. He promised never to destroy the world by flood again.

God gave Noah a special sign of this everlasting covenant. Find it in Genesis 9:13 and draw it here.

**The Story of the Tower of Babel**

Sin continued. The flood story was not the end. Some people used to build towers, called ziggurats, to honor their gods. In the story of the Tower of Babel, the people decided to build a tower for a different reason.

Read Genesis 11:4 and write why the people wanted to build their tower.

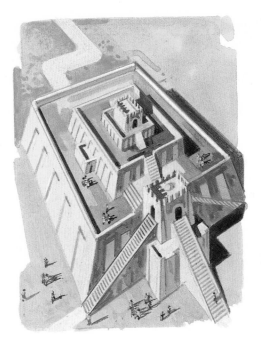

_____

According to the story, people throughout the whole world used to speak the same language. The Lord saw that the people building the tower were very proud. Because they had forgotten him, God confused their language. Then the people could no longer understand each other and could not complete their tower. They could not even live together and separately moved to various parts of the earth. Sin had divided them.

**Reconciliation—**
**A Return to God and an End to Conflict**

God did not leave people alone in their sin. He constantly offered them ways to return to him. Every sin separates us from God and our neighbor. Every effort to turn from sin helps heal this separation. This return to God and our neighbor is called **reconciliation.**

## Headlines

Newspapers often carry stories of sin and conflict. Think about relationships that were weakened or destroyed in the Genesis stories. Then fill in the chart below using the letters of the headlines.

**Psalm 100**

Cry out with joy to the Lord, all the earth.
Serve the Lord with gladness.
Come before Him, singing for joy.

Know that He, the Lord, is God.
He made us, we belong to Him,
We are His people, the sheep of His pasture.

Go within His gates, giving thanks.
Enter His courts with songs of praise.
Give thanks to Him and bless His name.

Indeed, how good is the Lord,
Eternal His merciful love.
He is faithful from age to age.

Grail Translation

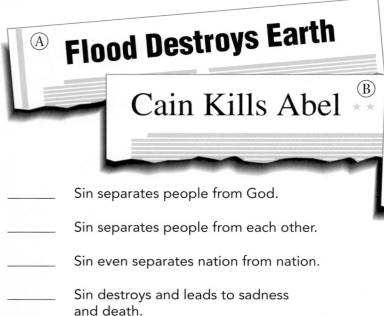

Ⓐ **Flood Destroys Earth**

**Cain Kills Abel** Ⓑ ★ ★

**TOWER CRUMBLES—** Ⓒ
World Divides

Ⓓ **Adam, Eve Disobey**

_____ Sin separates people from God.

_____ Sin separates people from each other.

_____ Sin even separates nation from nation.

_____ Sin destroys and leads to sadness and death.

**The Promise**

Ed saw Randy in the garage looking at his older brother's new mountain bike. "Hey, where's Bob?" he called as he walked toward Randy.

"Oh, he went somewhere with my dad," Randy replied. "He'll be back soon."

"Is that his new bike?" Ed questioned.

"Yeah, you like it?"

"Sure do. Are you going to ride it now?"

"Bob said it's a little tricky to handle. He told me to wait until he had talked to me about it. I can't wait to ride it."

"Why don't you? This is like my brother's bike and you've ridden his. Your brother won't care."

"But it's Bob's, and he told me not to."

"Aw, he'll never know. Let's try it out. You first," Ed suggested.

"Okay. I'll just take it down the driveway once." Randy started off with confidence. But then he hit a rough spot and swerved right into a tree. He wasn't going very fast, but the impact was enough to break the headlight. The front wheel was out of line, too.

How do you think Randy felt at that moment?

_____

How do you think Bob will feel?

_____

Ed called, "Are you all right?"

"I am, but just look at this bike!"

"Now what are you going to do?"

"What can I do? He'll see it when he gets home. I guess I'll just have to tell him what I did. Come on, let's put the bike back where he left it." The two boys put it into the garage and waited.

Bob and Mr. Sullivan returned a short time later. "Hi, boys," called Mr. Sullivan as he walked into the house. But Bob went over to his bike. Right away he saw the broken headlight. He turned to Ed and Randy, who were walking towards him. He could tell by the look on their faces what had happened.

What could Randy have done in the first place when Ed suggested riding the bike?

_____

In justice, what did Randy owe his brother?

_____

Bob was angry about the bike. The front wheel and headlight needed to be repaired. All that would cost money. Randy agreed to pay for it, even though he knew it would take him a while to save up the money. Then Bob said to Randy, "We can't ride it until I get that wheel fixed. But when it's done I'll show you how to ride it the right way."

Randy looked at his brother. "You will? You mean you're really going to let me ride it again?"

"Yeah, that's what I said."

For this ending to take place, what kind of person would Bob have to be?

_____

**A Forgiving Spirit**
Read the following stories. How would you end each story? In what ways could the people involved show forgiveness and kindness?

1. Linda's mother told her to dry the dishes. But Linda had made plans to meet several of her friends right after dinner. Besides, she always had to do the dishes while her older sister got to be with her friends. Linda yelled, "Why do I always have to do everything around here!" Then she ran out of the room.

2. José couldn't make baseball practice one day so he let George borrow his baseball bat. He only asked that George take care of it. At practice, as George hit the ball, he could hear the bat crack. It was hard to see the crack but the next time someone used the bat, it would splinter and break.

3. Louanne was with a group of girls who were talking about Marge, a new girl in their class who did not seem very smart. Although Louanne liked Marge, she did not want to be left out of the group. She joined in making fun of her. Then she took a piece of chalk and drew a picture of an ugly-looking girl on the side of the building and labeled it Marge.

4. Tom had forgotten to do his map for history homework. When he came in to school in the morning, he asked Rosie if he could borrow her homework. She gave it to him. After the papers had been handed in, Mr. Perry called them both into the hall. He asked them if they had copied. Rosie admitted they had. Both students received a zero.

5. Raymond was leaving the house to visit his friend in a neighboring apartment building. His seven-year-old sister came running after him, asking if she could go with him. Raymond said, "No, get out of here and leave me alone for once." He pushed her back into the house and closed the door.

## Things to Do at Home

1. As you watch television or read the newspaper, look for the effects of sin. Keep these intentions in your prayers.
2. You might like to read *Anne Frank: The Diary of a Young Girl.* It tells how this young Jewish girl remained hopeful in a very difficult situation.
3. Show gratitude and love to someone in your family. Be quick to apologize.
4. Pray Psalm 100 with a friend or member of your family.
5. Read the sin stories from the Bible.
   Adam and Eve: Genesis 3:1–24
   Cain and Abel: Genesis 4:1–16
   The Flood: Genesis 6:5–9:17
   The Tower of Babel: Genesis 11:1–9

## We Review

**What is sin?**
Sin is a person's free choice to turn away from God. It is the source of all evil.

**What are the effects of sin?**
Sin weakens or destroys a person's relationship with God and others.

**How did God respond to people when they sinned?**
When people sinned, God responded with love and mercy.

### Words to Know
sanctifying grace     original sin
sin     conflict
reconciliation

## We Respond

Thank you, Lord, for loving me so much.

Thank you, for always forgiving me.

When I trust you in all things, I learn true happiness.

Teach me to live a life filled with joy and hope.

## We Review

**Who's Who?**    Match the person with the description.

A. Abel
B. Eve
C. Mary
D. Satan
E. Person from Babel
F. Adam
G. Cain
H. Noah

_____ **1.** Would someday be crushed by the savior of the human race

_____ **2.** Offered the best of his flock to God

_____ **3.** Good person who was saved in the worldwide flood

_____ **4.** Killed his brother

_____ **5.** Blamed his sin on his wife

_____ **6.** First mother of the human race

_____ **7.** Tried to build a tower in order to be famous

**Word Challenge**    Choose a word from the rainbow to answer each clue. Then use the circled letters to work out the sentence at the bottom.

**1.** Source of evil: ___ ___ (1)

**2.** One effect of sin: ___ (2) ___ ___ (3) ___ ___ ___

**3.** Another effect of sin: ___ (4)(5) ___ ___ (6) ___ ___ ___

**4.** Cain and Abel: (7)(8) ___ ___ (9) ___ ___ ___

**5.** Sign of God's promise to Noah: ___ ___ (10) ___ ___ ___ ___

**6.** Creator of the world: (11) ___ (12)

**7.** Was built in Babel to show power and fame: ___ ___ (13) ___ ___

**8.** God's response to sinners: ___ ___ ___ ___ (14)

Rainbow words: brothers, mercy, rainbow, tower, God, sin, conflict, separation

Reconciliation is the return to a ___ ___ ___ ___ ___ and ___ ___ ___ ___ relationship with ___ ___ ___
                                    9  6  5  5  14        9  2  3  14                          11  2  12

and ___ ___ ___ ___ ___ ___ ___ ___ after it has been ___ ___ ___ k ___ ___ ___ ___ or destroyed by sin.
     1  4  10 11  9  7  2  8                            13  4  6      4  1  4  12

**Picture This!**    Draw a cartoon or comic strip of one of the sin stories.

**5**

# Our Family Album

Write the name of the missing person in each riddle.
Then write the number of the picture of that person.

**1**

I lived in Eden where life began.

Made in God's image, I'm _____, the first man.

Picture _____

**2**

I love my wife, but now I grieve!

I sinned with her, my lady _____.

Picture _____

**3**

My holy brother was a pain!

I murdered him! My name is _____.

Picture _____

**4**

A shepherd who gave to God his best,

I'm _____ sent early to eternal rest.

Picture _____

**5**

God said, "Now _____, an ark you must build

To escape from a flood. I won't let you get killed!"

Picture _____

## Puzzle Book

Complete the crossword puzzle. You can find the correct spelling of the answers in Unit 1 or in the glossary.

**Down**

2. Creator of the universe
3. One's free choice to turn away from God
4. Kind of book in the Bible that shows how God cared for the Israelites throughout history
5. First book of the Bible, which contains the creation accounts
7. People also known as Israelites
9. Saved from the flood because he was faithful to God

**Across**

1. Kind of book in the Bible that tells about the prophets and their messages
6. First five books of the Bible; word means five scrolls
8. Testament sometimes called the Christian Scriptures
10. Kind of book in the Bible that tells how a wise person lives
11. The perfect revelation of God
12. Testament sometimes called Hebrew Scriptures
13. Name given to the one sent to save us

## Notebook

Write the number of the correct definition after each word in the notebook.

1. Everything God made out of nothing
2. A gift from God by which we can think, judge, and know
3. A sign of God's covenant with Noah and the human race
4. What God called us to be toward life and the gifts of the earth
5. A gift from God by which we can freely choose

stewards _____

creation _____

free will _____

intellect _____

rainbow _____

# Scroll SCRAMBLE

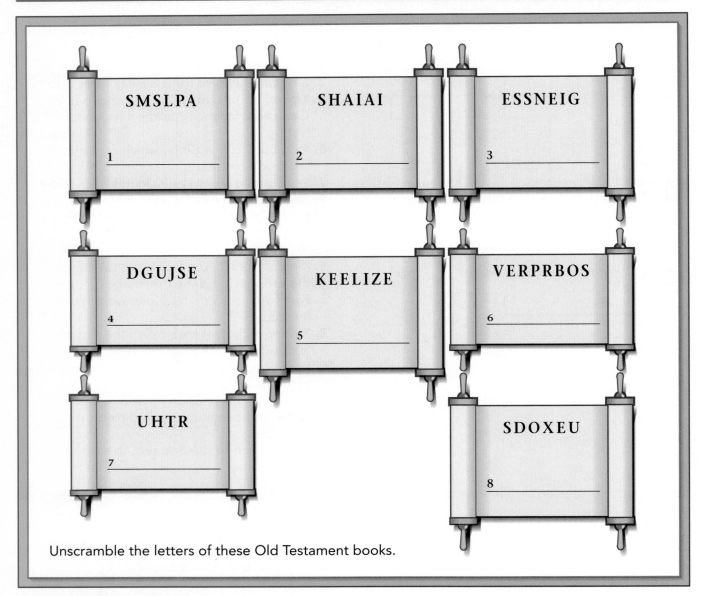

| | | |
|---|---|---|
| SMSLPA | SHAIAI | ESSNEIG |
| 1 _____ | 2 _____ | 3 _____ |
| DGUJSE | KEELIZE | VERPRBOS |
| 4 _____ | 5 _____ | 6 _____ |
| UHTR | | SDOXEU |
| 7 _____ | | 8 _____ |

Unscramble the letters of these Old Testament books.

## Which Book Is It?

Use your Bible's table of contents to find which books from Scroll Scramble match the descriptions below. Write their names.

**1.** First book in the Bible _____

**2.** Comes after the book of Psalms _____

**3.** The second book in the Pentateuch _____

**4.** The first book of the prophets _____

**5.** Two of the historical books _____

## Looking Back at Unit 1

In this unit, you have begun your study of the Old Testament, the first part of the Bible. It is through the Bible that God speaks to his people. The Bible is a mini-library of inspired literature. God inspired the authors to share his will for people and those truths about him that he wanted known.

The biblical authors told stories to explain the mysteries of creation and evil. These stories revealed that God created because of great love. God wanted to share love and life with the people he created. He asked them to take care of the things of the earth and to use them to bring joy to others. God wanted all to be happy, and he knew what would make them happy.

The sin stories tell us that people wanted to control their lives without God. With the first sin of pride and disobedience, the mystery of evil came into the world. As sin spread, people separated themselves from God and from one another. God never abandoned his people. He promised to send a redeemer to conquer sin and death.

## Living the Message

Can you give yourself a check (✓) for each statement?

_____ I am gaining skill in finding quotations in the Bible.

_____ I can tell the religious truths God teaches in the creation stories.

_____ I try to develop the gifts God has given me.

_____ I fight the effects of sin by trying to be a peacemaker.

_____ When I hear God's Word, I listen carefully and try to live according to it.

## Planning Ahead

God made you in his image and likeness, and what God made is very good. However, sin brings separation, conflict, and every type of unhappiness. Read the following verses from the Bible. Write what you will do to preserve the goodness and joy in God's creation.

Psalm 32:5

_____

_____

_____

Proverbs 14:21

_____

_____

_____

Ephesians 5:19–20

_____

_____

_____

Sirach 6:5

_____

_____

_____

# Celebrating God's Word

**Leader 1:**   We are gathered together in the name of the Father, and of the Son, and of the Holy Spirit.

**All:**   Amen.

**Leader 2:**   We have been created in the image and likeness of God, "who stretched out the heavens and laid the foundations of the earth" (Isaiah 51:13). We have been baptized into God's life. We are his people called to live in his love.

**All:**   Give thanks to the LORD, invoke his name;
   make known among the peoples his deeds!
Sing praise, play music;
   proclaim all his wondrous deeds!
Glory in his holy name;
   rejoice, O hearts that seek the LORD!
Rely on the mighty LORD;
   constantly seek his face.

Psalm 105:1–4

**Reader:**   A reading from the prophet Isaiah.
I, the LORD, your God,
   teach you what is for your good,
   and lead you on the way you should go.
If you would hearken to my commandments,
   your prosperity would be like a river.

Isaiah 48:17–18

The Word of the Lord.

**All:**   Thanks be to God. (*Pause for silent prayer.*)

**Song:**   "Your Word, O Lord"

### Your Word, O Lord
Mary Lou Skirbunt

Your word, O Lord, is the joy of my heart. I sing your prai-ses by night and by day, and walk with glad-ness a-long your way.

## Onondaga Creation Story

Anna loves to hear stories of her people, the Onondaga, a woodlands tribe of the Iroquois Federation. Like the Bible's story of creation, their creation story involves a tree.

An ancient chief and his wife lived in Skyland. Below Skyland there was a watery place populated by birds and animals who swim. In Skyland grew a great and beautiful tree that had roots facing in the four sacred directions. One night the chief's wife dreamed that the tree was uprooted. As the dream predicted, the chief did have the tree uprooted. While looking down through the hole left in Skyland, the chief's wife lost her balance and fell. As she fell, she clutched some seeds from the great tree and took them with her. Birds flew up to cushion her fall. Because the chief's wife could not live in the watery place, Muskrat offered to swim deep down in the water and bring back earth for her to stand on. When he brought back a pawful of earth, the animals wondered where to put it. A giant turtle came up from the waters and offered his shell as a resting place for earth. Muskrat placed the earth on the turtle's back, and it grew until it became the whole Earth. Then the chief's wife dropped the seeds she had been holding, and trees, flowers, and grass sprang up. Life began on the earth.

**Your family might plant a tree or adopt one growing in your yard or neighborhood. Create leaf prints of your tree by painting a leaf and then pressing it onto a sheet of paper. Make bark rubbings by placing paper on your tree and rubbing it with the side of a crayon. You might even keep a record of the changes on your tree, noting how it changes during the seasons. Here are some other tree-related family activities:**

- **As people in Switzerland and the Middle East do, plant a fruit tree when a child is born in the family.**

- **Enjoy reading together Shel Silverstein's book *The Giving Tree*.**

- **Make a list of items in your house that are made of wood.**

- **Start a leaf collection.**

- **Sit before a log fire eating fruit from trees and drinking sassafras tea.**

## The Cross

In Genesis a tree led to our downfall. Jesus saved us by the wood of the cross. The feast of the Triumph of the Cross is September 14.

Match the descriptions of crosses with their pictures.

_____ A Jerusalem cross has five crosses for the five wounds of Christ.

_____ A Fitchy (fixable) cross has a sword at one end so it could be planted by the crusaders.

_____ An Epiphany cross ends in three-leaf clovers, St. Patrick's symbol for the Trinity.

_____ A hope cross is made like an anchor, the symbol of our hope in Christ.

_____ The ankh, a loop over a T-shape, is the Egyptian symbol for eternal life.

_____ The Eastern cross has three cross-bars: one for the inscription, one for the crossbeam, and one slanted for the footrest.

_____ The papal (pope's) cross has three crossbars.

_____ The Celtic cross from the British Isles has a circle around the cross.

_____ The Maltese cross seen on Spanish coats-of-arms is from the island of Malta.

_____ The cross of suffering has a sword at each end.

_____ The Tau cross is shaped like the Greek letter T.

_____ The Cross Formy represents the wings of a bird, suggesting protection.

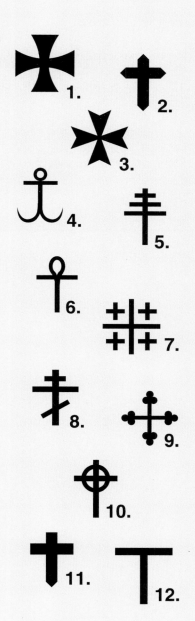

(Answers: 7, 11, 9, 4, 6, 8, 5, 10, 3, 2, 12, 1)

## Cross Quiz

✥ Is a crucifix displayed in your home?

✥ Do you ever wear a cross?

✥ When do you make the Sign of the Cross?

✥ Do you bless one another with the Sign of the Cross?

In the box create your own design for a cross.

# God Forms a
# Family of Faith

# Abraham Is Our Father in Faith

**6**

## God's Call and Abram's Response

based on Genesis 12

Have you ever been in awe of the power of the sea, the beauty of sunlight, or the strength of the wind? Many centuries before the coming of Christ, people wondered about these things. Nature impressed them greatly. Each element was a mystery to them. Many people worshiped the forces of nature as their gods. They offered prayers and sacrifices to these gods. They did not know the one true God. Faith is a supernatural gift from God.

  **M A P**

This map search will acquaint you with the names

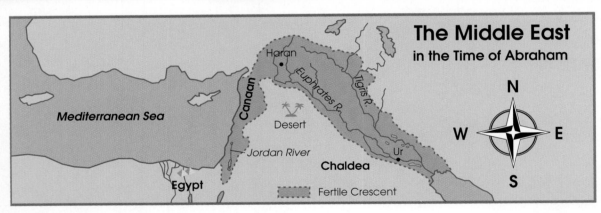

**The Middle East**
in the Time of Abraham

Haran

Euphrates R.

Tigris R.

Canaan

Mediterranean Sea

Desert

Jordan River

Ur

Chaldea

Egypt

Fertile Crescent

N W E S

Using the map from the time of Abraham, find each place and write its name on the line.

1. The city in Chaldea where Abram first lived

   Ur

2. The city on the Euphrates River where Abram later settled

   Haran

3. The land to which God called Abram

   Canaan

4. The area that included Canaan, Haran, and Ur

   Fertile Crescent

5. Two rivers in the Fertile Crescent

   Tigris and Euphrates

6. The sea to the west of Canaan

   Mediterranean Sea

In those times lived a man named Abram. God chose to reveal himself to the world through Abram. Early in his life Abram had traveled with his family and relatives from Ur in Chaldea to Haran. There he settled as a shepherd with his flocks. Then one day when Abram was seventy-five years old, God called him to make a journey to the distant, unknown land of **Canaan.**

God said to Abram:

"Leave your country, your family, and your father's house, for the land I will show you.

I will make you a great nation; I will bless you and make your name so famous that it will be used as a blessing."

Abram could not fully understand these words. He only knew in his heart that he must obey them at once.

As Abram set out from Haran on his journey to Canaan, he was also beginning another kind of journey, a spiritual journey. This journey would take him to a deeper and clearer faith in the one true God.

and locations of places in the story of Abraham.

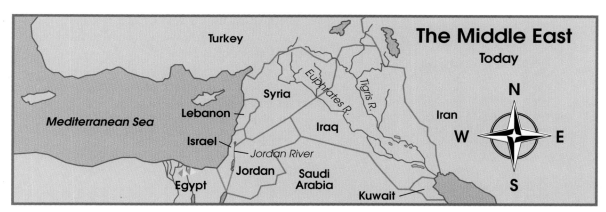

Use the modern map to list the countries located in the Fertile Crescent where Abraham journeyed.

_____   _____

_____   _____

_____   _____

_____   _____

## God's Covenant with Abram

based on Genesis 15, 17

After Abram's arrival in Canaan, God continued to encourage his trust and confidence. God said to Abram:

"Fear not, Abram! I am your shield; your reward will be very great."

Abram believed God, but he did not understand how all of God's promises could happen. He told God his problem:

"O Lord God, what good will your gifts be? You have given me no offspring; so one of my servants will be my heir."

God took Abram outside and said:

"Look up at the sky and count the stars, if you can. Just so shall your descendants be."

Abram again believed God, and God was pleased with Abram's faith. Then God made a very solemn agreement, called a **covenant,** with Abram. God said:

"No longer shall you be called Abram; your name shall be Abraham, for I am making you father of many nations. I will give to you and to your descendants the whole land of Canaan, and I will be their God. As for your wife Sarai, do not call her Sarai; her name shall be Sarah. I will bless her, and I will give you a son by her. You shall call him Isaac."

Within a year Sarah gave birth to a son, even though she and Abraham were very old.

Abraham was the first **patriarch,** or father and ruler of the chosen people. He was the man selected to receive God's promises and pass them on to his descendants. The name Abraham means "father of many nations." The changes in the names of Abraham and Sarah were signs that they were beginning a new way of life. Because of his faith and trust in God, we honor Abraham with the title Father of Believers.

We are believers. If Abraham is truly our father, then we must express our faith as he did: with prompt obedience and wholehearted generosity. If we live this way, then we will receive the rewards that God has promised to those who love him.

## Our Covenant with God

We humans are free to believe in God or not. God made a covenant with us when we were baptized. He promised to give us eternal life if we would believe in him and live according to those beliefs. We promised to renounce Satan, to believe in God, and to live as Catholic Christians. This was the beginning of our journey of faith.

We make this journey with God and with the whole Christian community. On the way, we live out our covenant with God and grow in our relationship with him. We do this whenever we pray, celebrate the sacraments, or give witness to our faith in Christlike words and actions.

Write something you will do to live out your covenant with God. The Holy Spirit, who helps us believe, will assist you.

_____

_____

_____

_____

_____

_____

### A Prayer of Faith

I will celebrate your love forever, LORD.
Age after age my words shall proclaim your faithfulness;
for I claim that love is built to last forever
and your faithfulness founded firmly in the heavens.
Happy the people who learn to acclaim you!
LORD, they will live in the light of your favor;
    they will rejoice in your name all day and exult in your righteousness.
    Once you said, "I will keep my love for him always.
    My covenant with him stands firm."

adapted from Psalm 89:1–2, 15–16, 19, 28 (JB)

This prayer of faith is part of a psalm that is a hymn to God's faithfulness.

Color a letter in the word _faith_ whenever you do an act to keep your covenant.

## A Challenge to Abraham's Faith

When Abraham accepted the call of God to leave Haran for Canaan, he did not know what the future would hold. God had chosen him, and that was enough.

Abraham's journey to Canaan meant a new beginning in his life. It was a great risk. He had to leave his homeland and his friends. He had to adjust to a new land and a new people. When he first went to Canaan, his knowledge of God was limited. In the years that followed, Abraham came to know God better. He expressed his faith in God and looked for ways to worship and serve him more generously.

Abraham saw the ways that Canaanites worshiped. They knew that life was great and mysterious; it had to be a gift from a powerful being. To honor this unknown source of life, the Canaanites followed a practice in which they killed their first-born children in a religious sacrifice. They made this offering in petition for abundant crops and herds and for blessings on their families.

When Isaac was born, Abraham might have wondered if his God expected him to sacrifice his son the way the Canaanites sacrificed their children to their gods. Sacrificing Isaac would have seemed impossible for Abraham. He loved Isaac, the son of his old age. And if he sacrificed Isaac, how would God keep his promise of making him the father of many descendants? Even so, Abraham was ready to do anything for his God.

The story of Abraham's trust in and love of God at this time in his life is told in the following playlet. The story had been told for many generations after the time of Abraham. It taught the chosen people that the one true God looks for a sacrifice of our wills rather than for a sacrifice of a human. We sacrifice our wills by saying no to things that would harm us and other people and by saying yes to loving actions even when we don't feel like it.

# Abraham's Sacrifice

based on Genesis 22

## Characters

God    Abraham    Angel    Isaac    Narrator

**Narrator:** Abraham had lived for many years in friendship with God. One day God called him.

**Voice of God:** Abraham, Abraham, where are you?

**Abraham:** Here I am, Lord.

**Voice of God:** Abraham, take your son Isaac, whom you love, and go to the land of Moriah. When you arrive, go to the mountain I point out to you and offer Isaac to me as a burnt-offering sacrifice.

**Narrator:** Although Abraham was saddened by God's command, he rose early the next morning. He saddled his donkey and went out with Isaac and two servants. On the third day of travel, Abraham saw the appointed place in the distance and spoke to his servants.

**Abraham:** Stay here with the donkey while Isaac and I go to the mountaintop to worship.

**Narrator:** Isaac carried the wood on his back. Abraham carried the flint and knife as they set off.

**Isaac:** Father, we have the knife, flint, and wood, but where is the sheep for the sacrifice?

**Abraham:** Son, God will provide the sheep for the sacrifice.

**Narrator:** When they reached the top of the mountain, Abraham built an altar and arranged the wood on it. He then tied up his son, Isaac, and put him on top of the wood. Just as Abraham reached out and took the knife to kill Isaac, an angel of God called out:

**Angel:** Abraham, stop! Do not harm your son, for now I know you fear God. You have not refused him your son.

**Narrator:** With great relief Abraham looked up and saw a ram caught by its horns in a nearby bush. Abraham knew that God did not want him to sacrifice Isaac. He took the ram and offered it in place of his son. Abraham had responded to God's command with faith. Because of his generous obedience, the Lord made this promise to him.

**Voice of God:** I swear by myself—it is Yahweh who speaks—because you have done this, because you have not refused me your son, your only son, I will shower blessings on you. I will make your descendants as many as the stars in the heavens and the sands of the seashore. In them all nations of the earth shall find blessing—all this because you obeyed my command.

**Narrator:** In not allowing Abraham to sacrifice Isaac, God taught his chosen people that he did not want human sacrifice. He also showed them that he rewards those who believe and trust in him with abundant blessings.

Abraham's faith in God was shown in his trust. God had led him to a new land, chosen him as a close friend, and given him a son. Abraham believed that God loved him, and trusted in God's goodness. God rewarded Abraham's faith and trust with a renewal of his promises.

Isaac would be with Abraham for many years to come. He would later marry Rebekah and have two sons. To them he would pass on the promises of God that he had received from Abraham.

Eventually a descendant of Abraham would be the Savior of the world. Through him all nations would be blessed.

## How Am I Like My Father Abraham?

Read the statements below. How would you truthfully complete your part?

1. Abraham obeyed God's call promptly. When my parents tell me to do something, I usually . . .

   ❏ obey promptly.
   ❏ do it later—sometimes much later.
   ❏ forget to do it.

2. Abraham generously left much of what he had when God called him to move. When I get something new and someone wants to try it out or use it, I usually . . .

   ❏ share generously.
   ❏ share but don't like doing it.
   ❏ say no and don't share at all.

3. Abraham trusted that God would keep his promises, even though it seemed hopeless. When I have problems, I usually . . .

   ❏ talk them over with God in prayer.
   ❏ talk them over with my parents or a trusted adult and then pray about it.
   ❏ get crabby or upset and don't pray at all.

Think over your answers. Is there room for improvement? What can you do about improving?

## Things to Do at Home

1. You may want to share the story of Abraham with your family. Other stories can be found in Genesis 13:1–13 and Genesis 18:20–33. What do these accounts add to your knowledge of Abraham?
2. With the help of family members, make a list of qualities that make a good and loyal friend. Which of these did Abraham show in his relationship with God? Which do you show towards your friends and family? You might want to share your list with your classmates.
3. Abraham was a man of faith who responded to God's call with generosity and prompt obedience. Ask your family members to tell about a time when they were called upon to practice great faith.
4. Make a covenant with a member of your family. Each of you should agree to do a certain favor for the other. After a few days, check to see how each person has kept his or her part. How is your covenant like that between God and Abram? How is it different?
5. Write the story of Abraham and Isaac as seen through Sarah's eyes.

## We Remember

**What does true faith in God lead to?**
True faith in God leads to complete trust in his goodness and prompt obedience to his call.

**What did God promise Abraham?**
God promised Abraham land and many descendants. He promised that all nations would be blessed through him.

---

### Words to Know

covenant        patriarch        Canaan

---

## We Respond

Lord, I believe in you. Increase my faith!

# We Review

**The Man of Faith**    Write the missing letters in the puzzle using the clues.

**1.** Abraham was the first and greatest _____ of the chosen people.
**2.** A covenant is a solemn agreement in which both parties make _____.
**3.** Today we honor Abraham as the Father of _____.
**4.** Sarah was the _____ of Abraham.
**5.** God called Abraham to the land of _____ and promised it to his descendants.
**6.** Abraham's son _____ carried on the promise.
**7.** The descendants of Abraham were to be as many as the _____ of the seashore.
**8.** Abraham had great _____ and trust in God.

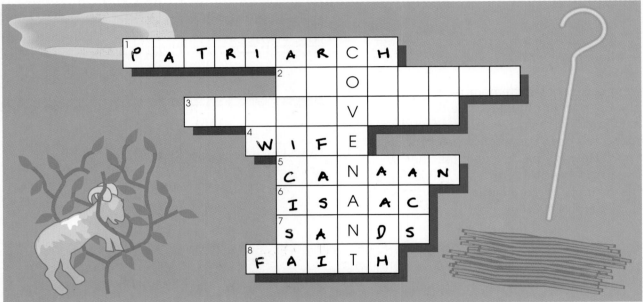

**Promises, Promises**    List four promises that God made to Abraham.

1. _____

_____

2. _____

_____

3. _____

_____

4. _____

_____

**Bonus**    Name two ways in which Isaac was like Jesus.

1. _____

_____

2. _____

_____

# Jacob Is Chosen by God

### A Plan of His Own

Boys and girls who have their hearts set on belonging to a team work very hard to make the team. They practice and spend hours working out. Being on that team is an important goal for them. They are willing to do almost anything in order to reach that goal. Everyone knows that only some will be chosen and that those who aren't chosen will be disappointed.

A biblical story tells us that there was a great deal of competition between Isaac's twin sons, Esau and Jacob. Even before their birth, God had told Rebekah that her younger son would play a special role in the life of his people. He was God's chosen one.

As the firstborn, Esau was to receive his family's **birthright.** This was the oldest son's right to the greatest part of the inheritance and to a special blessing from the father. The birthright was especially important in Isaac's family. Whoever received the birthright and special blessing would become a patriarch of God's chosen people. Though all of this was to go to Esau, it was very important to Jacob. He wanted it!

Jacob did not think he had a chance for this blessing unless he took matters into his own hands. One day Esau found Jacob cooking. Esau was very hungry and asked for some of the stew. Here was Jacob's chance! He said, "First, give me your birthright." Esau was so hungry that he agreed and even made an oath. Neither son told Isaac of this trade. What does this trade tell you about Esau?

## A Stolen Blessing

When Isaac was very old and nearly blind, he called for Esau to give him his blessing before he died. Rebekah overheard Isaac's words and told Jacob. Jacob was her favorite son. Rebekah wanted him to receive Isaac's special blessing. Instead of trusting that God would make Jacob the leader of his people, she felt that she would have to make it happen.

In your Bible read Genesis 27:1–29 to learn how Jacob got the blessing of the firstborn.

Then answer the questions below.

**1.** Why were Rebekah and Jacob able to fool Isaac? (verse 1)

_Isaac was blind._

**2.** How was Jacob disguised? (verses 15, 16)

_Jacob wore Esau's clothes and wore goats hair to feel hairy like Esau._

**3.** How did Jacob explain how he got the animal so quickly? (verse 20)

_He explained that God helped him._

**4.** Isaac had asked for Esau but was not certain which son had come. What confused Isaac? (verse 22)

_Jacob's voice confused Isaac but he smelt and felt like Esau._

**5.** What two things did Isaac ask for Jacob as he blessed him? (verses 28, 29)

_____

## Can Good Come from This?

Jacob had lied to trick his father into giving him the blessing that should have gone to Esau. God was not pleased with this deceit! Yet, because of his power and love, God would still bring good out of the situation. Jacob was his chosen one, and that choice would not be changed. It would be through Jacob and his family that the promise of a redeemer would be passed on.

Rebekah warned Jacob that Esau planned to kill him. She sent Jacob to stay with her brother Laban in Haran. On the way there, Jacob lay down to sleep one night at a shrine, using a stone for a pillow. He dreamed about a stairway leading from the ground to heaven with angels going up and down. (This stairway is usually referred to as **Jacob's ladder.**) The Lord appeared beside Jacob and renewed the promises he had made to Abraham. When Jacob wakened, he set up the stone as a memorial stone, marking the spot as a sacred place. Later he built an altar there and named the place Bethel.

## More Tricks!

Jacob stayed with Laban and eventually married his daughter Rachel, the girl he loved. But first he was tricked by Laban into marrying Rachel's older sister, Leah. Jacob's <u>sufferings</u> helped him become a better person. You might enjoy reading about this part of his life in Genesis 29:15–30.

After Jacob had worked twenty years for Laban, God told him to return to the land of his father, Isaac. Before he left, Jacob paid back Laban for his trick. He made sure that the livestock mated in such a way that he himself had the sturdy sheep and goats, while Laban had the weak ones! Jacob took his family and the livestock he had earned and journeyed back to Canaan. Because he was afraid that Esau was still angry, he sent his servants ahead with gifts for him. Then he took his two wives and eleven children across the river.

## A Blessing by Night

That night when Jacob was alone, a visitor came and wrestled with him until dawn. At one point the man wrenched Jacob's hip socket, but did not overcome him. He had to ask Jacob to let him go.

Find Jacob's reply in Genesis 32:27–29. Write it here.

_____

_____

Jacob's words showed both great faith and the importance of God's blessing. Jacob was willing to spend all his strength to receive it. He desired to have God act in his own life and through him in the lives of others. When the stranger saw this, he changed Jacob's name to **Israel.** It means "he has been strong against God." Jacob's new name was a sign of his new mission. He no longer thought only of himself. He was sent forth as the father of God's chosen people who would later be known as the **Israelites.**

Jacob's visitor did not give his name, but Israel realized that he had been visited by God himself. This divine visit assured Jacob that the blessing he had received from Isaac was truly his. He then returned to his homeland reassured that God was with him. From Jacob's twelve sons came the twelve tribes of Israel.

ISRAEL

JACOB

# Chosen for Mission

No matter how unimportant the activity, we know how good it feels to be chosen!

What is something you would want to be chosen for when you are an adult?

_____

Who would choose you? _____

How could you prepare now? _____

What would you need most to be successful? _____

God wants every person to be eternally happy with him. He chooses to be united with Christians during their lives here on earth. He gives them the mission of *continuing the life and work of Jesus.*

We do not know why certain people are chosen. God chooses freely, and, once he has chosen, he does not change his mind. Rebekah learned that her younger son was God's special choice even before his birth. You were also God's special choice from all eternity. You could have lived in a time or a place where you would have not known Jesus. But instead you were born into a Catholic or other Christian family.

The blessing that Isaac gave to his son Jacob was the sign that he was God's chosen one, a patriarch of his people.

What sacrament marked you as one chosen by God to be his child and a member of his Church?

_____

Jacob was weak and sometimes failed to live as God's chosen one. But God did not change his choice. Jacob knew God would always be there to help him. He had received the blessing of the divine visitor. He knew that this blessing would strengthen him to lead his people. You probably find times when you are not loving and kind. You do not continue the work of Jesus. But no matter how weak you are or how many mistakes you make, you will always be one of God's chosen people. God will always be ready to help you.

What two sacraments can you celebrate often to help you be a strong follower of Jesus?

_____

_____

## Living That Choice

Boys and girls are willing to work in order to be chosen for a team. It is even more important that they are willing to work and to practice after they are chosen.

To continue the life and work of Jesus wherever you are is a real challenge! It is very important to do things that will enable you to fulfill this mission. Life on this mission will not always be easy, but it will bring you real happiness.

## A Training Program for the Christian Mission

 **STUDY 1** Do all you can to come to know God. Learn how he wants his followers to live.

**EAT 2** Celebrate the Eucharist. Listen carefully to God's Word. Receive Communion and ask Jesus to make you strong for your mission. Celebrate the Sacrament of Reconciliation regularly. Ask Jesus to heal you and to help you grow strong.

**REST 3** Pray to God living within you. Listen to God speaking to you through the Scriptures, the Church, other people, and in your heart. Ask for the grace to do whatever the Holy Spirit asks.

**EXERCISE 4** Obey the commandments. Be ready to tell people that you follow Jesus. Try every day to be more like Jesus. Show his love and care to the people you meet. Be kind and loving to others even when it is hard. Try to help people who are poor, sick, and lonely as Jesus would. Be concerned about suffering people all over the world. Try to be a peacemaker.

---

Draw a picture or symbol to fit each part of your training program.

## What's Your Name?

Design and color your baptismal name in the box.

Three people you have studied so far have had their names changed by God as a sign of their special calling. Who are they?

_____

_____

_____

At baptism you were given your name. Your parents probably chose it, and it is the name by which God our Father called you to be a member of his family. That name is a sign of your mission. It reminds you to be Christ to everyone you meet.

Some people receive a new name at Confirmation, or when they become a priest, brother, or sister. It reminds them that God has asked them to spread his love in a special way. Other people take no new names at these times. They choose to repeat their baptismal names in order to recall their baptismal mission.

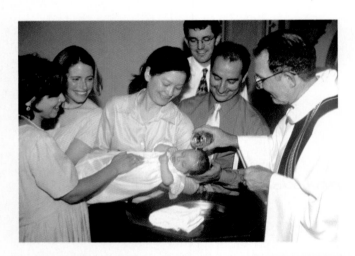

## Things to Do at Home

1. Jacob was afraid as he went to meet his brother Esau, and he prayed to God for help. Read Jacob's prayer (Genesis 32:9–13) and then write your own prayer asking God to help you.

2. In the morning ask for God's blessing. Then at night before you go to bed think about how you have continued the life and work of Jesus during the day.

3. Ask your parents why they chose your name for you. Prepare to share this with your class.

4. Jacob's story has colorful episodes. Draw one of them on a large sheet of paper. Your class might make a pictorial biography of Jacob.

5. The people God chooses are not perfect. Jacob had his faults and so do we. Find an example of a famous person, even a saint, who did much good despite a particular weakness. Write a report on him or her.

## We Remember

**Why was the birthright of special importance in Isaac's family?**

The son with the birthright would receive his father's special blessing and become the patriarch of God's people.

**What mission does every Christian receive at baptism?**

A Christian's mission is to continue Christ's life and work in today's world.

## We Respond

Write a prayer asking God to help you always to be faithful to your mission.

## We Review

**Jacob's Ladder** Climb the stairway by writing the missing words on the steps. Start at the bottom.

8. Our mission is to be like _____.

7. The _____ _____ were the descendants of Jacob.

6. Jacob had _____ sons.

5. God changed Jacob's name to _____.

4. In a wrestling match, Jacob's _____ was injured.

3. God renewed his promises in Jacob's dream at _____.

2. To fool Isaac, Jacob had to have _____ hands like Esau's.

1. Esau traded Jacob his birthright for some _____.

**A Flawed Hero**   Put a halo before every sentence that shows Jacob's goodness. Put an X before every sentence that shows his weakness.

X /  **1.** Jacob made a trade with Esau for his birthright.

X /  **2.** Jacob, disguised as Esau, received his father's blessing.

○ /  **3.** Jacob set up a memorial stone at Bethel.

○ /  **4.** Jacob worked for Laban even after he was tricked by Laban.

x /  **5.** Jacob tricked Laban out of the best livestock.

○ /  **6.** Jacob asked for God's blessing.

**Relatives**   Fill in the chart of Jacob's family.

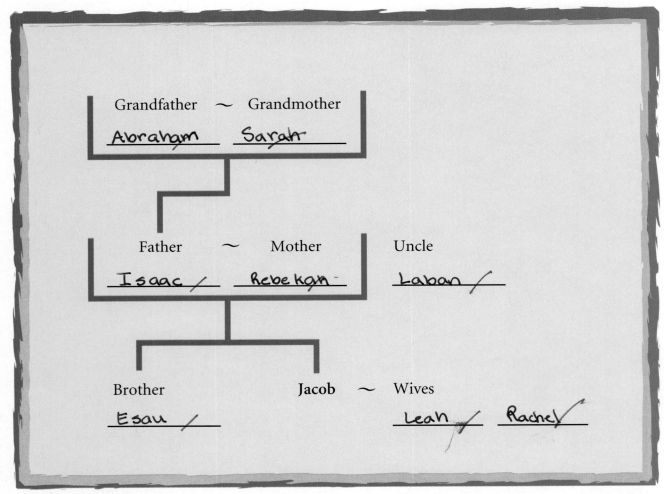

Grandfather  ~  Grandmother

Abraham    Sarah

Father  ~  Mother          Uncle

Isaac    Rebekah        Laban

Brother          Jacob  ~  Wives

Esau                Leah   Rachel

## Joseph–Son of Israel

based on Genesis 37

Israel experienced God's special plan for himself and his twelve sons through some unusual events. These events centered around Joseph, one of Israel's youngest sons. The life of Joseph reminds us that God provides for our needs and watches over us—God's loving **providence.**

Israel loved Joseph more than any of his other sons. To show this love, he had a fine long tunic made for Joseph. When Joseph's brothers saw how much their father loved Joseph, they were envious.

To make matters worse, Joseph told his brothers about a dream he had. "We were binding sheaves in the field when suddenly my sheaf stood up in the center. Your sheaves formed a ring around mine and bowed to it."

"Are you going to make yourself king over us?" his brothers asked. They hated Joseph all the more.

Again Joseph had a dream. He said, "I saw the sun, the moon, and eleven stars bowing to me."

This time even his father scolded him. "Are I, your mother, and your brothers to come and bow to the ground before you?"

One day Joseph's brothers were out tending their father's flocks. Israel told Joseph to go to his brothers to see if all was well with them and the flocks. His brothers saw him coming and plotted to kill him. "Here comes the man of dreams. Come on, let's kill him and throw him into a well. We can say that a wild beast devoured him. Then we shall see what comes of his dreams!"

Reuben, the eldest, objected. "We must not take his life. Throw him into that well, but don't kill him." So when Joseph came to them, his brothers took his splendid tunic and threw him into a dry well.

That night a caravan of traders passed by their camp. Judah asked, "What do we gain by killing our brother? Let us sell him to these Ishmaelites." So Joseph was sold for twenty pieces of silver. He was taken from Canaan to Egypt where he was sold as a slave to Potiphar, an official of the **pharaoh.**

Meanwhile, Joseph's brothers killed a goat and dipped Joseph's tunic in its blood. They sent the tunic to Israel with the message: "We have found this. See whether or not it is your son's tunic."

### Recall
1. Why did Joseph's brothers hate him?
2. What did Joseph's brothers do to him?
3. How was Israel led to believe that Joseph was dead?

## Dreams and Wonders in Egypt
based on Genesis 39, 40, 41

The Lord protected Joseph while he lived in Potiphar's house. Every work Joseph began was successful. Soon Potiphar put him in charge of all his possessions.

Joseph was a handsome man. When Potiphar's wife saw him, she fell in love with him. She wanted him for herself, but Joseph refused to commit sin with her for he had great respect for Potiphar and for God's laws.

Angry with Joseph, Potiphar's wife screamed and pretended that Joseph had tried to attack her. Potiphar became furious. He seized Joseph and threw him into jail.

Even in prison, Joseph won the respect and trust of others. He was put in charge of all the other prisoners.

Some time later Pharaoh's cupbearer and the chief baker were imprisoned for offending Pharaoh. Joseph was assigned to guard them.

One night both the cupbearer and the baker had strange dreams. The next morning when Joseph came to see them, he saw that they looked worried. He asked what was bothering them. They answered, "We have had strange dreams, but there is no one to interpret them."

Joseph replied, "Tell me your dreams."

The cupbearer in his dream had seen a vine with three branches filled with grapes. "I picked the grapes and squeezed them into Pharaoh's cup. I put the cup into Pharaoh's hand."

Joseph told the cupbearer that in three days he would be released and would again be cupbearer to Pharaoh. He asked the cupbearer to put in a good word for him when he got out. The chief baker, hoping for a similar interpretation, explained his dream. He had seen himself carrying three baskets. In the top one were baked goods for Pharaoh. Birds were pecking at the baked goods.

"In three days," Joseph told him, "Pharaoh will hang you."

Three days later the events happened as Joseph had predicted. But Joseph's attempts to be released were in vain. He remained in prison for two more years. Then Pharaoh had two dreams that no one in his court could explain. The royal cupbearer remembered Joseph and told Pharaoh about him.

So Pharaoh summoned Joseph. "I had a dream that no one can interpret, but I have heard that you can interpret dreams."

Joseph answered, "It is God who will give an answer."

Pharaoh began. "In my dream I was standing on the bank of the Nile. Seven cows, fat and sleek, came up out of the Nile. Behind them came seven other cows, ugly and scrawny. They ate the fat cows. In another dream, growing on one stalk were seven ears of corn, fat and healthy. But sprouting up after them came seven ears of corn, shriveled and thin and blasted by the east wind. These ears swallowed up the healthy ears of corn."

Joseph said that God had revealed to Pharaoh what he was going to do. In Egypt, there would be seven years of good crops. But those seven years would be followed by seven years of famine.

Pharaoh was so pleased with Joseph that he made him governor over all of Egypt. For the next seven years, Joseph collected and stored the abundant crops. When famine came in the following seven years, Joseph opened the storehouses to the people. All Egyptians needing food were told, "Go to Joseph!"

**Recall**
1. What happened while Joseph was in prison?
2. What interpretation did Joseph give to Pharaoh's dream?
3. What reward was Joseph given?

# A Family Reunited

based on Genesis 42–50

The famine Joseph had predicted was experienced everywhere. In Canaan, Israel's family needed food. They had heard of the stored grain in Egypt. So Israel sent all his sons to Egypt to buy food except the youngest, Benjamin, who was his favorite.

The ten brothers came to Joseph for grain and knelt before him. He recognized them immediately, but they did not know him.

Joseph accused them of being spies. They said they were not spies. They explained that they had left their father and brother at home. Joseph pretended he did not believe them. He kept one brother, Simeon, as a prisoner until they returned with the youngest brother as proof of their story.

When the brothers returned home and told Israel they would have to take Benjamin, he was very upset. Israel cried out, "Must you make me childless? Joseph is gone, Simeon is gone, and now you would take away Benjamin. My son is not going down with you!"

But soon they needed food and grain again. So Israel finally agreed to let them take Benjamin and return to Egypt.

Joseph received all his brothers. He had his servant fill their bags with grain and the money the brothers had paid for the grain. Joseph had his own silver cup put into his brother Benjamin's sack.

After the brothers left for home, Joseph sent his guard after them in search of the cup. When it was found with Benjamin, the brothers claimed innocence. But they were ordered to return to Joseph.

Joseph commanded that Benjamin stay with him as a slave. The brothers begged Joseph not to do this. Their father surely would die if Benjamin did not return.

Moved by their concern for their father, Joseph called them closer. "I am Joseph," he said, "your brother whom you sold into Egypt. God has sent me here to save your lives. Return quickly to your father and tell him to come down to me at once. Settle here in the region of **Goshen.** I will provide for you."

The brothers could hardly believe what they had heard. When they arrived home and told Israel, he was amazed. Immediately Israel, his sons, and their families went to Egypt. There they rejoiced to be with their brother.

The Israelites remained in Egypt. In time, their families grew large and prospered.

Years later, when Israel was about to die, he gave each one of his sons a blessing. Judah was promised he would become as powerful as a lion and rule over others. The **Messiah,** the one promised to deliver all people from sin, would come from **Judah's** family.

After Israel died, Joseph's brothers were afraid. They thought that Joseph might harm them for what they had done to him. So they went to him to ask forgiveness in their father's name. Moved by their words, Joseph responded, "Do not be afraid. Even though you meant to do evil, God planned that it would bring good. Because of what happened to me, many people have been saved. Do not worry. I will continue to care for you and your families."

### Recall
1. How had Joseph's dreams come true?
2. How did Joseph test his brothers?
3. Which son received Israel's special blessing?
4. What did Joseph answer when his brothers asked forgiveness?

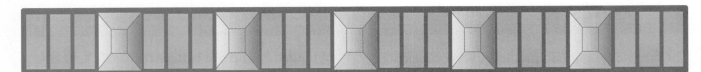

### Providence in Our Lives
Joseph took revenge on his brothers and caused his father pain. Jesus calls us to be more forgiving. In the end, though, Joseph could forgive his brothers because he trusted God. This trust helped him know that God would bring good out of all that happened. Through the events of Joseph's life, God arranged to provide food for Egypt and nearby countries.

God does the same thing in our lives. He guides all events of our lives so that when evil things happen to us, he makes them work for good if we cooperate with him.

Sometimes it takes a long time for us to see this. One way we can learn to see God acting in our lives is to think about the things that happen to us and others. Remembering that God loves us, we know that no matter what happens he can bring good from it. In prayer we ask God to help us trust and believe in his plan for our lives.

Can you recall a time when you felt God taking care of you in a special way? Write about it.

_____

_____

_____

_____

## Psalms of Trust

Several psalms speak of trusting in God. Pick one listed here. Read it in your Bible. Write one phrase of it in the space below. Add a design to make it look like a banner.

Psalm 23        Psalm 131        Psalm 121
Psalm 91:4–6    Psalm 62:1–2, 5–8

## We Remember

**What is providence?**
Providence is God's watching over us and caring for all our needs.

**What can we learn from the life of Joseph?**
From the life of Joseph we learn that God can bring good out of all things. We also learn how the Israelites came to live in Egypt.

### Words to Know
providence        Pharaoh
Goshen            Messiah

## We Respond

Lord, help me to love you more and more. Give me light that I may believe in your goodness and trust in your ways.

# We Review

**Joseph's Word Maze**   The following words will help you recall the story of Joseph. Find and circle each word in the maze. Then identify the word in a short phrase or sentence.

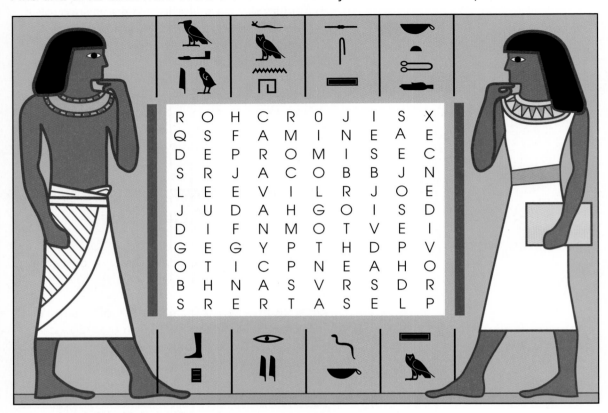

```
R  O  H  C  R  O  J  I  S  X
Q  S  F  A  M  I  N  E  A  E
D  E  P  R  O  M  I  S  E  C
S  R  J  A  C  O  B  B  J  N
L  E  V  I  L  R  J  O  E
J  U  D  A  H  G  O  I  S  D
D  I  F  N  M  O  T  V  E  I
G  E  G  Y  P  T  H  D  P  V
O  T  I  C  P  N  E  A  H  O
B  H  N  A  S  V  R  S  D  R
S  R  E  R  T  A  S  E  L  P
```

Joseph _____

Jacob _____

Judah _____

brothers _____

Egypt _____

caravan _____

famine _____

dream _____

promise _____

providence _____

**How Did It Happen?** Number these pictures so that they tell the story of Joseph in the right order.

④ Potiphar's wife wants Joseph for herself.

⑥ Joseph interprets the cupbearer's dream and the baker's dream

① Israel gives Joseph a gift which is a tunic with rainbow-like colors.

⑦ Joseph interprets the pharoah's dream about the seven fat and seven thin cows.

⑨ The Reunion of Joseph and his brothers.

③ Joseph is thrown into a hole by his brothers

⑧ Joseph gives food to the Egyptians during the famine.

② Joseph has a dream about his wheat his bowed to by his brothers' wheat.

⑤ Joseph is thrown in jail.

**Providence** There is a saying, "God writes straight with crooked lines." What does this mean? How is it true in Joseph's story?

This means that he allows bad things to happen, but makes good things come out of it. This is true in the story of Joseph. Joseph's brothers sell him into slavery but Joseph becomes Potiphar's assistant. Potiphar and his wife Joseph in jail, but he interprets the pharoah's dream and becomes his right-hand man.

# 9

# God Forms a Family of Faith

**Then and Now**

Each of the following incidents is taken from an Old Testament story in this unit. After reading each example, give a similar incident from the practice of faith today.

1. Abraham responded with faith by doing what God told him to do. What can we do to express our faith today?

_____

_____

2. Abraham was willing to sacrifice his son, Isaac, if God wanted him to do this. What might a Christian sacrifice for his or her faith?

_____

_____

3. In the story of Jacob and Esau, Esau chose to trade his birthright for a dish of food. For what might a Christian be tempted to trade God's grace?

_____

_____

4. The brothers of Joseph did not want to leave Benjamin in Egypt. They were concerned about their father and did not want to bring him this sorrow. How can we show concern for our parents?

_____

_____

5. Many difficult things happened to Joseph, but he still trusted God. After his brothers had treated him so cruelly, he gave them food and forgave them. How can we show we forgive those who hurt us?

_____

_____

# A SCROLL PUZZLE

Complete the puzzle using the word box.

## Across

**2.** Joseph _____ his brothers and gave them food.

**3.** God's watching over us and caring for our needs is called _____.

**6.** The one promised by God to deliver all people from sin is called the _____.

**8.** The father and ruler of God's people was called a _____.

**9.** When we rely on God, we have _____ in him.

**10.** When God made a covenant with Abram, God changed his _____.

## Word Box

| | | |
|---|---|---|
| covenant | patriarch | baptism |
| providence | Messiah | faith |
| trust | forgave | name |
| Canaan | | |

## Down

**1.** An agreement between God and his people is called a _____.

**4.** God made a covenant with us at our _____.

**5.** When we believe in God and his Word, we have _____.

**7.** _____ is the land promised to Abraham and his descendants.

Read each description and write the name of the person who fits it.

1. He was the first patriarch of God's people. He is also the Father of Believers.

   _____

2. He was Abraham's son. God promised that through his descendants his promise would be fulfilled.

   _____

3. He received the birthright from his father, Isaac. Then his name was changed to Israel.

   _____

4. She received a message from God that her younger son, Jacob, would lead God's people.

   _____

5. He was Isaac's older son, who sold his birthright for a little bit of food.

   _____

6. He was sold to traders by his brothers. After they came to him in Egypt, he forgave them.

   _____

7. In Israel's blessing, he received the promise that the Messiah would be his descendant.

   _____

8. He was the king of Egypt who made Joseph the governor.

   _____

**Family Tree**  Fill in the family tree of faith.

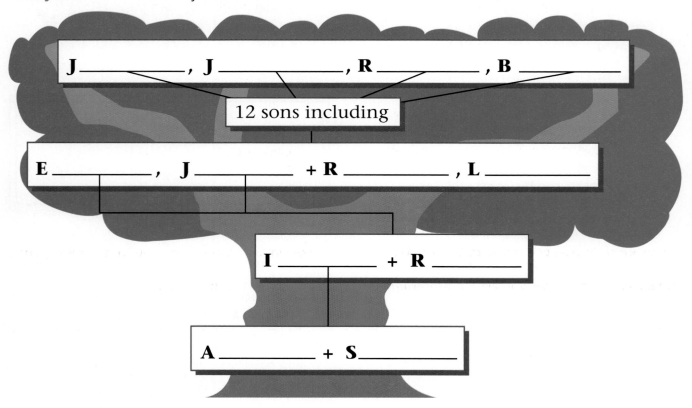

## An Encouraging Letter

Ted broke his leg in a bicycle accident. He will be in the hospital for a few weeks. He will miss the soccer games he was scheduled to play.

Imagine you are a friend of Ted's and write him a letter. Encourage him by telling him how God's providence could bring good from his accident.

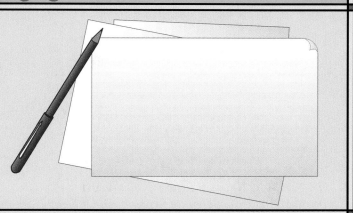

## Looking Back at Unit 2

In this unit you have met your fathers in the faith, the patriarchs. These men, Abraham, Isaac, and Jacob, were the ones to whom God chose to reveal himself. From their families God formed his chosen people. He promised to send his own Son as a member of this people to save all from the power of sin.

When this unknown God began to reveal himself to Abraham, he asked for wholehearted obedience. Abraham obeyed promptly and generously, trusting completely in God's goodness. We hear little of Isaac, but the stories of Jacob and his family are vivid examples of God's providence.

We, too, have been chosen by God, and this choice was marked by our baptism. Our special mission is to continue the life and work of Jesus wherever we are. We can do this with complete trust in God's providence. We know that in every situation God can draw us closer to him.

## Living the Message

Can you give yourself a check (✓) for each statement?

❏ **1.** I can tell the stories of Abraham, Isaac, Jacob, and Joseph.
❏ **2.** I take time to think how I am fulfilling the mission given to me at baptism.
❏ **3.** I try to show my faith in God by prompt, generous obedience to his calls.
❏ **4.** I trust God even when things go wrong, since I know God can bring good even from evil.
❏ **5.** I frequently pray to God and tell him of my faith, my hope, and my love.

## Planning Ahead

For all eternity God chose you to belong to him in a very special way. God chose you for the mission of carrying on the life and work of Jesus. In Scripture we read, "I have called you by name: you are mine" (Isaiah 43:1). Think how you will respond to God's choice. Write your response below.

_____

_____

_____

_____

# Celebrating God's Presence

**Introduction**

**Reader 1:** Truly God is in this place! This is a dwelling place for the Lord. It is holy and special to us. Let us celebrate!

**Leader:** God comes to us every day and brings us dawn and life. God greets us in the smiles of our families and friends. God speaks to us deep in our hearts because God loves us so much.

**Song** (*Procession: Bible, candles*)

**Readings and Responses**

**Leader:** In the Old Testament we read of God speaking to the people he chose. These people would mark in a special way the place where God spoke to them.

**Reader 2:** A reading from the book of Genesis. (*Read Genesis 12:7.*)

**Leader:** Let us pray.

**All:** God, come to us today. Speak to us and help us trust in your Word. (*Silent prayer*)

**Leader:** When God appeared to Jacob in a dream, Jacob named the place Bethel, which means "house of God."

**Reader 1:** A reading from Genesis. (*Read Genesis 28:10–22.*)

**Leader:** Let us pray.

**All:** Father, we meet you in Scripture. We meet you in your Son, Jesus Christ. We meet you in our hearts where you speak to us.

**Presentation of Symbols**

**Leader:** We have our own stones to mark God's special message to us. We bring these as reminders that God is truly present in our lives.

(*Hold your prayer stone in your hand and extend your arms toward the altar or enthroned Bible as the reader prays.*)

**Reader 2:** This is a special place. This is a special time. Lord, help us remember your loving care for us. Make each of our hearts a "Bethel"—a place where you live. May we pray to you. May we love you. May we share that love with everyone in the world.

(*Carry your prayer stone to the altar and place it by the Bible and candles.*)

**Litany of Love**

**Leader:** We love you, Lord, for you have revealed yourself to us.

**All:** I will praise the Lord all my life. I will sing praise to my God forever.

**Reader 1:** You created us, bringing us the joy of life. You are close to us in times of trouble and pain.

**All:** I will praise the Lord all my life. I will sing praise to my God forever.

**Reader 2:** You have a plan for our lives. In your providence, you care for us and those we love.

**All:** I will praise the Lord all my life. I will sing praise to my God forever.

**Reader 1:** May we be rooted in Christ and built up in him. May we grow strong in faith and be filled with gratitude.

**All:** I will praise the Lord all my life. I will sing praise to my God forever.

**Song**

# Christmas Customs from Different Cultures

Adopt any of these customs to make Christmas special in your family:

**Japan: *Fish*** The people of Japan, who live on islands, often use images of fish as decorations. For Christians the fish has a religious meaning. It is an ancient symbol for Christ because the initials of the phrase "Jesus Christ, Son of God, Savior" are *ICHTHYS* in Greek. This is the Greek word for *fish*. Use paper bags or envelopes to make fish. Draw a fish so that its mouth is at the fold. Cut it out double, leaving the halves connected at the mouth. Add ribbon or tissue to the tail and fins, draw eyes and scales, and add glitter. Hang the fish on your tree.

***Germany: Christkindl*** *Christkindl* is German for Christ Child. People draw names for a Christkindl, a person for whom they will secretly pray and do favors during Advent. They prepare for Jesus by showing love for others.

***Poland: Opłatki*** *Opłatki* is a wafer of bread similar to a Communion host that is stamped with a nativity scene.

On Christmas Eve a piece of it is cut into two circles. Both circles are notched from one edge to the center. The notches are slid into each other to make a globe, or *Swiat,* to represent the world. This is hung above the dinner table as a reminder of the presence of Christ with the family at meals. The evening meal, usually meatless, consists of special foods including poppyseed cakes and a large piece of opłatki that is broken and shared with a blessing at the beginning. On the table is a plate that has salt and bread on it and a dollar under it symbolizing good fortune.

## Austria: Lebkuchen

Here is an Austrian recipe for "bread of life," a traditional European Christmas treat.

4 whole eggs
1 lb. brown sugar
2 cups flour

1 teaspoon cinnamon
1/4 lb. almonds, finely chopped
2 oz. lemon peel cut fine

Beat eggs and sugar until fluffy. Mix flour and cinnamon with the nuts and lemon peel. Combine the mixtures. Bake in two greased 10" 3 15" pans at 375°F for 25 minutes. When cool, frost with white frosting. Cut into squares.

## Spain: Wreath Cookies

These cookies can be tied to the Christmas tree with ribbon or colored thread and eaten off the tree.

3 egg whites
3/4 cup confectioners' sugar
1 tablespoon cornstarch

Beat egg whites until stiff. Add 3/4 of the sugar gradually. Beat until marshmallowy. Mix cornstarch and remaining sugar and fold into egg white mixture. Put the batter into a pastry tube or a rolled wax paper tube and pipe it onto a greased pan or a pan lined with wax paper or baker's parchment. Shape the batter into wreaths. Bake at 275°F for 45 minutes.

# Who's Who?

Match the pictures with the people.

Abraham  •

Sarah  •

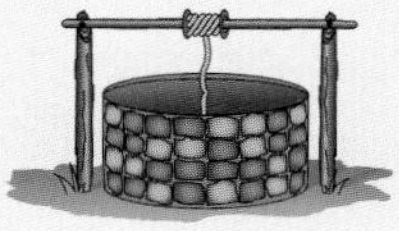

Isaac  •

Rebekah  •

Jacob  •

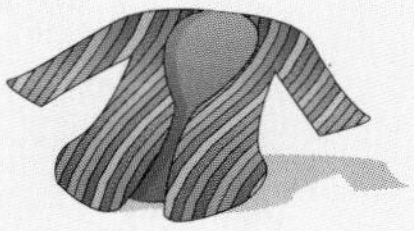

Esau  •

Joseph  •

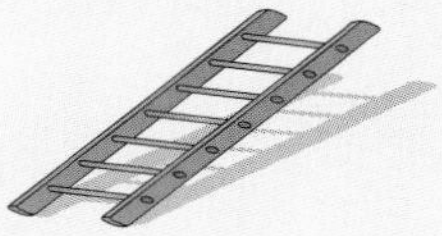

Rachel  •

Judah  •         **• fourteen years**

(Answers: Abraham/stars, Sarah/baby, Isaac/knife and wood, Rebekah/well, Jacob/ladder, Esau/bowl of stew, Joseph/coat, Rachel/fourteen years, Judah/lion)

**Hope**

Use the code to discover what the patriarchs and the chosen people were responsible for passing down through the generations:

| | | |
|---|---|---|
| 1 = a | 4 = h | 7 = o |
| 2 = e | 5 = i | 8 = p |
| 3 = f | 6 = m | 9 = r |

| | |
|---|---|
| 10 = s | |
| 11 = t | |
| 12 = v | |

$\overline{11}$ $\overline{4}$ $\overline{2}$  $\overline{8}$ $\overline{9}$ $\overline{7}$ $\overline{6}$ $\overline{5}$ $\overline{10}$ $\overline{2}$

$\overline{7}$ $\overline{3}$  $\overline{1}$  $\overline{10}$ $\overline{1}$ $\overline{12}$ $\overline{5}$ $\overline{7}$ $\overline{9}$

**Bible Smile**

Where is tennis mentioned in the Bible?

*When Joseph served in Pharaoh's court.*

(Answer: The promise of a savior.)

# God Guides
# the Chosen People

# God Rescues the Chosen People from Slavery

**10**

### Moses, a Man with a Mission

based on Exodus 1–10

Moses is one of the most important men of the Old Testament. God chose him to free his people from slavery in Egypt. The story of Moses' mission is told in Exodus, the second book of the Bible.

For several hundred years, the rulers of Egypt remembered that Joseph had saved them from famine. In time, however, a Pharaoh who did not know about Joseph ruled Egypt. He saw that there were many strong Hebrews, and he feared they might try to take over Egypt. Pharaoh forced the Hebrews into slavery and placed Egyptian slave drivers over them. The Hebrews had to work in the fields, make bricks, and build great cities for the Egyptians.

When the number of Israelites continued to increase, Pharaoh ordered that newborn Hebrew boys be drowned. Hearing this, one Hebrew woman hid her newborn son for three months. When she could no longer safely hide her baby, she placed him in a basket and left him among the reeds along the Nile River. His sister Miriam waited nearby to see what would happen.

Soon Pharaoh's daughter came down to the river with her maids. Noticing the basket among the reeds, she sent one of them to fetch it. When she

opened the basket, she saw the baby boy crying. She knew it was a Hebrew child and felt sorry for him. Miriam stepped forth and asked if she could get an Israelite woman to nurse the baby. Pharaoh's daughter agreed, and Miriam went to get her own mother.

When the baby no longer needed to be nursed, his mother took him to Pharaoh's daughter. The Egyptian woman adopted him and named him Moses, which meant "drawn from the water."

Moses was brought up as a prince at Pharaoh's court. He grew up to be a strong, well-educated man. But he knew he was a Hebrew, and it disturbed him to see his people suffer.

One day Moses saw an Egyptian strike a Hebrew. In anger, Moses killed the Egyptian and quickly buried him in the sand. Pharaoh found out about it and sought to put Moses to death. So Moses fled to Midian. There he met the Midianite priest Reuel and went to live with his family. After a time, Moses married one of Reuel's daughters. For many years Moses worked as a shepherd for his father-in-law.

## God Calls

Meanwhile the Hebrews prayed to be freed from their slavery. It was while Moses was tending the sheep grazing on Mt. Sinai, also called Mt. Horeb, that God spoke to him. Moses saw a bush flaming with fire but not burning up. When he went to investigate, God called his name and told him to remove his sandals for he was on holy ground.

God said, "I have been listening to my people who are suffering greatly in Egypt. I have heard their cries. I will rescue them and lead them to a land flowing with milk and honey. I will send you to Pharaoh to lead my people out of Egypt."

Moses made all sorts of excuses. First he asked, "Who am I to go?" God said, "I will be with you." Then Moses asked, "When the Israelites ask me who sent me, what shall I tell them?" God replied, "I am who am. I am the God of your fathers Abraham, Isaac, and Jacob." Next Moses said, "I am a slow speaker and cannot speak well. Isn't there someone else better able to speak for you?" But God answered, "I will assist you, Moses. Your brother Aaron will go with you and speak for you."

Finally, Moses did what God asked and left Midian for Egypt. He met Aaron on the way and explained their mission. Moses and Aaron went before Pharaoh. They delivered God's message: "Thus says the Lord, the God of Israel: Let my people go. They are to celebrate a feast to me in the desert." But Pharaoh refused to let the Israelites leave their work to offer sacrifice to Yahweh. Instead, Pharaoh ordered the slave drivers to work the Israelites harder. No longer would they be given the straw they needed to make bricks. Now they would have to gather their own straw and still make as many bricks.

The Israelites were angry and complained to Moses. He saw their distress and pleaded with the Lord, "Lord, why do you treat this people so badly? My going to Pharaoh has only made matters worse."

The Lord answered, "Now you shall see what I will do to Pharaoh. Forced by my hand, he will send the Hebrews away. I remember my covenant with the Israelites. I will bring you to the land I promised your fathers."

## Ten Plagues

At God's command, Moses went back to Pharaoh. Aaron threw down his staff, and it became a snake. Pharaoh's magicians threw down their staffs, and these became snakes also. But Aaron's staff swallowed the magicians' staffs. This showed that God's power would swallow up Pharaoh's power, which he had abused.

Then Moses warned Pharaoh, "The Lord has sent me to tell you to let my people worship him in the desert. If you refuse, I will strike the water of the river and change it to blood. All the fish will die, and the water will be unfit for anyone to drink."

Pharaoh ignored Moses. When Aaron stretched out his staff and struck the river, the Nile turned red. But Pharaoh was not impressed, for the Nile had been polluted before.

Then, at God's command, Moses stretched out his arm, and a **plague** of frogs came upon the land. Frogs swarmed everywhere: in beds, in ovens, in mixing bowls. Pharaoh called for Moses and

Aaron. He said, "Pray to your God to get rid of these frogs, and I will let your people go to worship him." So Moses prayed. The frogs died, but Pharaoh did not keep his word.

Moses predicted more plagues, but Pharaoh would not listen. Gnats and then flies covered the land. Plagues were sent: disease among the animals, boils on the people and animals, great hailstones, locusts, and days of darkness. Each plague was a sign that God was speaking through Moses, but Pharaoh refused to recognize God.

Finally God told Moses to warn Pharaoh about a final, terrible plague. If Pharaoh refused to let God's people worship him, every firstborn in the land would die. Pharaoh did not believe this would happen; he still would not let the Israelites leave his land.

## The Mission of Moses

Answer the following questions.

What mission did God give to Moses?

_____

_____

How did Moses feel about his mission?

_____

_____

How did God help Moses when things were difficult?

_____

_____

_____

## Your Mission

God is with you as he was with Moses. Write a prayer telling God you believe this.

_____

_____

_____

God has a special mission or good work for you today. Write what you think it is.

_____

_____

God wants you to prepare now for a special mission in life. Write what you could do to prepare for it.

_____

_____

# Exodus, a Night to Remember

God promised to protect his people from the terrible plague. Moses gathered the Israelites and told them how to get ready for escape. This escape is called the **Exodus.**

On the appointed night, each family gathered to eat a spotless lamb whose blood had first been sprinkled on their doorpost. They ate the lamb roasted, and with it they ate unleavened bread (bread made without yeast) and bitter herbs. They ate with sandals on their feet and staffs in their hands, ready for flight.

After midnight, cries of mourning came from the houses of the Egyptians. All the firstborn had died, even Pharaoh's son. But death had passed over the Israelite houses marked with the lamb's blood.

Pharaoh sent for Moses and Aaron. "Leave at once," he said. "Go and worship the Lord as you have asked. Take your flocks and herds and go." The Egyptians urged the people to leave. They gave them silver, gold, and clothing.

So the Israelites, led by Moses and Aaron, left Egypt. The Lord went before them. By day a column of cloud guided them on their journey, and by night a column of fire. God was truly with his people, leading them to freedom.

Some days after the Israelites left, Pharaoh changed his mind. He ordered his soldiers to capture the fleeing Israelites. By the time the Israelites reached the Red Sea, they could see the Egyptian soldiers coming in their chariots. All hope seemed lost! The Israelites cried out, and Moses said,

 "Fear not! Stand your ground, and you will see the victory the LORD will win for you today. These Egyptians whom you see today you will never see again. The LORD himself will fight for you."

Exodus 14:13–14

Moses raised his staff as Yahweh directed him to do. The pillar of cloud came between the Egyptians and the camp of Israel. The night passed without the army coming any closer. A strong wind blew all night and made a dry path through the water. The Israelites safely crossed the sea. When the Egyptians tried to follow, the Lord clogged the wheels of their chariots. Yahweh told Moses to stretch out his hand over the sea again. Moses did as God commanded, and the Egyptians in their chariots were drowned.

The Israelites knew that it was God who had saved them, and they sang his praises. Miriam led the women in dancing, singing, and playing tambourines:

 "Sing to the LORD, for he is gloriously triumphant; horse and chariot he has cast into the sea."

Exodus 15:1

## The Jewish Passover

Ever since the Exodus, for more than three thousand years, the Jewish people have remembered the night when their houses were "passed over." They celebrate the event each year in the feast of **Passover.**

There are many preparations for Passover. Houses are cleaned very well. Tables are set with the best tablecloths, plates, wineglasses, and silver. Candles are placed on the tables, too. There is a special family meal called a **seder.** *Seder* is the Hebrew word for "order of service." In the seder, families praise God and tell again the story of his saving love. Foods that symbolize the hardships the Israelites endured in Egypt are carefully arranged on the seder plate.

## The Christian Passover

Jesus celebrated the Passover each year and recalled with his people how God had freed them from slavery. At his last meal, Jesus raised the bread and wine. He prayed a prayer of praise and thanks for all God had done for his people. He said, "Do this in memory of me." But Jesus' meal was more than a memory of freedom; it was a gift of himself.

From that day on Jesus' followers have celebrated the sacred meal in remembrance of him. His suffering, death, and resurrection brought about complete freedom for all God's people. Jesus himself was the lamb whose blood saved the world. We celebrate his saving love at every Mass. There we are set free from sin and death.

## The Eucharist

Each Mass is a celebration of the great mystery Jesus left us as an everlasting covenant. The Mass has two main parts: the **Liturgy of the Word** and the **Liturgy of the Eucharist.** Together they form one act of worship.

During the Liturgy of the Word, God speaks to his people today. We hear the story of our salvation. We experience God's love for us and for all people as it is recorded in Scripture. The Scripture readings used at Mass are found in a book called the Lectionary. The **Lectionary** has readings for all the days of the year. There are readings for special times, like Easter. There are others for the saints honored throughout the year. There are readings for Masses celebrating the sacraments, special occasions, and votive Masses. **Votive Masses** celebrate the mysteries of the Lord or honor Mary and the saints outside of the assigned days.

In the Liturgy of the Eucharist, Jesus, as the new Moses, makes present his saving acts. He offers himself to the Father for us. We join in his sacrifice. Then he feeds us with the bread and wine that is himself. We are united and strengthened as God's people.

## Becoming God's People

It is said that when some sculptors look at a block of stone, they can see the beautiful statue trapped in it. Their hands can create a masterpiece from the stone. We are like that stone. We are masterpieces that want to be freed.

Listening to the Word, celebrating Christ's offering of himself for us, joining him in that offering, and sharing in the holy meal bring us life. Every Eucharist can change us. Usually this doesn't happen suddenly. Great things require time and care.

Those who open themselves to God will be filled. There is grace and power in the words of Scripture. There is grace and power in the Eucharistic sacrifice—the banquet of the new covenant.

How will you know if you are becoming the masterpiece you are meant to be? There are many signs. God's Word will come to mind unexpectedly. You will find the strength to begin to think through your actions and responses. You will talk to God more. You will be more concerned about the happiness of others. Slowly your view of life and the world will change—you will mature. You will be a happier person, more at peace.

The eucharistic celebration is not just remembering what God has done in the past. It is also celebrating what God is doing right now, right here, in you.

## Things to Do at Home

1. Read more about how God called Moses and saved the Israelites in Exodus 1–15.
2. Do research on the Jewish celebration of Passover. Write a report telling how the following are used in the celebration.

matzoh     bitter herb     haroset
wine     seder place     Haggadah

3. Plan with your family to have a seder celebration at home or to join with another family or group for this celebration.
4. Read your Bible to find the answers to the following questions.

What two cities in Egypt were built by Hebrew slaves? (Exodus 1:11)

_____

How many years had the Israelites been in Egypt? (Exodus 12:40)

_____

Why did God lead the people by a roundabout way to the Red Sea? (Exodus 13:17–18)

_____

_____

5. Prepare in a special way for your celebration of the liturgy this week. Pay close attention to the readings for the Mass. Listen for the message God has for you.

## We Remember

**What is the Exodus?**
The Exodus is the event in which God led the Israelites out of Egypt to freedom.

**What is Passover?**
Passover is the Jewish feast that celebrates God's freeing the Israelites from slavery.

**What do we celebrate at the Eucharist?**
At the Eucharist we celebrate the great mystery of Jesus' sacrifice and the holy meal that unites us, the new people of God, with him and one another.

### Words to Know

| | |
|---|---|
| plague | Exodus |
| Passover | seder |
| Lectionary | votive Mass |
| Liturgy of the Word | |
| Liturgy of the Eucharist | |

## We Respond

Give thanks to the LORD, who is good,
    whose love endures forever.
Psalm 118:1

# We Review

**The Great Escape**    Cecil B. De Mille made a famous movie of the Exodus called *The Ten Commandments.* Pretend you are in charge of the props for this movie. Match the props with the scenes that require them.

**A.** lamb, bread, herbs

**B.** burning bush

**C.** frogs

**D.** chariots

**E.** basket that floats

**F.** sheep

**G.** bricks

**H.** red water

_____ **1.** First days of Moses' life

_____ **2.** Hebrew slaves forced to labor for Egypt

_____ **3.** Moses goes to Midian because of his crime

_____ **4.** God speaks to Moses

_____ **5.** The first plague

_____ **6.** Another plague

_____ **7.** Passover meal the night the firstborn die

_____ **8.** Death of the Egyptians in the Red Sea

Identify the characters in the movie.

**A.** Moses

**B.** Aaron

**C.** God

**D.** Miriam

**E.** Pharaoh's Daughter

**F.** Reuel

**G.** Pharaoh

**H.** Hebrews

**I.** Egyptians

_____ **1.** "I am who am."

_____ **2.** The chosen people; descendants of Abraham

_____ **3.** Moses' sister

_____ **4.** Woman who adopted Moses

_____ **5.** Ruler who would not let the slaves in his land go into the desert to worship their God

_____ **6.** A poor speaker through whom God sent plagues to Egypt and rescued his people

_____ **7.** Moses' brother

**Three Sacred Meals**    Read each phrase and write the letter of the meal it matches. Phrases may have two answers.

**A.** Passover          **B.** Last Supper          **C.** Eucharist

_____ **1.** The celebration of the Jewish Passover by Jesus and his apostles

_____ **2.** The Christian commemoration of Jesus' saving acts

_____ **3.** The sacrifice of the Lamb of God on the cross

_____ **4.** Eaten in memory of God's saving his people from slavery in Egypt

_____ **5.** Called seder meal

_____ **6.** Includes readings from the lectionary

_____ **7.** Roasted lamb is eaten

_____ **8.** Brings about God's saving his people from sin and death

# God Gives Us the Law

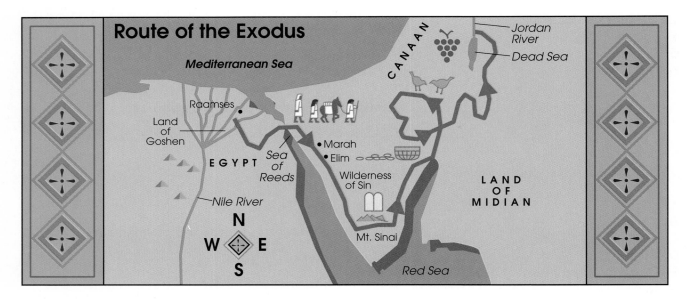

**Route of the Exodus**

Mediterranean Sea

CANAAN

Jordan River

Dead Sea

Raamses

Land of Goshen

EGYPT

Sea of Reeds

• Marah
• Elim

Wilderness of Sin

LAND OF MIDIAN

Nile River

Mt. Sinai

N
W   E
S

Red Sea

## Struggles in the Wilderness

based on Exodus 16, 17

Free from the Egyptians, the Israelites set out for the Promised Land. The direct route was dangerous. On that route the Israelites would have met enemies. Because they were not ready to defend themselves against attacks, God had Moses and Aaron lead the people by a longer, more indirect, route.

The Israelites' journey to the Promised Land was a difficult one through the wilderness. They were used to city life in Egypt and were not prepared for the hardships of the wilderness.

## At Marah in the Desert

The Israelites traveled three days without finding water. Finally they reached Marah, an oasis, but the water was so bitter that no one could drink it. When the people grumbled, Moses cried out to the Lord. God pointed out some wood and told Moses to throw it into the water.

When Moses obeyed, the water became fresh. Then God laid down a law for the people, saying, "Listen carefully to the Lord your God and do what is right in my eyes. Keep all my commandments, and I will be your healer."

## The Manna and the Quail

After the Israelites were refreshed, they set out again. They reached the Wilderness of Sin, which is between Elim and Sinai, almost two months after they had left Egypt. Once more they complained to Moses and Aaron: "Would that we had died at the Lord's hand in Egypt, as we sat by our fleshpots and ate our fill of bread! But you had to lead us into this desert to make the whole community die of famine!" Again Moses spoke to the Lord. God sent **quail** in the evening and manna in the morning to feed his people. The people found **manna** on the ground every day except the Sabbath. Manna was white flakes that tasted like wafers made with honey. The Israelites ate this bread for the rest of their journey.

## The Water from the Rock

One night the Israelites came to a campsite that had no water. Again they complained to Moses. Again Moses told God about the people's complaints. God directed Moses to take his staff and, in front of the people, strike one of the large rocks nearby. When Moses did as God had commanded, water flowed from the rock. Once again God showed love and care for his people.

The Israelites had much to learn before they would be ready to enter the Promised Land. God guided them as they wandered in the wilderness for forty years. Years later when they looked back, they remembered God's loving care for them. They had learned that they could trust God's plan for them.

Many of the psalms praise and thank God for his loving care. Find Psalm 111 in your Bible. Write verse 5 here.

_____

_____

## Our Journey to Heaven

Like the Israelites, we are on a journey. We must learn to trust God and to follow his directions. We must remember that God loves us and is constantly with us. Then our journey through life will be a happy one. God is good and wants us to enjoy the blessings he has prepared for us.

Match the experiences of the Israelites with ours. Draw lines from the sentences in the first column to those that match in the second column.

**The Israelites' Experiences**

**1.** God saves them by leading them through the waters of the Red Sea.

**2.** God speaks to them through Moses.

**3.** Life in the wilderness is difficult.

**4.** God feeds them with manna and quail

**5.** God makes his presence known in different ways.

**Our Experiences**

• In this life we must often face hardships.

• God feeds us with the Eucharist.

• God saves us through the waters of Baptism.

• God speaks to us through Jesus, through Sacred Scripture, and through his Church.

• God is present in his Word, in the sacraments, and in the good examples of those around us.

If you've ever gone camping, you know how important it is to have a guidebook. A good guidebook tells you how to get ready for your trip. It tells you what clothing, food, and supplies to pack and how to provide shelter.

A camper's guidebook helps you master the skills you need to have a good time. It explains how to light a fire and how to protect yourself from dangers. It has checklists to help you have a safe, enjoyable trip.

God, who loved his people, gave them guides to help them on life's journey.

### A Covenant with Yahweh

based on Exodus 19–25

When the Israelites reached Mount Sinai, Moses climbed the mountain where God had first spoken to him. This time God offered the Israelites a covenant. He gave Moses **commandments** and said that the Israelites would be his people if they followed his law. The people were grateful for these guides. They responded, "Everything the Lord has said, we will do!" Then they offered a sacrifice. The animal's blood that was sprinkled on the altar and on them sealed the covenant.

### A Reminder of the Covenant

Later God gave Moses the laws of the covenant written on tablets of stone. He told Moses to give the people a visible reminder that he was with them. "Build me a sanctuary," God said, "so that I may dwell among them." The Ten Commandments were to be kept in a special chest called an **ark** or the **ark of the covenant.** The ark was to be housed in a **Tent of Meeting,** a portable sanctuary.

God promised to speak with his people when they came before the ark of the covenant. The ark was a sign of God's presence. It was a reminder of the covenant God had made with his people.

Moses stayed on the mountain for forty days. The people, not knowing what had happened to him, went to Aaron and asked him to make them a god. Aaron collected gold from them and then fashioned a calf. The Israelites sacrificed to it and began celebrating. When Moses came down from the mountain, he saw the calf and the people dancing. In his anger, he threw down the tablets and broke them. Then he melted down the calf and ground it into powder.

Moses prayed to God for forgiveness for the people. He called the people stiff-necked, which means stubborn or haughty. He spoke to God as a friend. God renewed the covenant and replaced the broken tablets. This would not be the last time that the Israelites fell into the sin of **idolatry,** the worship of false gods. Surrounded by pagan neighbors, they would often give in to the temptation to be like them. They would break their covenant in which they promised to love and adore only Yahweh, the one true God.

The covenant with God on Sinai was an important event in the Israelites' journey to the Promised Land. By giving them the law, God showed his people how to live in love. Obeying the commandments would bring them peace and lead them safely to the end of their journey.

## God's Covenant with You

God has made a covenant with you. He has chosen you to be his and to show his love to the world. But God leaves you free. You can decide for yourself what kind of journey you want to make.

## Destination: Heaven

Think of life as a hike to God our Father. Fill in this plan and the guide for your spiritual hike.

Who will be your guide?

_____

What will help you map your way?

_____

Who will be your fellow hikers?

_____

How can they help you follow the trail God has shown you?

_____

## A Hiker's Guide

**1.** Use the proper kind of footgear: virtues or good habits. What virtues or good habits would help you feel comfortable and cheerful on the hike?

_____

**2.** Take plenty of good food. What food could nourish you and give you the spiritual strength you need?

_____

**3.** Take equipment you'll need along the way. What will help you get to your heavenly home?

_____

**4.** Be alert for dangers along the trail to heaven. What could harm you or cause delays?

_____

**5.** Know first-aid skills for spiritual hurts. How can you help yourself or others who are spiritually hurt?

_____

**6.** Obey rules for spiritual hikers. How should you show love and respect for people and things on the way?

_____

## Things to Do at Home

1. Make your hiker's guide into a booklet and design the pages. Share it with the class.
2. Make a replica of the ark of the covenant. This was a gold-plated box. On top was a throne flanked by two cherubim (angels) who covered it with their wings. Inside were manna and the tablets of the Law.
3. A time capsule is a collection of familiar objects that are preserved in one period to show people of the future how those of another time lived. Imagine that you were one of the Israelites who experienced the Exodus. What would you include in your time capsule?
4. On a piece of sandpaper use crayons to depict a scene or symbol from the Exodus. Your art could be part of a bulletin board in your classroom or Lenten display in your parish.
5. Discuss with your family the "Duties of a Catholic Christian" listed under "Things Every Catholic Should Know" on pages 4 and 5 of your book. How do you carry out these Church precepts (laws) that every Catholic must follow?

## We Remember

**What promises were made in the covenant between God and his people?**

In the covenant, God promised the Israelites that they would be his people. The Israelites promised to do everything the Lord had said.

### Words to Know

| | |
|---|---|
| quail | Tent of Meeting |
| manna | ark of the covenant |
| idolatry | |

## We Respond

Think of a definite time when you can praise and thank God each day. Write your prayer time here.

_____

# We Review

**Moses' Log**    Suppose Moses had kept a log, or record, on the journey to Canaan. Fill in the blanks.

To avoid _____, we are taking a difficult route to Canaan. This was our third day without water. We finally reached _____, but the water there was bitter. At God's command, I threw _____ on the water, and it became sweet.

It's been two months since we left. The people long to return to Egypt, where they ate well. This evening God sent _____, and we were able to have fresh meat. This morning God fed us in an amazing way. When we awoke, white flakes were covering the ground. They were like sweet wafers. We called them _____.

Tonight we had to camp at a place without water. Again the people complained. God had me strike a _____ with my staff, and water flowed out.

What a tremendous gift God has given us! Today on Mt. _____ he gave us his Law. We sealed a covenant with God by offering a sacrifice and sprinkling its blood on the _____ and on the people.

Today God instructed me to build a visible reminder of his presence with us. We will make a chest called an _____ and keep it in a _____.

After forty days with God on Sinai, I brought down the tablets on which he had written out the Law for us. To my horror, the Israelites were worshiping a _____.

They had already fallen into the sin of _____.

**Covenant Terms**    A covenant is like the two sides of a coin. Write God's promise on one side of the coin and the Israelites' promise on the other side.

# 12

# We Live the Commandments Today

## A Sign of Love

Everyone wants to be happy, but people have different opinions about what brings true happiness. What about you? Write at least three things that make you happy.

1. _____

_____

2. _____

_____

3. _____

_____

The search for happiness was very real for the Israelites. They had escaped from a foreign country where they had been treated cruelly. They had journeyed through harsh desert.

Yet the Israelites had their belief in Yahweh to support them. They wanted to be his chosen people. That is why they were filled with joy when God made his covenant with them at Sinai. For the Israelites, the commandments were a sign of God's love. They were part of their recipe for happiness. People would look at the Israelites and know that their God was close to his people.

Why did the Israelites love the law so much? First of all, the commandments showed them how to be free from ignorance and selfishness. Many of the laws were known to them before they received the commandments. God has implanted in the heart of each human being natural laws as a guide. With the giving of these laws, the Israelites were assured that obedience to these laws would lead to happiness.

Second, their obedience would be a way to unite them to Yahweh. Since God would not force them to obey, their free response would be a sign of their love.

Finally, these commandments would unite the Israelites and set them apart from all others as the people of God. The law would help them live together in peace. It would help them live according to God's plan for them.

The Israelites often expressed their gratitude to God in songs and praise.

Your commandments fill me with
delight.
I love them deeply.
I stretch out my hands to your beloved
commandments.
I meditate on your statutes.
I rejoice in your promise
like someone on finding a vast
treasure.
I keep your decrees.
They are the joy of my heart.
adapted from Psalm 119:47, 48,
162, 167, 111

# YOU SHALL LOVE

The commandments are often divided into two groups. One group addresses our relationship with God. The other group addresses our relationship with others. When Jesus spoke of the law, he used this division. All God's laws call us to protect and promote our own lives and the lives of others! Guided by the Holy Spirit, the Church tells us how God's laws apply from age to age.

**1**
I, THE LORD, AM YOUR GOD. YOU SHALL NOT HAVE OTHER GODS BESIDES ME.

**2**
YOU SHALL NOT TAKE THE NAME OF THE LORD, YOUR GOD, IN VAIN.

**3**
REMEMBER TO KEEP HOLY THE SABBATH DAY.

**4**
HONOR YOUR FATHER AND YOUR MOTHER.

**5**
YOU SHALL NOT KILL.

**6**
YOU SHALL NOT COMMIT ADULTERY.

**7**
YOU SHALL NOT STEAL.

**8**
YOU SHALL NOT BEAR FALSE WITNESS AGAINST YOUR NEIGHBOR.

**9**
YOU SHALL NOT COVET YOUR NEIGHBOR'S WIFE.

**10**
YOU SHALL NOT COVET ANYTHING THAT BELONGS TO YOUR NEIGHBOR.

Read Mark 12:30–31. Write the words of Jesus that summarize the first group.

_____

_____

_____

_____

Write the words of Jesus that summarize the second group.

_____

_____

LOVE

summarizes all the commandments.

_____

We use the word *love* so often that sometimes we forget what it really means. The commandments remind us that love makes demands on us. They help us express our love in practical ways. They help us learn to live in peace with one another.

Read these stories. Underline the names of the people who show they understand the meaning of love.

 Tanya and Courtney had promised to be best friends always. They were on the same swim team and shared many hobbies. But Tanya had other friends who disliked Courtney. When she was with these other girls, Tanya would ignore Courtney.

 Carlos liked to be with his friends. He enjoyed entertaining others by making up jokes and stories about people in the neighborhood. He would mock teachers, old people, and even friends. Soon very few of the boys wanted to be real friends with him.

 Kristen's longtime friend, Antoinette, moved to California with her family. Kristen set aside time each week to write to her. At first Antoinette answered the letters right away. But eventually the letters stopped coming, even though Kristen had continued to write.

How would you describe a loving person? Finish this statement:

When people say they love us, we expect them to

_____

_____

_____

## Loving God

Like the Israelites, we can express our love for God by obeying the commandments. Loving God means we respect him, speak to him, listen to him, and speak reverently about him. Loving God means wanting to spend time with him in prayer and worship.

In his goodness God created all things. In Jesus he has revealed his tremendous love for us. To trust in people or in things more than in God shows we do not really know and love him.

Discuss: How does belief in any of the following show a lack of trust in God?

✢ superstitions, good luck charms
✢ astrology charts
✢ fortune tellers, palm readers
✢ chain and prayer letters
✢ ouija boards
✢ seances, spiritualism

## The Language of Love

God wants us to "keep in touch." He wants us to keep him in our lives. We can refer to this "keeping in touch" as prayer. Prayer can be simple and spontaneous.

*Sharing love with family and friends often leads to feeling our Father's care.*

*The words of a song may make us think of God.*

*Talking to God before we go to sleep and when we wake up keeps us in touch with God.*

*A beautiful, crisp autumn day may help us turn our hearts to God.*

*Visits to church and celebrating the Eucharist help us remain close to God.*

## The Power of a Name

Our names are special. They identify us as unique. God's name is special, too. Out of love we try to honor God's name.

Read the following words and definitions. If the word describes a respectful use of God's name or the gift of speech, place a (✓) in front of it. If the word describes a disrespectful use, place an X in front of it.

_____ **1.** blessing—a prayer asking God to make someone or something holy

_____ **2.** oath—calling on God to witness to the truth of what someone says

_____ **3.** perjury—lying while under oath; asking God to witness a lie

_____ **4.** cursing—calling down evil on someone or something

_____ **5.** swearing—taking an oath

_____ **6.** blasphemy—speaking against God in a hateful manner

_____ **7.** profanity—speaking of a blessed person, place, or thing with disrespect

_____ **8.** prayer—lifting up the mind and heart to God

## Special Times of Love

We enjoy being with those we love. We look forward to spending special times with them. God knew his people needed these special times, and so he invited them to observe the **Sabbath,** the holy day. This day would be a time to rest, to forget about ordinary matters and everyday problems. It would be spent trusting in the Father's love and care.

This day was also the time for the community to come together and renew their relationship with God. It is the same for us. We are not alone on this journey to heaven. We can find joy and strength in worshiping God with the Church at Mass. This is our greatest form of prayer.

By Church law Catholics offer this special worship in **Sunday Mass.** Sunday reminds us of the creation of the world by the Father, the resurrection of Christ, and the coming of the Holy Spirit on Pentecost. Every Sunday is a little Easter because we celebrate the Lord's resurrection. Other days set aside for special celebration are called **holy days of obligation.** They are listed in "Things Every Catholic Should Know" on pages 4 and 5. On these days Church law obliges us to honor Jesus, Mary, or the saints at the Eucharist. Which one will you celebrate next?

## The Life of Christ— The Life of the Church

The life, death, and resurrection of Jesus are remembered and celebrated in the Church throughout the year. These celebrations make up the liturgical year, or church year. See the diagram of the **liturgical year** on page 95.

The early Christians celebrated only one feast: Easter. Soon they began to include a celebration of Christ's birth. Easter and Christmas were celebrated with special readings from the Scriptures. The weeks before these two great events were spent in preparation. The time before Christmas is called **Advent;** the time before Easter is called **Lent.**

**Ordinary Time** is the time between the seasons of Christmas and Lent, Easter and Advent. During Ordinary Time the readings center on the teachings of Jesus and his life.

Eventually a whole calendar of feasts and celebrations for the church year was formed. The liturgical year begins with the First Sunday of Advent and ends with the Feast of Christ the King.

The Sunday readings are divided into three cycles: A, B, and C. It takes one year to complete each cycle. After three years, the community has heard the most important readings from Scripture. Again and again, we recall God's plan of salvation and his overwhelming love for us.

**Friendship Survey**

Think about . . .
   who your best friend was last year.
   who your best friend is this year.

How would you finish these sentences?

1. When I get upset with my friend, I usually . . .

   ✤ pretend nothing is the matter.
   ✤ tell my friend how I feel and try to settle our problems.
   ✤ talk behind my friend's back.
   ✤ ignore my friend for a while and make friends with others.

2. When my friend wants to do one thing and I want to do something else, I usually . . .

   ✤ argue about it, trying to convince my friend to do it my way.
   ✤ give in and do whatever my friend wants.
   ✤ sometimes do what I want; sometimes do what my friend wants.

3. When my friend wins a game or a contest, or scores better on an assignment than I do, I usually . . .

   ✤ feel very happy.
   ✤ feel bad I didn't do as well.
   ✤ congratulate my friend right away.
   ✤ feel a little angry and jealous.

Check (✓) how you rate as a friend.

   ❏ Ever-faithful
   ❏ Need improvement
   ❏ Running about average
   ❏ Not worth having

## A Heart for Others

Friends. Everyone wants to have them. We like to have others around and to share our thoughts and feelings with them. We need to know we are loved. We need to know others accept us and are willing to be patient with us. Sooner or later we discover that love is a two-way street. We must give if we wish to receive.

Jesus understood our need to share and be with people. He was aware of the difficulties that come with living with others. So he gave us the example of his own life to show us how to love. He gave us other guidelines also.

Read Matthew 7:12. What title is given to this section?

_____

Write Jesus' advice here.

_____

_____

# THE GOLDEN RULE IN ACTION

What does it mean to treat others as you would like to be treated? Here's your chance to find out! After each sentence below write what you would do to treat others as you would like them to treat you. Then finish the concluding sentence.

**1.** I don't want other people to lie to me.

_____

**2.** I don't want people to damage or steal things I own.

_____

**3.** I don't want others to talk behind my back or tell others about my mistakes and faults.

_____

**4.** I don't want others to copy my work and take credit for the work I do.

_____

**5.** I want loyal friends and a family that loves me in spite of my faults and mistakes.

_____

**6.** I want people to thank me when I do things for them and notice when I try my best.

_____

**7.** I want people to apologize when they hurt me and to make peace with me.

_____

**8.** I want to be included in a group at lunch and outside at games.

_____

**9.** I want others to respect me enough that they will not use crude or embarrassing language when I am around.

_____

I want to be the kind of person who  _____

*If that's what you want, start today!*

As you make decisions in life, ask yourself:

✠ What does God ask of me in his commandments?
✠ What would Jesus do?
✠ How should I act if I am trying to follow the Golden Rule?

And if at first you don't succeed, try, try again! That's what matters!

## A New Commandment

On the night before he died, Jesus gave his followers a new commandment. It was a command of love. This love was to be the sign of the Christian. The Ten Commandments demanded love, too. But now Jesus demanded more.

*Our love . . .*

*must be like his love for us.*
*is to be given to all, even enemies.*
*is willing to make sacrifices for others.*
*may mean a share in carrying the cross.*
*will lead us to the Father.*

Write the new commandment found in John 13:34–35.

_____

_____

_____

Some people follow the rules and keep the commandments, but do not really love. Jesus spoke out against this empty kind of loving. God wants our hearts.

## Things to Do at Home

1. Get ten 3-by-5-inch cards. Write a commandment on each card and its number on the back. Use the cards to help you memorize the commandments. After you know them all by heart, mix the cards and put them in the correct order. Then recite them to one of your parents, a teacher, or a classmate. When you can recite them all without help, ask the listener to place a check (✔) in the box below.

   ❏ Parent
   ❏ Teacher
   ❏ Classmate

2. Interview your parents or other adults to find out how their families spent Sunday when they were children. Compare Sunday customs of today with those of years ago.

3. For one day try to keep track of all the acts of love you observe from the time you get up in the morning to the time you go to bed. If possible, jot them down on a sheet of paper. Share your observations with someone. Then include a prayer of thanks at the end of the day for all the goodness in your life.

4. Words are important. Think of the way you speak to others. Do your words bring others happiness or do they hurt others?

5. Memorize one of the following Scripture passages: Mark 12:29–31; John 13:34–35; Matthew 5:1–10.

6. Listen carefully to the lyrics of several popular songs. Make a list of those that show a true understanding of love and friendship and those that do not. Then try to write your own song or poem on the same theme.

## We Remember

**What are the two great commandments?**
The first great commandment is that you shall love the Lord your God with all your heart, with all your soul, with all your mind, and with all your strength. The second is that you shall love your neighbor as yourself.

**What new commandment did Jesus give at the Last Supper?**
At the Last Supper Jesus said, "I give you a new commandment: love one another. As I have loved you, so you also should love one another." (John 13:34)

---

### Words to Know

| | |
|---|---|
| oath | blasphemy |
| perjury | liturgical year |
| cursing | Advent |
| swearing | Lent |
| profanity | Ordinary Time |
| holy days of obligation | |

### Words to Memorize
the Ten Commandments
the holy days of obligation

---

## We Respond

"No one has greater love than this, to lay down one's life for one's friends."

John 15:13

Lord, I will try to remember your special love for me today. I will try to show my gratitude for this love by

_____

_____

## We Review

**A Test of Love**   Draw a heart on the line before each true sentence.

_____ **1.** The Ten Commandments were a sign of God's love.
_____ **2.** The Israelites resented having to keep the Ten Commandments.
_____ **3.** The commandments led to true happiness.
_____ **4.** The commandments united the Israelites.
_____ **5.** God's law made the Israelites like all other peoples.
_____ **6.** It is not enough to follow the commandments; we must do so out of love.

Choose one of the Ten Commandments. Tell how it shows love of God or love of others.

_____

_____

_____

_____

_____

_____

_____

**What's the Law?**   Match the laws with their identification.
**A.** The Ten Commandments
**B.** The two great commandments
**C.** The Golden Rule
**D.** Jesus' new commandment
**E.** Love

_____ **1.** Love God and love your neighbor as yourself.
_____ **2.** This law was given on Mt. Sinai.
_____ **3.** It summarized all the commandments.
_____ **4.** Treat other people as you would like to be treated.
_____ **5.** Love one another as Jesus loves us.

**The Liturgical Year** Here is a diagram of the liturgical year. Refer to it as you do the following activities.

**1.** Color Advent and Lent violet.

**2.** Color the seasons of Ordinary Time green.

**3.** Leave Christmas and Easter white.

**4.** The longest season of the liturgical year is

_____.

**5.** The new Church year begins on

_____.

**6.** The year ends on the feast of

_____.

**7.** What does the Church recall and celebrate during the year?

_____

_____

**8.** Name two holy days of obligation.

_____

_____

_____

**9.** What are we obliged to do to celebrate that day?

_____

# God's People
## Learn God's Way

**13**

### Learning to Live as God's People

Most of us do not like to wait. We want what we want NOW! If we have to wait a long time, we often become impatient. We may begin to complain about those who keep us waiting.

We are not too different from the Israelites. They wanted the Promised Land immediately! But they were not yet ready. The fulfillment of God's plan for them took many years in the desert. After spending more than a year at Sinai, they were on their way again, following the cloud, the sign of God's presence, to Canaan.

### A Fearful People

based on Numbers 13, 14:1–38

When the Israelites reached Canaan, Moses sent out a leader from each of the twelve tribes to survey the land. After forty days they returned, two of them carrying a branch with a cluster of grapes. The scouts reported, "We went into the land to which you sent us. It does, indeed, flow with milk and honey, but its people are fierce. The towns are fortified and strong!" Caleb of the tribe of Judah proclaimed, "We ought to seize this land. We can do it." Moses and Aaron agreed.

Read Numbers 13:31–33 to learn how the other men described the land and people of Canaan. Write their description in your own words.

_____

_____

How would you have felt after hearing about Canaan?

_____

Would you have decided to march into the land? Why or why not?

_____

The people were filled with fear. They wanted to choose a new leader and return to Egypt. Joshua, another leader who had surveyed Canaan, joined Caleb to defend Moses and Aaron. They said to the people, "If the Lord is pleased with us, he will lead us into this land and give it to us. Do not rebel against the Lord. Do not be afraid of the people of this land; the Lord is with us." The people did not listen and threatened to stone them. They had made their decision: they would not march against Canaan.

Suddenly the glory of the Lord appeared at the Tent of Meeting. God asked Moses, "How long will this people insult me? How long will they refuse to believe in me despite the signs I have performed among them?" God said he would strike them with sickness and disown them.

Moses prayed on behalf of the people. God agreed not to destroy them. In his mercy, he forgave them but let them suffer the results of their sins. They would not see the land that God had promised their fathers. Instead they would spend forty years in the wilderness, moving slowly to the east side of Canaan. Only Caleb and Joshua, who had followed God faithfully, and some of the young children would live to enter Canaan.

## A Complaining People

based on Numbers 20:1–13

During these years of wandering, the people could not quite put their faith totally in the Lord. Each time they met a problem, they grumbled and complained. They blamed Moses and Aaron. They wished they were back in Egypt—or even dead. But God understood his people. Whenever Moses prayed for them, the Lord provided for them in some new way.

Can you recall two ways in which God provided for his complaining people?

_____

_____

_____

_____

When the Israelites arrived at Meribah, they complained that it did not have figs, vines, or pomegranates. They complained because there was no water to drink. Moses and Aaron again pleaded with the Lord. God told Moses to call the people together and to cause water to flow from a rock by striking it with his staff. Moses questioned whether God would have mercy on the rebels.

Then he struck the rock twice, perhaps because his faith was weak. God did answer Moses' prayer, but he was not pleased. The Lord spoke to Moses and Aaron, "Because you were not faithful to me in showing forth my sanctity before the Israelites, you shall not lead this assembly into the land I will give them."

The reason for God's displeasure seems to be Moses' lack of faith in God's unfailing love for the people. In any case, this story shows that we must accept the results of our actions and decisions.

### Real or Fake?

How useless is fake money! We call it counterfeit. It has no buying power, and it can bring a lot of trouble. The same is true of counterfeit Christians. They do not have the joy and peace of Christ. Instead, their sins bring sorrow to themselves and others.

People expect Christians to act as Christians, to make decisions according to the teachings of Christ. Are you a real Christian, or are you a counterfeit one? People can tell by looking at the choices you make. God has chosen you to be one of his special people. When others see the choices you make, are they able to recognize you as one who follows Jesus?

### A Power to Judge

How do you know that stealing is wrong and that telling the truth is right? Some things are wrong by nature. Not even a good intention or certain circumstances will ever make these evil things good. All people have the power within themselves to judge how good or bad an act is. This power is **conscience.** Our conscience is a wonderful gift. We should educate it according to the teachings of Christ and act according to our conscience's advice.

In some ways, conscience can be compared to a computer. If a conscience is fed accurate data and is in good working order, it makes correct and good judgments. If it is fed the wrong data, it will not be able to make correct judgments. If a computer is ignored, it will soon break down and be unable to do its job. So, too, if our conscience is ignored over a long period of time, it will not be able to make good decisions. There is, however, a big difference between conscience and a computer. A computer is a machine. Conscience is a power of a human being and can be guided by the Holy Spirit.

### Decision-Making Vocabulary

To learn how a computer works, we must study some computer terms. To learn how conscience works, we must also know the meanings of some important words.

**Obligations** are duties we have because we have agreed to them and accepted certain rights and privileges. Because we are God's people and agree to do what he wants, the Ten Commandments are obligations for us.

*When Beth agrees to baby-sit for her neighbor, Mrs. Schultz, she has certain obligations. Can you name some?*

**Principles** are truths we believe in strongly enough to act on them. They help us decide how to act in different situations. Jesus gave us many principles in his Sermon on the Mount and at the Last Supper.

*Beth has principles she believes in. One is that she must keep her word. Now she has been invited to go skating on the same night she has agreed to baby-sit for Mrs. Schultz. What decision will she make if she really lives by her principles?*

**Consequences** are the results of choices. Sometimes we can be sure of consequences; at other times we cannot. Sometimes we can be sure of only some of the consequences.

*What consequences can Beth be sure of if she keeps her word and baby-sits for Mrs. Schultz? What will happen if she chooses to go back on her word? What are some consequences she cannot be sure of?*

## Making a Decision

All people have decisions to make. People who want to follow Jesus will ask the Holy Spirit to guide them in making their decisions.

Conscience helps us make decisions in particular situations. We decide if we have any *obligation* to make one special choice. We then ask ourselves if our *principles* demand a certain choice. Finally, we look at the possible *consequences*. We ask if a choice would weaken our friendship with God or be harmful to us or others. After we do this, conscience makes its judgment. Conscience always judges in favor of what it sees as good.

After conscience has made its judgment, we can choose to follow its decision or ignore it. Feelings or desires can oppose our choice if we let them.

*If Beth is fearful that she will not be invited to go skating again, she may choose to go back on her word. She may even decide to lie about the reason she cannot baby-sit.*

*If Beth is a good skater and wants to impress her friends, she may decide to go back on her word and go skating instead.*

What feelings or desires could lead Beth to go back on her word?

_____

What feelings or desires could lead Beth to keep her word?

_____

_____

Once we have made a decision and acted on it, conscience goes back to work. It informs us whether our choice was good or bad. If we have chosen the good, we will be at peace. If conscience tells us the choice was not good, we will be uneasy and unhappy. This uneasy feeling is good. It is a warning signal that we are going away from God. It helps us realize we must follow our conscience to find real happiness.

As you can see, conscience is a big help in daily decision making. We must remember to listen to and follow its judgment. When we follow the judgment of a good conscience, we become more like Jesus. Then people will recognize us as true Christians, not counterfeits.

## Conscience at Work

Read each of the following situations and answer the questions.

The other boys make fun of Dominic because he will not go to the deli with them. His dad has forbidden him to go because drugs are passed around there. Dominic is tired of being made fun of. He does not intend to take any drugs. His dad is out of town.

What obligation will help Dominic decide if he will go to the deli?

_____

What commandment requires this of him?

_____

What decision do you think Dominic should make? Should he go to the deli just this one time? Give a reason for your choice.

_____

_____

Judy has gone camping. She has planned to be home to go to Mass Sunday evening. On the way home someone suggests stopping to visit a girl who lives close to camp. Because it is already late, Judy knows the visit would cause her to miss Mass.

Judy has an obligation to go to Mass every Sunday if it is possible. She believes that there are times when she is responsible to speak and not keep silent. Should she speak up now?

_____

What will the consequence be if Judy does not say that she wants to get home for Mass?

_____

Tell two things that might happen if she does say that she wants to go home now.

_____

_____

All Steve's friends have decided to spend Saturday at the mall. Everyone is to bring enough money to buy lunch and to play the pinball machines. Steve wants to go, but he has been saving his money to send to some poor children. They need winter clothes.

What do you think Steve should decide?

_____

What Christian principle or obligation can help him decide?

_____

## Things to Do at Home

1. Show your parents the "Decision-Making Vocabulary." After watching a TV program together, discuss the decisions that were made. Were the people aware of their obligations? Do you know any of the principles on which they based their decisions?
2. Look at the Sermon on the Mount (Matthew 5–7) and pick out at least three principles that are very important in the life of a real Christian.
3. After looking at the newspaper or watching the news on TV, spend at least five minutes praying for sinners. Ask God to forgive them and to help them make up for their sins. Pray Moses' prayer (Numbers 14:13–19) if you wish.
4. The law required Israelites to tithe or give ten percent of all they owned for religious purposes. You might make a decision to give ten percent of any money you receive to the Church or to the poor.

## We Remember

**How does our conscience help us with our decisions?**
Conscience helps us to make decisions based on our obligations, principles, and consequences.

## We Respond

Write a prayer asking the Holy Spirit to teach you to make Christlike decisions.

_____

_____

                                        .

_____

## We Review

**Decisions, Decisions!**    Analyze the Israelites' decisions not to go into Canaan, using the vocabulary you learned.

1. The Israelites should have known what to do because they had a power within themselves to judge how good or bad an act is. This power is _____.

2. The Israelites had promised to do whatever God asked. When God asked them through their leaders to go into Canaan, they had an _____ to do so.

3. The Israelites knew that God was with them and would help them and that therefore they could trust God. They should have acted on this _____.

4. Whenever the Israelites did not follow God's Law, they suffered. They should have considered this _____ when they decided not to go into Canaan.

5. As they wandered in the desert and realized they had made the wrong decision, the Israelites' _____ probably bothered them.

**Spies**   Complete this rap about the arrival at Canaan. Then say it together with a group.

When the chosen people came to the Promised _____,

Their leader named _____ made this demand,

"Let twelve men go, one from each tribe,

To scout the land. May they come back alive."

The spies were gone for forty days.

On their return they had nothing but praise:

"Canaan's flowing with milk and _____.

Look at these grapes. But this isn't funny:

The people are _____ and their towns are strong.

If we value our lives, we'll move right along."

Only Joshua and _____ with Moses and Aaron

Trusted God enough to be quite daring.

"We can do it," they said. "Let's attack."

"No way," said the others. "To Egypt! Turn back!"

So for forty long _____ they had to wander.

Their bad decision is something to ponder.

**Rewards**   Answer these questions.

**1.** Why were Joshua and Caleb the only two original Israelites privileged to enter the

Promised Land? _____

_____

**2.** According to the Bible, why wasn't Moses allowed to enter Canaan? _____

_____

## A Bronze Serpent

based on Numbers 21:4–9

Have you ever seen a snake gliding near you? How did you feel? How did you act? Do you know which snakes are poisonous? Many people are fearful of snakes, even those that are harmless. They do not trust any snake.

Throughout the Israelites' years in the wilderness, God had provided for their needs. But now they had grown tired of the manna God had given them. They said, "We are sick of this tasteless food." They complained about Moses and even about God.

The Bible tells us that God sent serpents among them. The bites of these snakes caused death. Only after many had died from poisonous bites did the people realize their sinfulness.

The people went to Moses and admitted that they had sinned by speaking against him and against God. They asked him to intercede for them so that God would save them from the snakes. Moses prayed, and God answered his prayer. He told Moses to make a bronze snake and to put it on a pole where the people could see it. People who had been bitten by a snake came to see the bronze serpent. They had faith in God's power to heal them. These people lived. They were healed of the terrible snakebites.

## Christ's Saving Death

Hundreds of years later, when the Gospel of John was written, this story was remembered. John tells us about a conversation between Jesus and Nicodemus. In this conversation, Jesus refers to Moses and the bronze serpent.

 And just as Moses lifted up the serpent in the desert, so must the Son of Man be lifted up, so that everyone who believes in him may have eternal life.

John 3:14–15

Who is the Son of Man? _____

How was the Son of Man lifted up?

_____

What happened when people looked at the serpent Moses lifted up?

_____

_____

What will the Son of Man do for us now because he has been lifted up?

_____

The lifting up of the snake hinted at what would later happen to Jesus. We say it **prefigured** Jesus. The healing of the people who looked at the bronze serpent prefigured the healing of those who would believe in Jesus.

When Jesus was lifted up on the cross, he offered a perfect sacrifice of obedience to the Father. He offered his sacrifice in the name of all sinners, totally making up for sin. But we must have faith in his sacrifice.

Some things we can do to show our faith in the sacrifice of Jesus are

✢ being sorry for sin.
✢ being willing to make up for sin.
✢ trying to live according to the law of love.
✢ trying to become more and more like Jesus.

With faith like this we will become reconciled to God. Our friendship with him will grow.

## Rejoicing in Our Redeemer

We can be healed and reconciled with the Father because Jesus was lifted up on the cross. We can also share in his resurrection and ascension into glory. We rejoice with him. We praise him. We thank him for his death, which is the promise of our life.

Read the following poem and complete the last two statements.

### Look at the Crucifix

If you would like to know God,
   look at the crucifix.

If you wonder how much he wants you in heaven,
   look at the crucifix.

If you wonder what you are worth,
   look at the crucifix.

If you _____,
   look at the crucifix.

If you _____,
   look at the crucifix.

# A Thanksgiving Song

Praise is rightfully yours,
   God, in Zion.
Vows to you must be fulfilled,
   for you answer prayer.

All flesh must come to you
   with all its sins;
though our faults overpower us,
   you blot them out.

Happy the man you choose, whom you invite
   to live in your courts.
Fill us with the good things of your house,
   of your holy Temple.

Psalm 65:1–4 (JB)

## Reconciliation in Our Lives

Sin is the worst evil in the world. It is the cause of many other evils. It caused the death of Jesus, but by his death Jesus broke the power of sin. His sacrifice has the power to help us overcome sin in our lives. Through Jesus our friendship with God can be restored and strengthened.

We know that everyone is weak. Even though we love God and try to serve him, we sin. Our sins do not bring happiness. They damage our relationship with God, with other people, and even with ourselves.

God recognizes our weakness and is not surprised by our sins. He always loves us and wants to give us his forgiveness. All we need to do is turn to God, express our sorrow, and promise to do better. Then we will be reconciled. Our friendship with God will grow stronger.

## Receiving Forgiveness

God in his goodness has given us several ways to be reconciled with him when we have sinned. They are

✠ the Sacrament of Reconciliation (Penance).
✠ an act of love.
✠ an act of contrition.
✠ the Eucharist.

The following paragraphs explain each of these ways of being reconciled. After each section identify the type of reconciliation being described.

 When we have said or done something that hurts a friend, we feel unhappy until we say, "I'm sorry. Will you please forgive me?" If this is true with our friends, it should be even truer with God. As soon as we recognize that we have sinned, we should ask his forgiveness. God's answer will not be heard with our ears, but we will know it in our hearts: "Your sins are forgiven" (Luke 5:20).

 Sometimes we want to do more than say we are sorry when we hurt others. We want to do things that show that we are sorry. We want to love them and help them. We can also be reconciled with God by doing things that show how much we love him.

 In the Eucharist we remember that Jesus loved us enough to suffer and die for us. He offered this sacrifice to restore us to perfect friendship with his Father. In every Mass Jesus offers this same sacrifice for us. As we participate we express our sorrow for anything we have done to separate ourselves from the Father. We ask Jesus to help us make up for our sins and to become more like him. The Penitential Rite can remove our sins if we are truly sorry.

The fullest sign of God's forgiveness comes when Jesus gives himself to us in Holy Communion. He who is all holy takes away anything that separates us from himself.

 When we confess our sins with sorrow, we can be sure that Christ will heal us. He will restore our relationship with God no matter how serious our sins are.

## What to Confess

A person who commits a mortal sin should ask God's forgiveness immediately in his or her heart. Then the person must also confess the sin in the Sacrament of Reconciliation. Until this is done he or she may not receive Communion.

A mortal sin should be confessed with enough information to let the priest know how serious the sin is. We must also confess the number of times we have committed each mortal sin.

We have committed a **mortal sin** only if

✢ we have done something which is *seriously* wrong,
✢ we *knew* it was seriously wrong, and
✢ we *freely* and *willingly* chose to do it.

If one of those conditions is missing, the sin is not mortal. A serious sin is not always a mortal sin. If the person did not know that something was seriously wrong, it was not a mortal sin. If something happened so quickly that a person did not really have time to choose freely, it was not a mortal sin.

**Venial sins,** lesser sins, can be forgiven in other ways, but it is good to confess them in the Sacrament of Reconciliation. We receive special help to overcome them in this sacrament. The priest can help us to get at the roots of our sins and bad habits.

## Healing and Growth

God has given us the Sacrament of Reconciliation to help us overcome sin. Through this sacrament our mortal and venial sins are forgiven. The wounds in our minds and wills caused by sin are healed. The life-giving power of this sacrament, grace, remains with us in our daily life. It strengthens us so that when we are tempted again, we will be more likely to say no to temptation and yes to God.

The Sacrament of Reconciliation helps us know ourselves better. Examining our conscience is like looking in the mirror. We see the times we have accepted God's **grace** and have done what he asked. We see our good habits and our bad habits. We see where we are weak and where we are strong.

Looking in this mirror regularly will help us know if we are growing in love for God and others. Each time we receive forgiveness in the Sacrament of Reconciliation, we grow stronger in God's life and love. This sacrament helps us correct our bad habits and form good ones. It helps our conscience recognize the good and strengthens our will to choose it.

As the good becomes a habit, we grow in **virtue.** A virtue is a habit of doing something good. We do it because it is what God wants for our own happiness and the happiness of others.

## Name the Virtue

As young people described below overcome their sins, they will grow in virtue. Choose the virtue each young person will be putting into his or her life.

consideration     truthfulness     humility     obedience     patience     generosity

Sam gets plenty of money to spend every week. He buys everything he wants but does not share with anyone. Then he sees that he has been very selfish. He decides to put one-fourth of his spending money in the poor box at church this month. He will grow in the virtue of

Raymond turns the volume of his radio up very loud after school. He realized that he has been very thoughtless because he knows the noise gets on his mother's nerves. He is going to try to remember to keep the volume low. He is growing in the virtue of

_____.

_____.

Maryann got in the habit of lying in order not to be punished. She knows this is wrong and is trying to tell the truth even if she will be punished. She is growing in the virtue of

Frank always gets good grades without studying. He brags to Dave, who usually gets Ds on tests even when he studies hard. Frank recognizes that he has been very proud. He offers to help Dave with his math every night. Frank is growing in the virtue of

_____.

_____.

Julie gets very angry every time her brother teases her. If she tries to laugh instead of getting angry, she will grow in the virtue of

**What about You?**
What is one virtue you have?
What is your worst bad habit?
What virtue could take its place?

Think of two ways you can practice that virtue. Decide what you will do today.

_____.

## Things to Do at Home

1. Think of each member of your family. What is each person's most outstanding virtue? Thank God for the goodness each person brings into your life.
2. Ask someone you know and love to tell you what he or she thinks is your most outstanding virtue. Thank God for this gift and try to make it grow even stronger. Ask God to help you with his grace.
3. Ask for an old missalette from your church. Cut out the prayers of the Mass that call us to reconciliation. Put each one on a card and label it. Explain each one.
4. Memorize Psalm 65 and pray it whenever you think of God's loving forgiveness.

---

### Words to Know
prefigure    virtue       grace
venial sin   mortal sin

### Words to Memorize
an act of contrition

---

## We Remember

**What are four ways of being reconciled with God?**
Four ways of being reconciled with God are the Sacrament of Reconciliation, an act of contrition, an act of love, and the Eucharist.

**What is a virtue?**
A virtue is a habit of doing something good—something that God wants us to do.

## We Respond

Choose one virtue you want to have in your life. Each evening when you examine your conscience, think about how you have practiced that virtue during the day.

## We Review

**From Death to Life**    Use the clues to fill in the acrostic.

1. This sacrament celebrates the sacrifice of Jesus that saved us.
2. The serpent that Moses made hinted at or _____ what Jesus would do.
3. The serpents appeared and bit the Israelites after they had _____.
4. Jesus' death on the cross _____ us with the Father.
5. Both the serpent in the desert and Jesus brought _____ to wounded people.
6. The Israelites were healed of their snakebites when they looked at the _____ serpent on the pole.
7. When we sin, God is always ready to _____ us if we are sorry.

__ __ __ H __ __ __ __ __

__ __ E __ __ __ __ __ __ __

__ __ __ __ A __ __ __ __

__ __ __ __ __ __ L __ __

__ I __

__ __ __ N __ __

__ __ __ G __ __

**Forgiveness Facts**   Supply the missing information.

Four ways to be reconciled with God:

The Sacrament of _____

An act of _____

An act of _____

The _____

Three conditions that all must be present for a mortal sin:

We've done something that is

_____ wrong.

We _____ it was seriously wrong.

We _____ and willingly

_____ to do it.

Four reasons to celebrate the Sacrament of Reconciliation:

Through it, mortal and venial sins are

_____.

The wounds in our minds and wills caused by sin are

_____.

We receive _____, power that
strengthens us against temptation.

We replace bad habits with good ones that are called

_____.

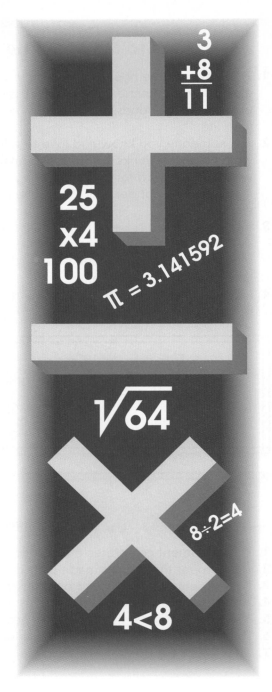

## Moses—A Great and Wise Leader

based on Deuteronomy 31, 32, 34

Suppose you and your friends want to form a basketball team. What is one of the first things you will do? Choose a captain, a leader. That person will be the one to get the team organized and to make decisions.

Moses was the leader of the Israelites for many years. He received authority, or the right to lead, from God. He helped organize the tribes into a nation. He spoke to God for the people and made decisions based on God's word and God's law. Moses served the people by caring for their needs. He led them through the desert until they came to the plains of Moab. Canaan was close by.

After giving the people many instructions, Moses told them that he was about to die. He reminded them of all the Lord had done for them. God had delivered them from the Egyptians. He had given them food and drink in the desert and had watched over them with loving care. Moses also reminded the people to keep the law of God.

Then Moses called Joshua, a military leader, and in the presence of all the people said to him, "Be brave and steadfast, for you must bring this people into the land which the Lord swore to their fathers he would give them."

Encouraging the people to love God and listen to his word, Moses spoke a blessing to each of the twelve tribes. Then he went up Mount Nebo alone. There God showed him the Promised Land, saying, "This is the land that I swore to Abraham, Isaac, and Jacob that I would give to their descendants. I have let you feast your eyes upon it, but you shall not cross over."

Moses died at an old age and was buried in the valley of Moab. For thirty days the Israelites mourned his passing. As a true leader, Moses had obeyed God as he served the people. He had taught them how to walk in the way of the Lord. Scripture tells us that there has never been such a prophet in all of Israel as Moses, the man whom the Lord knew face-to-face.

## Joshua— A Strong and Fearless Leader

based on Joshua 1

After the death of Moses, Joshua became the leader of the Israelites. He was filled with the spirit of wisdom, for Moses had laid his hands upon him. The name *Joshua* is the same as the name *Jesus.* It means "God saves." The Lord spoke to Joshua, saying:

"Prepare to cross the Jordan here, with all the people, into the land I will give the Israelites. . . . Be firm and steadfast, taking care to observe the entire law which my servant Moses enjoined on you. Then you will have success. Do not fear, for the LORD, your God, is with you."

adaptation of Joshua 1:2, 7–9

Joshua immediately called together the officers of the people. He ordered them to go through the camp and tell the people to get ready to cross the Jordan in three days. Now Moses had already given land on the east bank of the Jordan to three tribes. Joshua called for the men of those tribes. He told them that even though they already had their land, they were to cross the Jordan and help win the rest of the land.

The Israelites believed that God was with Joshua, and they followed his directions. All prepared to cross the Jordan and enter the Promised Land.

## Great Leaders

Both Moses and Joshua were good leaders for God's people. Skim page 111 and find leadership qualities that Moses showed. List some of them.

_____

_____

_____

What happened to Joshua when Moses laid hands on him?

_____

_____

The Lord told Joshua how to be a good leader. Reread God's words to Joshua and underline all the qualities God mentioned.

## The Promised Land at Last!

based on Joshua 3–6 and 24

When preparations to invade the Promised Land were completed, Joshua broke camp. He then led the people to the banks of the Jordan as God directed. There they camped to make the final preparations for crossing the river. On the third day, the people were told that they were to follow the priests carrying the ark of the covenant. Joshua said to them, "Sanctify yourselves, for tomorrow the Lord will perform wonders among you."

The next day Joshua directed the priests to take up the ark of the covenant, lead the Israelites to the river, and walk right in. As soon as the priests set foot in the Jordan, its waters stopped flowing! Perhaps at that moment God caused a landslide to stop the waters for a time. In any case, God kept his promise that the people would be able to cross the river on dry ground. The priests stood with the ark of the covenant to one side of the pathway across the Jordan. After all the people had crossed the river, they followed. Then the waters of the Jordan again flowed freely. This reminded the Israelites of how their fathers had walked on dry ground through the Red Sea. It was a sign to them and to all who would come after them that God is powerful. He is always with his people.

## The Battle of Jericho

When the tribes in Canaan heard of God's care for his people, they were afraid. The first city to be attacked by the Israelites was **Jericho.**

Each morning for six days the priests took up the ark of the covenant. Seven priests carrying ram's horns marched in front of the ark. In front of them marched specially selected troops. Once each day they circled the walled city of Jericho in this manner, with the priests blowing the ram's horns. On the seventh day they marched around the city seven times. On the seventh time around the city, Joshua commanded the people to shout, for the Lord had given them the city and everything in it.

As the horns blew and people shouted, the wall collapsed, and Israelites stormed the city. Word of Joshua's success spread throughout the land.

## Victory

It was no easy job to conquer Canaan. The people living there were strong and experienced in war. The Israelites had poor weapons and no regular army. Yet one city after another fell to the Israelites under Joshua's command.

After they had conquered the land, the Israelites assembled in Shiloh where they set up a tent to house the ark of the covenant. This was a place of worship for them and a reminder of God's continued presence among them. Here, before the tent, Joshua divided the land among the tribes that had not yet received a part, except for the tribe of Levi. The **Levites** were the priests, and the Lord was to be their inheritance. They were given cities in the lands of the other tribes, which they would serve. Can you find each tribe's land on the map on the next page?

Before he died, Joshua called all the tribes together in Shechem. By this time other people had joined them. He reminded the Israelites of the goodness that God had shown to them. He pointed out that the Lord had kept his promise. He had given them the land of Canaan. Joshua then asked the people to decide which gods they would serve. They said, "We will serve the Lord, our God, and obey his voice." Joshua renewed the covenant. Then he sent the people to their own lands, the lands promised to them as the descendants of Abraham.

## Using the Map

Locate the following places on the map. Be prepared to tell the importance of each place.

Canaan        Moab         Nebo
Shechem       Shiloh       Jericho
Bethlehem

Answer the following questions.

What natural feature borders the Promised Land on the

east? _____

west? _____

north? _____

south? _____

What two main bodies of water are in it?

_____

_____

What river connects the seas?

_____

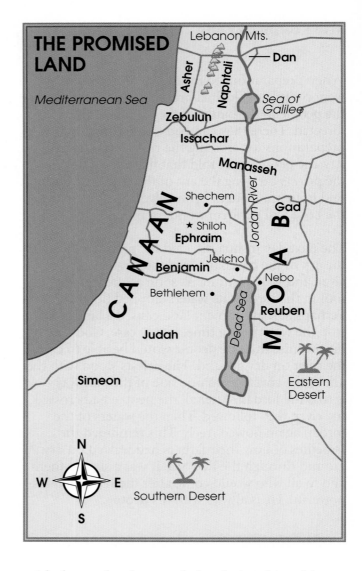

### Reaching Heaven

We, too, have a promised land. It is heaven. Like the Israelites, we journey every day in hope of one day reaching our goal.

God sent the Israelites a leader, Joshua, to bring them to their homeland. To us he sent his very own Son, Jesus Christ, who suffered, died, and rose from the dead in order to open the gates of heaven.

The Israelites wandered many years in the desert before they were ready to enter the Promised Land. If we die without having made up for our sins, we cannot go directly to heaven. Instead we must first be purified in **purgatory.** This painful experience of separation from God readies us to live with him forever.

Those Israelites who were not faithful to the true God never reached the Promised Land. So it is

with those who destroy their relationship with God through serious sin and do not repent before death. Such sin prevents a person from knowing the joys of heaven.

Before the Israelites could possess Canaan, they had to fight many enemy tribes. We, too, have enemies. We have to fight our own selfishness and pride. We also have to fight hate, distrust, impurity, dishonesty, and other forms of evil in the world about us. God can give us the strength to conquer these enemies and enter into the Promised Land.

The Israelites had the ark of the covenant as a sign of God's constant presence. We have something much greater. We have God's own divine Son in the Eucharist. We have his words and teachings in the Gospels. We have his presence in the Church and in the sacraments.

We receive the guidance and grace of Christ through his representatives on earth:

✝ The Holy Father: Christ's representative, the visible leader of the Church;

✝ the bishops: Church leaders in the different dioceses;

✝ the priests and deacons: Church leaders in the parishes of each diocese.

God shows us the way to heaven and gives us the means to get there. As members of God's Church we must follow its laws. If we live in obedience, we will one day enjoy life with God forever.

## Church Leaders

Write the correct words to complete each sentence below.

**1.** God gave us his own _____ to be our leader on our way to heaven.

**2.** The visible head of the whole Church who represents Christ is the

_____ .

The name of our present one is _____ .

**3.** Church leaders who take care of dioceses are the _____ .

The name of our diocese is _____ .

The name of our diocesan leader is _____ .

**4.** Church leaders who take care of parishes are the _____ .

The name of our parish is _____ .

The name of our pastor is _____ .

The names of our associate pastors are _____ .

The name of our deacon is _____ .

**5.** How can we show respect for Church leaders? _____

_____

## Things to Do at Home

1. Every person is meant to be a leader. He or she can lead by giving good example. Brainstorm with your family to see how many ways you can think of in which ordinary persons can become leaders. Share your list with your classmates.
2. Moses and Joshua were good leaders because they prayed. Discuss praying together as a family with your family members if you do not already do so. Some questions you might ask are: Is it possible to set aside a time once a week to pray together? What suggestions do you have for this time of prayer?
3. During family prayer time, remember to pray for the leaders of the Church. You might invite your parish priest or deacon to your house for dinner.
4. Learn the traditional song "Joshua Fought the Battle of Jericho."

## We Remember

**Who leads us to our promised land the way Joshua led the Israelites to Canaan?**
Jesus and his representatives in the Church lead us to heaven.

### Words to Know
Jericho
Levites
purgatory

## We Respond

Thank you, Lord, for showing us the way to heaven. Thank you for giving us leaders to guide us there. Bless especially our Church leaders. May they lead us in your way. Amen.

## We Review

**Two Homelands**    Fill in this chart comparing the Promised Land of Canaan to our promised land.

|  | Canaan | Heaven |
|---|---|---|
| People promised the homeland |  |  |
| Leader |  |  |
| How God is present with his people |  |  |
| Time of Formation, testing and preparation |  |  |
| Enemies to be overcome |  |  |
| Helps given by God |  |  |

**People and Places**   Identify the following, using the words in the ram's horn.
Words may be used more than once.

**1.** Greatest prophet of Israel _____

**2.** Tribe of priests that did not receive part of the land _____

**3.** City in Canaan where the Israelites renewed their covenant _____

**4.** Led the people into Canaan _____

**5.** City whose walls fell when the Israelites blew horns and shouted _____

**6.** Died on Mount Nebo _____

**7.** Represents Christ as visible head of the Church _____

**8.** Place where the Israelites kept the ark of the covenant _____

**9.** River the Israelites crossed to enter Canaan _____

**10.** His name means "God saves." _____

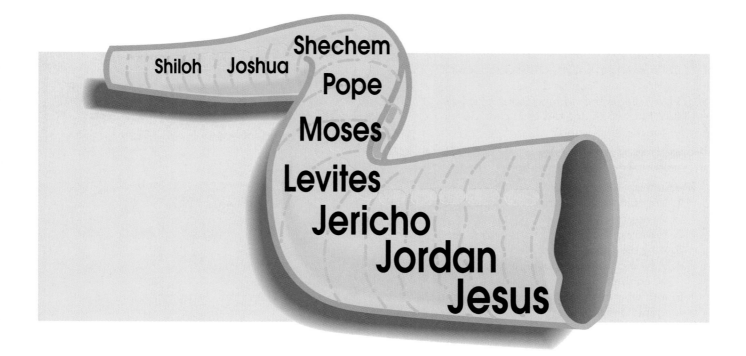

Shiloh   Joshua   Shechem   Pope   Moses   Levites   Jericho   Jordan   Jesus

# God Guides the Chosen People

## To the Promised Land

Use paper sandals for markers. Flip a coin. For heads, move two blocks. For tails, move one block. Choose a question from the list that matches the color of the block you land on. If you answer correctly, stay in the block. If you answer incorrectly, go back one block. The one who enters the Promised Land first wins. You could play with a die instead of a coin.

### Easy
1. What book of the Bible contains the story of the mission of Moses?
2. Who was the sister of Moses?
3. What was the first city of Canaan taken by the Israelites?
4. Who was to speak for Moses?
5. What is the name of the family meal celebrated on the feast of Passover?
6. Who became the leader of the Israelites after the death of Moses?
7. How long did the people wander in the desert?
8. From what mountain did God show Moses the Promised Land?
9. What was the last and worst plague?
10. What two things did God provide for food in the desert?

### Difficult
1. What was God's reply when Moses asked who he was?
2. How did the Lord guide the Israelites on their journey?
3. How is the Eucharist like the celebration of the Jewish Passover?
4. In what book do we find the Scripture readings that are used at Mass?
5. What are the two main parts of the Mass?
6. What do the foods used at the Passover feast symbolize?
7. What three things should we consider when making a decision?
8. Why did the Israelites love the law so much?
9. Where was the ark of the covenant housed?
10. What are the first three commandments?

### Medium
1. Why did Pharaoh force the Hebrews into slavery?
2. How was the bronze serpent like Jesus?
3. Why did Moses flee to Midian?
4. How did the Israelites remember the night when their houses were passed over?
5. Into what two groups are the commandments divided?
6. When does the liturgical year begin? When does it end?
7. What are the two great commandments?
8. What two things does our conscience do?
9. What was the chest called from which God spoke to the people?
10. What sin did the people commit right after making the covenant?

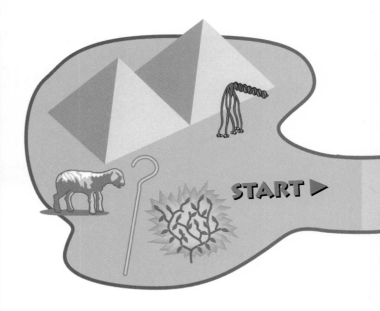

START ▶

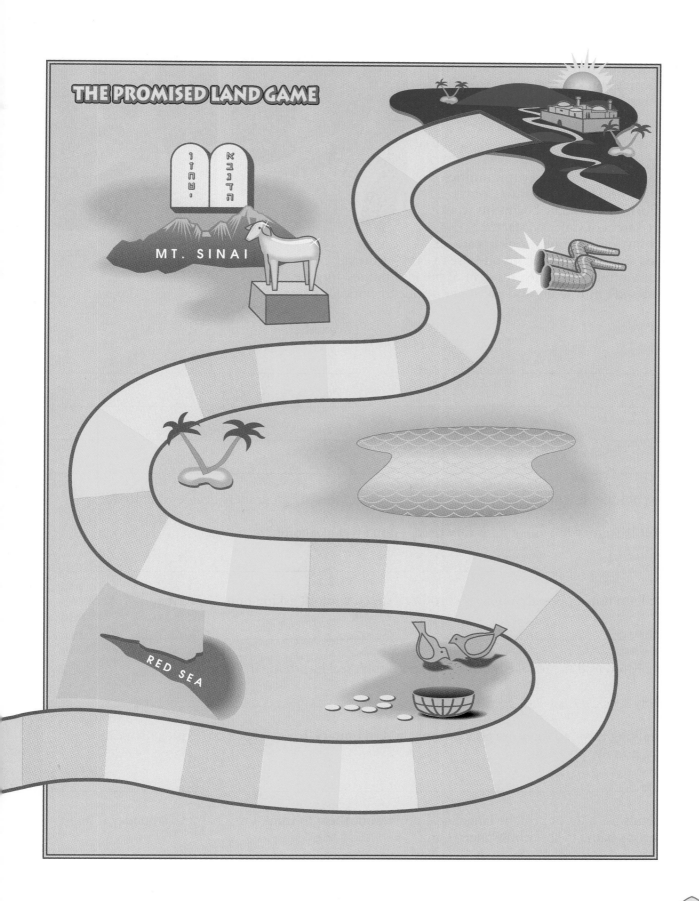

THE PROMISED LAND GAME

MT. SINAI

RED SEA

## Living the Commandments

Decide which of the two great commandments the people are following and put their names under the correct heading. Add names of other people you know. Be ready to tell why you chose the people you did.

1. Arthur Simon started Bread for the World, which works for changes in law to aid the hungry.
2. Jean Vanier, who founded communities for people who have disabilities, prays each morning before he begins his work.
3. Mother Teresa of Calcutta started a community of religious sisters to care for the poor and sick who had no one else to care for them.
4. Corazon Aquino, once the president of the Philippines, forgave her husband's murderers and asked her people to work for peace.

Love God

_____

_____

_____

_____

Love Others

_____

_____

_____

_____

Write the commandment and its number that would help these sixth graders decide what to do:

1. Linda: It is Sunday morning. I am very tired. I don't feel like going to church.

   Number _____: _____

2. Victor: I am not supposed to play my brother's stereo without asking him. I used it and broke it.

   Number _____: _____

3. Marcia: Mom told me to take out the garbage. I don't feel like doing it.

   Number _____: _____

4. I am walking through the store after school and I'm hungry. It would be easy to pick up a candy bar and put it in my pocket.

   Number _____: _____

5. My friends use a lot of profane language. I don't want them to think I'm a baby, so someday I might use Christ's name to show how angry I am.

   Number _____: _____

## Looking Back at Unit 3

In this unit we have accompanied the Israelites as they left a life of slavery in Egypt and journeyed to the Promised Land. This was a strange way of life for the Israelites, who were a fearful, complaining people. They often failed to respond to God's love. However, God was faithful to his word. He had chosen this people to belong to him in a special way. He had made a covenant with them. God promised that he would be with them to care for them no matter how hard things would become. He asked them to live according to his law of love. Everyone would then recognize that they belonged to him.

When they failed to keep their part of the covenant, God was always ready to forgive them. He loved them and cared for them constantly. Their task was to repent and turn toward God's mercy. Through the leadership of Moses and Joshua, God finally led his people to the Promised Land.

We are God's people also. He asks us to live by his law. Jesus, his Son, gave us a new commandment, "As I have loved you, so you also should love one another" (John 13:34). God asks us to base our decisions on his law and on the principles we learn from Jesus. When we fail to do this and commit sin, Jesus will always reconcile us with his Father if we are truly sorry.

## Living the Message

Can you give yourself a check (✓) for each statement?

❏ **1.** I can tell several of the stories about what happened while the Israelites wandered for forty years in the wilderness.
❏ **2.** I can explain how the commandments are a sign of God's love.
❏ **3.** I understand how my conscience helps me to make decisions.
❏ **4.** Before making a decision, I try to stop and think about my obligations, principles, and consequences.
❏ **5.** I have decided to celebrate the Sacrament of Reconciliation regularly in order to be reconciled with God and grow in virtue.

## Planning Ahead

Jesus gave us many principles to guide our lives. Look up the following references. Choose three that you will try especially hard to follow in your life. Number them, and, on the corresponding lines below, write each passage in your own words. Memorize the words of Jesus.

| | |
|---|---|
| Matthew 6:1 | Matthew 6:19 |
| Luke 11:9 | John 8:47 |
| Matthew 6:14 | Luke 6:27–28 |
| Luke 14:10–11 | John 15:17 |

**1.** _____

_____

**2.** _____

_____

**3.** _____

_____

# Rejoicing in God's Guidance

## Introduction

**Leader 1:** Lord God, you have guided your people in many wonderful ways. You led them through the wilderness as a pillar of cloud during the day and a pillar of fire at night. You made them a holy nation when you gave the Law of Sinai. You gave them good, strong leaders. You continue the loving care of your people today, Lord. You are leading us through the wilderness of this earth to the glory of your eternal kingdom. You are always with us. We have come together to praise and thank you for your goodness.

**Song** (*One that thanks or praises God for his loving care*)

## Procession

**Leader 2:** Lord, you have spoken to us in your holy Word. We rejoice in that Word and proclaim that you alone are our God.

(*Everyone joins the procession led by students carrying the Bible and candles.*)

## Readings and Responses

**Leader 1:** The Torah tells of God's loving care for his people. Let us listen now to God's command to Moses in a reading from the book of Deuteronomy.

**Reader:** A reading from Deuteronomy 31:19–22. (*Read from the Bible.*)

**Leader 2:** Psalm 119 praises God for guiding us on our way to eternal life with him. Let us listen to some of the verses of this psalm. After each verse, please respond by saying, "Proclaim the name of the Lord. O tell the greatness of our God."

(*Students read verses selected from Psalm 119. All repeat the response.*)

## Prayers of Thanks and Petition

**Leader 1:** Eternal Father, you are the Lord our God. You have taught us how to live as your people. Listen now to our prayers of praise and thanksgiving.

**Leader 2:** For the leaders of the Church—the pope, the bishops, priests, and deacons who lead us to you,

**All:** We praise you and give you thanks.

**Leader 3:** For the Sacrament of Reconciliation in which you forgive our sins and give us your grace,

**All:** We praise you and give you thanks.

**Leader 4:** For your commandments which you gave us out of love so that we could love you more,

**All:** We praise you and give you thanks.

**Leader 5:** For your Holy Word which reveals your goodness and love,

**All:** We praise you and give you thanks.

## Conclusion

**Leader 6:** Let us now stand and pray the great prayer which Jesus himself taught us to pray.

**All:** Our Father . . .

**Song** (*A joyous hymn of praise*)

# FAMILY FEATURE

## Kwanzaa

Like a growing number of African-Americans, the Carlton family celebrates Kwanzaa for seven days: from December 26 to January 1. *Kwanzaa* is a Swahili word that means "the first." It refers to the harvest of the first crops. The festival celebrates the values or principles needed by the community to harvest the first fruits. On each day of Kwanzaa the Carlton family celebrates one of the seven principles of nation building:

### Seven Principles of Kwanzaa

| | |
|---|---|
| December 26 | Umoja (oo-MOH-jah): Unity, coming together |
| December 27 | Kujichagulia (koo-jee-cha-goo-LEE-uh): Self-determination, control of your own life |
| December 28 | Ujima (oo-jee-MAH): Working together and responsibility |
| December 29 | Ujamaa (oo-jah-MAH): Cooperative economics, sharing profits |
| December 30 | Nia (NEE-ah): Purpose |
| December 31 | Kuumba (koo-UM-bah): Creativity |
| January 1 | Imani (ee-MAH-nee): Faith |

About a week before Kwanzaa, the Carlton family decorates the house. Mrs. Carlton covers a low table with a cloth of red, black, and green, which are the colors used for Kwanzaa. On this she places a woven straw mat with stripes of the same colors. On one side she puts a straw basket of mixed fruit and vegetables. In the center she places a candleholder with seven candles, one black, three red, and three green, that represent the seven principles and celebrate the unity with the ancestors who embody these principles. The first candle lit is the black candle, which stands for umoja, or unity, and is placed in the center of the candleholder. Another symbol used in this celebration is corn. An ear of corn is placed on the mat to represent each child in the family. On the table Mrs. Carlton places gifts that will be given to her children on the last day. A gift given during Kwanzaa is called zawadi (zah-WAH-dee).

At the feast called Karamu the Carlton family, their relatives, and next-door neighbors share in a feast. They drink from a unity cup symbolizing the acceptance of the seven principles and the dedication to carry them out during the coming year.

You might join in the celebration of Kwanzaa in your community this year or use some of its aspects at home. Watch the newspaper for Kwanzaa recipes and try them with your family, remembering the principles they represent.

**Bible Smile**

What happened to the frogs after the first plague?

*They croaked.*

African gold mask belonging to the Queen Mother. Musée National des Arts Africains et Oceanieus, Paris, France.

# On the Way to Becoming a Nation

Work this crossword puzzle.

**Across**
3. Feast celebrating the Exodus
5. Idol made by the Israelites
7. Its blood saved the Israelites.
10. An agreement with God
12. It parted for the Israelites.
13. Bread God sent
18. River Israelites crossed
19. Chest where God was
20. God's leading the Israelites out of Egypt
23. River that turned to blood
25. Number of plagues
26. Leader of the Israelites
27. Mount where Moses died
28. God led Israel as a column of _____.
29. Number of years the Israelites journeyed
30. Where the ark was kept

**Down**
1. Leader who took Moses' place
2. Where water came from
4. The Promised Land
6. One of the plagues
8. Sign of God's presence that burned
9. First city the Israelites took
11. What God revealed to Moses
14. Moses' brother
15. Birds Israelites ate
16. Moses' sister
17. A bronze one saved the Israelites.
21. Mountain where God gave the commandments
22. Canaan: land of milk and _____
24. Land where Israelites were slaves

(Answers: 1. Joshua, 2. rock, 3. Passover, 4. Canaan, 5. calf, 6. frogs, 7. lamb, 8. bush, 9. Jericho, 10. covenant, 11. name, 12. sea, 13. manna, 14. Aaron, 15. quail, 16. Miriam, 17. serpent, 18. Jordan, 19. ark, 20. Exodus, 21. Sinai, 22. honey, 23. Nile, 24. Egypt, 25. ten, 26. Moses, 27. Nebo, 28. fire, 29. forty, 30. tent)

UNIT
4

# God Leads the Chosen People

# God Protects the Israelites through Judges

## 17

## Challenges in Life

Everything always goes wrong!

Everyone is mad at me.

I'm always making mistakes.

I get so embarrassed!

Why should I even try?

I can't do anything right.

I'll never make the team.

Do these sound familiar? These feelings are natural and everyone experiences them at times. They are a normal part of growing and living. They are challenges to be met. We can learn a lot about ourselves when things don't go as we had hoped.

Growing up can be exciting. There is so much to learn and to discover. We look forward to new experiences and more responsibilities. But along the way there are also rough spots. We make many mistakes. We sometimes fail. How frustrating and painful this can be!

### Problems in the Promised Land

Many of our experiences are like those of the Israelites. They, too, had growing pains. They knew what it was like to fail and to have to start over again. The pattern of failing and beginning again runs throughout the Book of Judges.

When the Israelites entered Canaan, the Canaanites were mainly farmers. The Canaanites knew more than the Israelites knew about crafts and the land, but they did not know Yahweh and all that he had revealed. Instead, they worshiped Baal, a pagan god. They believed he would protect their crops and bring a good harvest.

Because of the Canaanites and other groups, the Israelites did not take over the land quickly and completely. Sometimes they fought battles, and sometimes they settled peacefully.

After many years, the tribes of Israel were spread out over a large area. Some tribes were cut off by mountains or unfriendly people. No longer were the Israelites a united family. They were not organized under leaders like Moses or Joshua.

Besides all this, there was much to learn about living in the Promised Land. Once the Israelites had been desert travelers. Now they had to plow the soil and plant crops. Once the ark of the covenant had been in their midst. Now they had to make yearly trips to Shiloh in order to celebrate together. There were so many changes in their lives!

How did the Israelites deal with these changes? For one thing, they made many mistakes. They often forgot the Lord and all he had done for them. Instead, they turned to Baal just as their Canaanite neighbors did. The Exodus seemed so far away!

But then the Israelites found their lives in danger. Invading tribes threatened to take their land. During these struggles the Israelites realized they had forgotten the Lord. Since God had always protected them, they called to him. They wanted to be forgiven and protected once again.

## An Answer to Prayer

God answered the prayers of the Israelites by sending leaders to save them from their enemies. These men and women were called **judges.** They were not judges as we know them today. They did not sit in courtrooms clothed in long black robes. These judges were usually strong military leaders in times of emergency. They were leaders of their tribes who were respected for their victories. People came to them for advice and to settle arguments.

The judges were gifted with a power by God called a **charism.** A charism is a special gift of God given to a person for the good of others. The judges had charisms that helped them defeat Israel's enemies.

At times these judges did not seem holy. Their lives and ways were rough. But they did protect the Israelites and remind them to be faithful to Yahweh. The time from the death of Joshua to the beginning of the rule by kings is called the period of the judges. This was probably from about 1250 B.C. to 1020 B.C., a little more than two hundred years. Twelve judges are named in the Book of Judges.

## The Story Repeats Itself

The Book of Judges shows a pattern in the lives of the Israelites. Read the given references and number the steps of this pattern. Then write the key words, which are printed in italics, on the correct steps.

_____

Step Four: Judges 3:9,11

_____

Step Three: Judges 3:9

_____

Step Two: Judges 3:8

_____

Step One: Judges 3:7

_____ The Israelites turned to the Lord for help. *(SORROW)*

_____ The Israelites displeased the Lord; they turned from him and worshiped false gods. *(SIN)*

_____ The Lord sent a deliverer, a judge, to save his people by defeating the enemy. *(SALVATION)*

_____ The Israelites were attacked by enemies. *(SUFFERING)*

Now read Judges 3:12. What step are the Israelites repeating? _____

## Fresh Starts

It took a great deal of *courage* and *honesty* for the Israelites to admit their mistakes, but they knew God was with them to help them. They could look forward to the future with *hope.* They *relied on God* and were eager to make a fresh start.

How about you? After you've made a mistake, what do you do? Use the italicized words in the paragraph to describe how you can make a fresh start after you have made a mistake. Write the steps here.

_____

_____

_____

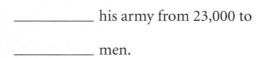

# ISRAELITE HALL OF FAME

Some of the judges have become famous. Their stories tell of fantastic battles and acts of courage. The Israelites were proud of their heroes. When the people retold their stories, they would forget or exaggerate some of the facts. But those who heard the stories understood their message and found strength and hope. Whenever the Israelites found themselves in trouble, they looked back at their history. They remembered how they had turned from the Lord. They also recalled those who brought them back to God. Then they could deal with new problems.

## Deborah: A Faith-Filled Woman

Judges 4, 5

Deborah was a judge and prophet of Israel. Seated under Deborah's palm tree, she advised the Israelites who came to her for judgment. One day Deborah told Barak, "God commands you to march on Mount Tabor. He will deliver Sisera into your hands." Sisera had led the Canaanite army against the Israelites for twenty years. Barak would not go to battle without Deborah, so she went with him and ten thousand men. They put every Canaanite soldier to death except for Sisera, who had fled on foot. He, however, was tricked by Jael. Jael invited Sisera into her tent, fed him, and then killed him while he slept.

Deborah took great risks and trusted in the Lord. After the battle she praised God for all he had done for his people through her, Barak, and Jael.

## Gideon: An Obedient Judge

Judges 6–8

Gideon was a nobody. His family was the poorest in the tribe. Nonetheless, he was called by God to defend his people from the Midianites. Gideon responded childishly by putting God to a test. He put woolen fleece on the ground and asked for signs that God would save Israel. First he asked to have dew come on the fleece while the ground was dry. Then Gideon asked to have the fleece remain dry while dew fell on the ground. God humored Gideon and did as he asked. Then to show that trust in God leads to victory, God gave Gideon special directions for his army. Read Judges 7:2–8 and complete this summary of what Gideon was told to do:

_____ his army from 23,000 to

_____ men.

You might wish to read about the battle in Judges 7:16–22.

## Samson the Strongman

Judges 13–16

The colorful story of the judge Samson is larger than life. It was handed down about a hero who fought the Philistines. These seacoast people, after whom Palestine was named, were longtime enemies of the Israelites. According to the Bible, Samson took them on single-handedly.

✤ Against his parents' advice, Samson married a pagan girl. At his wedding he bet the guests that they couldn't answer a riddle he made up. When his Philistine bride told her relatives the answer, Samson reacted with pride and selfishness and killed thirty Philistines to pay off the bet he lost.

✤ When Samson's bride was given to another man, Samson caught three hundred foxes. He fastened torches to their tails and set fire to the Philistines' crops. A thousand men came to capture Samson. He slew them all with the jawbone of a donkey.

From his birth Samson was under a vow not to drink or cut his hair. As long as this vow was kept, the Spirit of God gave him great strength. One day Samson fell in love with Delilah. The Philistines paid her to find out the secret of Samson's strength. Samson told her. Then, while he slept, Delilah had his hair cut, leaving him powerless. The Philistines seized him, blinded him, and put him in prison.

At a festival in honor of the Philistine god, Samson was brought out to amuse the people. By this time his hair had grown. He pushed against the pillars of the building where the Philistines were gathered. The building collapsed and killed them all, including Samson.

## Ruth, the Foreigner

Book of Ruth

The story of Ruth takes place during the time of the judges. Its message is that God loves all people. Its heroine, Ruth, was not Hebrew. She was a Moabite married to a Hebrew man whose family had come to Moab during a famine. When Ruth's husband, his father, and his brother died, Naomi (Ruth's mother-in-law) wished to return to Israel. Read what Ruth said to Naomi in Ruth 1:16–17.

Write two reasons why it would be difficult for Ruth to go with Naomi.

_____

_____

_____

In Israel Ruth gathered grain with the poor for Naomi and herself. The landowner, Boaz, a good man, made sure that she had enough. In those days the nearest relative of a deceased man had the right to the man's land and his widow. Boaz was related to Naomi's family, but he wasn't the nearest relative. One day Naomi told Ruth to go to Boaz while he slept and lie down at his feet. Boaz would understand that he was to ask for the right to the land and to Ruth.

Ruth did as Naomi said. Boaz then found the man who was legally entitled to the land and to Ruth. Before a court the man surrendered his rights to Boaz. Boaz married Ruth and God blessed them with a son. This son became the grandfather of King David, the ancestor of Jesus. Ruth stands out as a model of loyalty and faith. Even someone who was not Hebrew could become a part of God's plan of salvation.

## Special People in Our Lives

All of us admire certain people. We respect what they do and value their opinions. We try to imitate their actions or style of dress. Sometimes we don't even see their weaknesses or failings.

These people are our heroes or heroines. They may be parents, older brothers or sisters, teachers, sports players, performers, or friends. They may be people we have never really met, such as people from history. Or they may be people very close to us.

We may become like the people we admire without even being aware of their influence.

⚜ Are the people I respect honest and brave, or do they have only attractive physical qualities?
⚜ Do my heroes and heroines stand up for what is right, or do they avoid such conflicts?
⚜ How do these people react to difficult situations? Is it with violence or with calmness?

### Heroes and Heroines of Tomorrow

People we admire can inspire us to stretch ourselves and do more than we ever dreamed possible. Because of them we may discover our own strengths, beauty, and worth. The gifts God gave us may grow. Then we, too, can inspire others. The power of good example is mighty. It can change people deeply. Even after many years it may be remembered and be helpful to others. It is a joy to know that our goodness can encourage and support others.

Think of someone you admire, someone you would like to imitate. What is it about this person that you like the most? How has this person personally helped you grow in life? What does he or she value as important?

## Things to Do at Home

**1.** Interview your parents, grandparents, older friends, or relatives. Find out about their heroes and heroines. Ask these questions:

Who is someone you really admired?
Why did you admire him or her?

How did this person affect your life?

Did you learn anything about life and about yourself from this person? What?

Do you still admire this person?

**2.** Below are the names of twelve judges. See if you can pronounce them.

| | | | |
|---|---|---|---|
| Othniel | Deborah | Jair | Elon |
| Ehud | Gideon | Jephthah | Abdon |
| Shamgar | Tola | Ibzan | Samson |

**3.** Read Judges 8:22–23 to find out what Gideon said when the people asked him to rule over them. Tell why you think he was a good leader.

**4.** Imagine you are a writer. Write an article to help people who have made serious mistakes or have failed. Your title is "How to Make the Most out of Failure" or "The Brighter Side." Include examples and three positive ideas.

## We Remember

**Who were the judges?**
The judges were people sent by God to save his people. They often fought battles and encouraged the Israelites to be faithful to Yahweh.

### Words to Know
Judges          charism

## We Respond

I am special. God has gifted me in many ways. One of my best qualities is

_____

_____

I can give a good example by

_____

_____

_____

## We Review

**The Pattern**    This is the pattern of the Israelites' lives during their first two centuries in the Promised Land. Fill in the blanks.

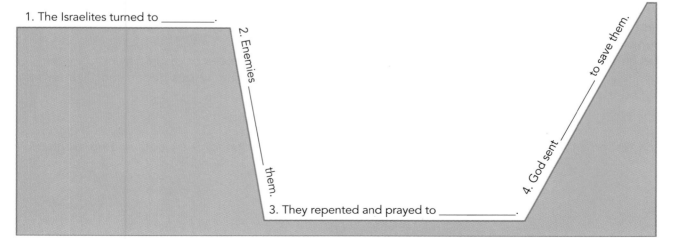

1. The Israelites turned to _____.

2. Enemies _____ them.

3. They repented and prayed to _____.

4. God sent _____ to save them.

**A Whole New World**   Match the Israelites' old way of living with their new experiences in Canaan.

**Old Life**

_____ **1.** Lived together under Moses and Joshua

_____ **2.** Had the ark of the covenant in their midst

_____ **3.** Had no land to fight over

_____ **4.** Were desert travelers

**New Life**

**A.** Had unfriendly neighbors

**B.** Tribes separated and not united under a leader

**C.** Had to learn to farm

**D.** Had to make yearly trips to Shiloh where the ark of the covenant was

**Crossword Puzzle**   Complete the following crossword puzzle and then follow the final direction.

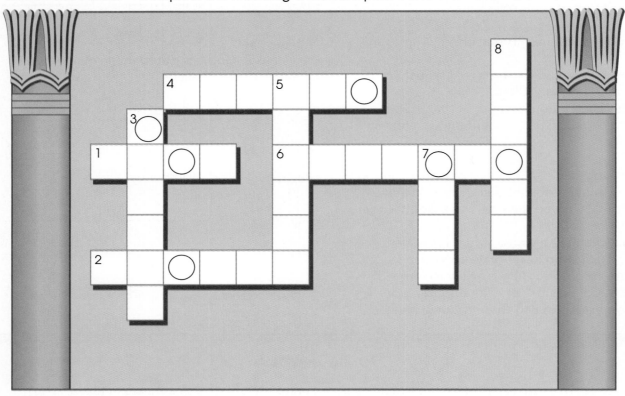

**Across**
1. The name of a pagan idol
2. A judge known for his tremendous physical strength
4. Men and women sent by God to defend the Israelites
6. She led the Israelites into battle against the Canaanites.

**Down**
3. Name of the Promised Land
5. He led a small army and defeated the Midianites.
7. She was an ancestor of the Savior.
8. The time of the judges began shortly after his death.

Use the circled letters to write the name of a gift from God that is given for the good of others.

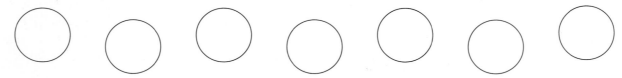

# 18

# The Lord Gives the Israelites Kings

## God's Revelation to Samuel

based on 1 Samuel 1–4, and 7

The last and greatest judge was Samuel. He was judge over all Israel, not only one or two tribes. Samuel made just and wise decisions. The people knew he was a prophet, someone who spoke God's word to them. They loved and respected him and usually did what he told them.

Even as an infant Samuel was special. His mother, Hannah, had prayed for a child for a long time. She promised God that if she had a baby, she would offer it to him. A few years after Samuel was born, she took him to the Temple to be dedicated to the Lord and left him there. God blessed her with five more children.

As a boy, Samuel heard God's call in his sleep and answered with a generous, "Here I am, Lord." God gave Samuel the first of many hard tasks. He was to tell Eli, the priest who was his teacher, that God was not pleased with Eli. Eli had failed in his

duties as a father. His sons were blaspheming God, but Eli did not correct them. He let them do whatever they wanted, even if what they did wasn't good. God told Samuel to warn Eli that he and his sons would be punished for their sins. Although Samuel was afraid to tell Eli God's message, he did as God asked. Eli realized that Samuel was speaking for God, and he answered, "He is the Lord. He will do what he judges best."

Many years later, the Israelites were fighting the Philistines. Eli's sons were killed, and the Philistines captured the ark of the covenant. When Eli heard that the sign of God's presence had been captured, he fell backward off his chair and died of a broken neck.

Samuel then became judge of Israel. For many years he led the Israelites back to Yahweh. He offered sacrifices and prayed for them. He was a spiritual leader, not a military one. Through Samuel, God prepared his people for kings.

## The Demand for a King

based on 1 Samuel 8

In his old age, Samuel appointed his sons as judges over Israel. However, they could never be good leaders, for they were not faithful to God. The Israelites needed a strong leader to unite them as they struggled to bring justice to the land. The countries around them had kings, so the people told Samuel that they, too, wanted a king.

At first, Samuel objected. Kings in other countries were treated like gods. Samuel warned the Israelites that kings could easily get too powerful and become corrupt. They could force people to work for them and levy taxes. But the people would not listen. They said only a king could unite them and lead them to victory against their enemies. So Samuel prayed for guidance. As he listened to God, he knew in his heart that God was telling him to grant the people's request.

## Saul and David as Kings

based on 1 Samuel 10–2 Samuel 5

God inspired Samuel to anoint Saul. Saul was tall, handsome, and courageous. He was also a good soldier. Samuel poured oil over Saul's head as a sign that God had chosen Saul as ruler. God would send him his spirit to help Saul rule in God's name.

At the beginning of his rule as king, Saul was a great military leader. He united and led the people against other nations. But as time went on he forgot that he was called to rule in God's name, not his own. Several times Saul did not listen to the messages of the Lord that Samuel brought him. Instead he did what he wanted.

Saul was no longer a fit ruler for Israel, and Samuel told him that his kingdom would not last. The Lord had chosen another man to lead his people, a man who would carry out his will.

Saul ruled for about ten more years. When he was no longer open to the Spirit of the Lord, an evil spirit filled him. Saul became moody and difficult to live with. Some of his servants thought that soothing music would help him feel better. They suggested that David, a shepherd boy from Bethlehem, play the harp for him whenever he was troubled. That was how David, who was to be the second king of Israel, came to work for Saul. David's music calmed Saul, and Saul became very fond of David. Saul's son Jonathan and David became best friends. Eventually Jonathan prevented Saul from killing David.

The poem on the next page tells of David and some of his experiences while he was serving Saul. Read it and fill in the blanks with a word that rhymes with the last word in the line above it.

# DAVID — THE SHEPHERD KING

The first king of Israel, a man named Saul,
Was not living up to his God-given _____.

So Samuel went to anoint a new king
And in Bethlehem town found a lad who could _____.

The boy was brought in from watching the sheep.
He was handsome and strong; the Lord's law he did _____.

His music was good. His mind was quite sharp.
He surely could soothe King Saul with his _____.

Then a Philistine giant delivered a taunt.
But young David's courage nothing could _____.

David faced tall Goliath and killed him quite dead—
Slung a stone to his forehead, then cut off his _____.

The people admired young David's brave deed,
And soon he began Saul's army to _____.

News went around of David's great feats;
Soon people were cheering the lad in the _____.

King Saul heard the people and with jealousy filled,
He wouldn't be happy till David was _____.

Saul tried to pin David by spear to the wall,
But David was lucky and not hurt at _____.

Saul's madness young David could not understand,
But he knew that to live he must leave the _____.

He fled through the hills with King Saul close behind,
Until one encounter changed angry Saul's _____.

For as Saul, God's anointed, slept with spear at his head,
David could have killed him but chose life _____.

Although David's men wanted him to attack,
He just stole Saul's spear and then quickly moved _____.

'Twas then that Saul realized a fool he had been,
For David was loyal—more so than most _____.

God blessed the lad David who did the right thing.
He lived many years and became a great _____.

## The Uses of Oil

Have you ever had sore muscles? If so, you might have rubbed oil on the aching part of your body. Soon the oil's soothing effects would have relieved your pain. Athletes in ancient Greece rubbed their bodies with oil to prepare for their races. The penetrating oil gave them a feeling of new strength and enabled them to run better.

Oil has many important uses. It strengthens and heals. It gives light and warmth. Oil powers some of our greatest machines. Mixed with perfumes, it fills the air with a fragrance that delights all who are near it.

## Anointing with Oil

Because of oil's wonderful effects, people began to use it in religious ceremonies. The words and actions used in a religious ceremony are called a **rite.** One rite of the Israelites showed their respect for the ark of the covenant. They kept a lamp burning before the ark at all times. Oil made from crushed olives was used in the lamp.

The people used oil to dedicate persons or things to God. For instance, Jacob poured oil over the stone he set up to mark Bethel as a holy place. The pouring or rubbing on of oil in rites is called **anointing.**

## Marked with God's Seal

People who had been chosen by God for special work were anointed. The anointing was a sign that God's Spirit was with the chosen one. Those who were anointed could count on strength from God to do his work.

Moses anointed Aaron when he consecrated him to God as a priest. Among God's anointed ones were the men chosen to be kings of the Israelites. The kings were anointed to carry out God's saving plan.

A sacred oil used in sacramental anointing today is called **chrism.** The word *chrism,* like *Christ,* comes from a Greek word that means "anoint."

Chrism is made by mixing olive or vegetable oil with perfume. Its fragrance reminds us that all who are anointed with it should fill the world around them with the Spirit of God. Chrism is used in Baptism, Confirmation, and the ordination of priests and bishops.

On Holy Thursday (or another suitable day) a special Mass, called the Chrism Mass, is celebrated in each diocese. During this Mass the bishop consecrates chrism and blesses the other oils that will be used by the Church for anointing and healing. Priests from the diocese concelebrate with the bishop. Then they carry the holy oils to their parishes.

You, too, have been anointed! Immediately after the waters of Baptism made you a member of the Church, you were anointed as priest, prophet, and king. You were chosen to pray, proclaim God's words, and lead. During the anointing, everyone prayed that you would always live as a good member of the Body of Christ. When you are confirmed, you are anointed with the words, "Be sealed with the gift of the Holy Spirit." Holiness ought to shine through you on all you meet.

## Oil in Scripture

Read your Bible and match each fact with the verse from the Bible that talks about it.

_____ Exodus 27:20–21

_____ 1 Samuel 9:16

_____ Leviticus 8:12

_____ John 1:41

_____ Exodus 29:36–37

_____ 1 Samuel 24:7

**A.** Moses ordained Aaron by pouring chrism on his head.

**B.** Olive oil is to burn perpetually in a light in the Tent of Meeting.

**C.** The word Messiah means "the anointed one."

**D.** God told Samuel to anoint Saul as king of Israel.

**E.** David would not harm Saul because the anointing had consecrated him to the Lord.

**F.** An altar is anointed as a sign that it is sacred and consecrated to the worship of God.

**Psalm Prayer**

The LORD is my strength and my shield;
in him my heart trusts.
I was helped, my heart rejoices
and I praise him with my song.

The LORD is the strength of his people,
the stronghold where his anointed find salvation.
Save your people; bless Israel your heritage.
Be their shepherd and carry them for ever.

Psalm 28:7–9 Grail Translation

## Sister Thea Bowman: A Fighter for God

God still calls forth leaders and gives them charisms to guide his people. Sister Thea Bowman is a good example. She grew up in a poor area of Mississippi. Inspired by the Sisters who taught her, she became a Catholic at the age of ten and eventually joined the Sisters. Gifted with a beautiful voice and a dynamic personality, Sister Thea spread the message of God through performing.

In her lively public appearances Sister Thea combined singing, gospel preaching, prayer, and storytelling. Her programs were aimed at breaking down racial and cultural barriers. She encouraged people to talk to one another so that they could understand and love one another. She taught that everyone should try to work out differences and should strive together to make a better world.

In 1985 Sister Thea learned that she had terminal bone cancer. She prayed "to live until I die—to live fully." Clearly she was given this grace. When not confined to bed by pain, Sister gave programs seated in a wheelchair with a red racing stripe, a gift from Pittsburgh Steeler Dan Rooney. Because she had lost her hair in chemotherapy treatments, Sister wore a colorful bandanna. When the United States bishops met in 1989 and discussed Black Catholics, Sister Thea was a key speaker. By the end of the meeting some bishops were moved to tears as, at her invitation, they stood, joined hands, and sang "We Shall Overcome."

Sister Thea lived with love and laughter, following her grandfather's advice, "You might go down, but go down fighting!" She fought evil, especially prejudice, suspicion, hatred, and things that drive people apart. Sister Thea fought for God and God's people until her death in March 1990.

How can you be a fighter for God?

## Things to Do at Home

1. Pray that the leaders of our country will follow God's ways and make wise and just decisions.
2. Read the biography of a leader. Be ready to share
   - ✤ how that person showed concern for others.
   - ✤ what you liked best about the way the leader worked with others.
   - ✤ some difficulties the leader faced.
3. What do you think it means to be "loyal to the royal in you?" Write a paragraph about the idea.
4. Read more about the friendship between David and Jonathan in 1 Samuel 18:1–5; 19:1–7; 20. What qualities of friendship do the two men show?

## We Remember

**What is anointing?**
Anointing is pouring or rubbing oil on a person or thing to dedicate that person or thing to God.

**Why were kings anointed?**
Kings were anointed as a sign that God had chosen them to rule in his name.

### Words to Know
chrism            rite            anointing

## We Respond

"Living the truth in love, we should grow in every way into him who is the head, Christ."
Ephesians 4:15

## We Review

**A Royal Debate**   Fill in Samuel's balloons with his reasons against having a king.
Fill in the people's balloons with their reasons for having a king.

**Who Am I?**   Match each person with his or her description.

**A.** Samuel

**B.** Saul

**C.** David

**D.** Jesse

**E.** Hannah

**F.** Eli

**G.** Jonathan

**H.** Goliath

_____ **1.** I was a judge and a priest whose sons were a disappointment.

_____ **2.** I was in line for the throne, but my best friend got it instead.

_____ **3.** I was a large Philistine who was killed by a boy.

_____ **4.** I was the first king of Israel, who lost the throne because of disobedience.

_____ **5.** I was the father of eight sons, the youngest of whom became king.

_____ **6.** I longed for a son. When he came, I gave him to the Lord.

_____ **7.** I was a shepherd who became a great soldier and then the greatest king of Israel.

_____ **8.** I was the last judge of Israel who anointed two kings.

**Marked for Mission**   Can you fill in the missing words to complete the acrostic? Use the clues below.

__ A __ __ __ __ __

__ __ N __ __ __ __ __ __ __ __

O __ __ __ __ __ __ __ __

__ __ __ I __ __

__ __ N __ __ __ __ __ __

__ __ T __

✢ The first anointing, which sets people apart as members of the Body of Christ

✢ The anointing that seals the Christian with the gift of the Holy Spirit

✢ The anointing that consecrates a man to the service of God and the Church

✢ The fragrant oil used in Baptism and Confirmation

✢ To set apart as sacred, as being dedicated to God

✢ The words and actions used in a religious ceremony

# God Rules through David and Solomon

**19**

## David's Leadership

*based on 2 Samuel 5–8, 11–19*

People who assume public office have goals in mind. They usually express these goals in their campaign promises. Their success is measured by how well they achieve their goals.

As King of Israel, David had goals to unite his country and to make it strong. He showed his gift of leadership, obeying God's law and serving his people. He was able to lead the army in conquering new lands for Israel, to unite the people, and to build up their confidence.

David made **Jerusalem** the capital of his newly united kingdom. With a great celebration he brought the ark of the covenant to the tent he had set aside for it. David himself led the happy crowds, dancing before the ark as it was brought into the city. The presence of the ark in Jerusalem led the people to refer to their capital as the Holy City, as well as the City of David. They came there often to worship God. This helped unite the people into one great nation.

## David's Sin

David was a great king and warrior, but he was not perfect. He allowed his feelings to lead him into sin. While David's men were out of the city waging a war, he saw a very beautiful woman named Bathsheba. He fell in love with her from the moment he saw her and asked his servants to find out who she was. They told him she was the wife of one of his soldiers, named Uriah. David got Bathsheba pregnant and wanted her to be his wife. He ordered his army's commander to place Uriah in the front line. There the fighting would be fierce, and Uriah would surely be killed. David's orders were carried out, and Uriah was killed. After Bathsheba mourned the death of her husband, she became David's wife. God was very displeased with what King David had done.

Would David have chosen to sin if he had thought about any of these things?

- ✦ his obligations to God and the people
- ✦ his principles as a leader of God's people
- ✦ the consequences of his action

## David's Sorrow

The Lord sent the prophet Nathan to David to tell him this story.

In a certain town there were two men. One was rich, the other poor. The rich man had many animals. The poor man had only one lamb, so that lamb was very important to him. One day the rich man had a visitor. He didn't want to take an animal from his own flocks for a meal, so he took the poor man's lamb instead.

Then Nathan asked David how he would judge this case. David, angry at the story, demanded, "Tell me who this rich man is. He deserves to die."

Nathan answered, "You are that man! You have been given everything from the Lord, and yet you had Uriah killed in battle so that you could also have his wife. The Lord God is angry with your sin, and it will bring you suffering."

At once David realized his sin, but he also knew that God is very merciful. He repented for offending God, for being unjust to Uriah, and for the bad example he gave his people. Nathan told him God had forgiven him, but the son to be born to David and Bathsheba would die. Soon after he was born, David's son became very sick. David fasted and prayed, hoping that his child's life would be spared, but on the seventh day the boy died.

David learned well the lesson of God's love and forgiveness. When his son Absalom rebelled against him, David remained loving and forgiving. He earned one of the greatest compliments given to anyone in the Hebrew Scriptures. God called David "a man after my own heart and mind."

## David—Noble in Failure

Discuss the following questions with a small group. Record your answers on the lines.

**1.** Why was David's sin so serious?

_____

_____

**2.** Why did David repent?

_____

_____

**3.** What harm did his sin cause? _____

_____

**4.** How should we accept others when they make mistakes?

_____

**5.** How can we make up for our failures?

_____

_____

## David's Love for God

It is believed that David wrote some of the prayer-songs, or psalms, in the Book of Psalms. These are full of praise, love, and gratitude for God's great kindness. Some psalms, though, carry the message of sorrow for offenses and ask for God's forgiveness.

Here is a psalm David might have written. Why would it be a good one to pray before the Sacrament of Reconciliation?

### Psalm 51

Have mercy on me, God, in your
    goodness;
  in your abundant compassion
    blot out my offense.
Wash away all my guilt;
  from my sin cleanse me.
A clean heart create for me, God;
  renew in me a steadfast spirit.
Restore my joy in your salvation;
  sustain in me a willing spirit.
My sacrifice, God, is a broken spirit;
  God, do not spurn a broken,
    humbled heart.

Psalm 51:3–4, 12, 14, 19

Once David desired to build a great temple to house the ark of the covenant. He expressed this wish to Nathan, but Nathan, speaking for the Lord, said

"I will make you famous. I will establish a house for you. Your son will build a house for me. I will favor him with many gifts. Your family and your kingdom will last forever, and your throne will stand firm."

Nathan's prophecy came true. David's son Solomon built a temple for the Lord. And one member of David's royal house was Jesus Christ, whose kingdom has no end.

## Do-It-Yourself Penance

A true penitent is not only sorry for sins and failure but tries to make up for them. Think about each incident given below. Decide in what way the boy or girl could make up for the wrong that was done and write it on the lines.

1. Carol was shopping for her mom at the supermarket. When she reached the candy aisle, no one was around, so she took some candy bars and pocketed them.

_____

_____

_____

_____

2. Lou was with a group of boys from the neighborhood. They planned a contest to see who would take a dare. Lou was challenged to smoke some marijuana. He took the dare.

_____

_____

_____

_____

## In the Footsteps of David

based on 1 Kings 1–6, 8, 10–11

When King David was old, he commanded that his son Solomon be anointed as the next king. After his anointing, Solomon took his place on David's throne. Before David died, he instructed his son, "Take courage and be a man. Keep the mandate of the Lord, your God, following his ways . . . that way you may succeed in whatever you do."

David had ruled over Israel for more than forty years. When David died, he was buried in the city of Jerusalem, the City of David.

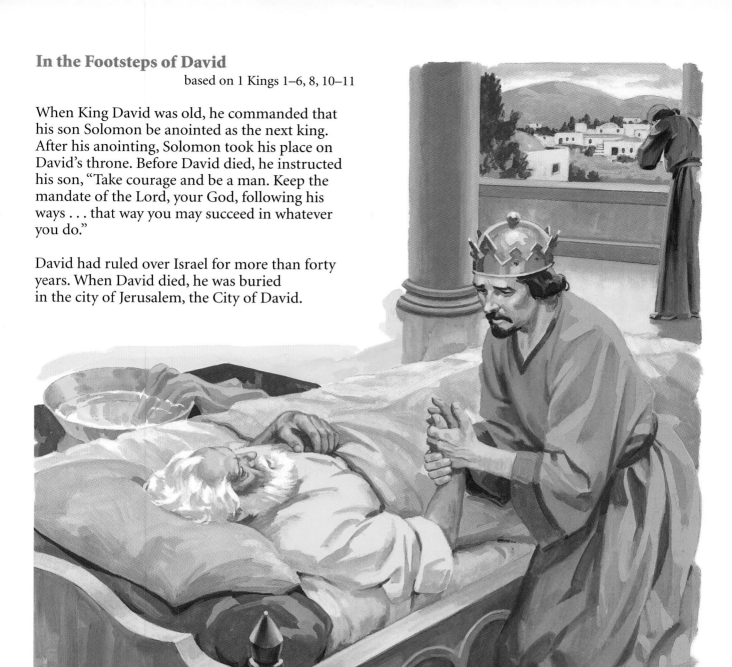

## Solomon, a Wise King

Solomon loved the Lord and followed the commands of his father, David. One night the Lord spoke to him in a dream, "Solomon, ask a favor of me, and I will give it to you."

Solomon answered, "I am a mere youth, not knowing at all how to act. I serve you in the midst of the people whom you have chosen, a people so vast that it cannot be numbered or counted. Give your servant, therefore, an understanding heart to judge your people and to distinguish right from wrong."

The Lord was pleased with Solomon and said:

"I do as you requested. I give you a heart so wise and understanding that there has never been anyone like you, and after you there will come no one to equal you. In addition, I give you what you have not asked for—such riches and glory that among kings there is not your like. And, if you follow me by keeping my commandments as your father David did, I will give you a long life."

# The Wisdom of Solomon

## Characters

**Narrator**    **Woman 1**    **Woman 2**    **Solomon**    **Guard**

**Narrator:** One day two women came to King Solomon. Each one had given birth to a baby.

**Woman 1:** Your Majesty, this woman and I live together. One night, soon after the birth of our sons, her son died. Later that night, after I was asleep, she took my son and put her dead son next to me. In the morning I was shocked to see my baby dead. When I looked more closely, I saw it wasn't really my child—it was hers!

**Woman 2:** That's not true! The living baby is mine. The dead one is hers. Her baby was smothered during the night!

**Solomon:** Guard, bring me a sword.

**Guard:** (*Bending on one knee*) Here you are, Your Majesty!

**Solomon:** Since you can't decide whose baby this is, we'll cut it in half and give each of you a part.

**Woman 1:** Oh, no, Your Majesty! Please don't kill the child! Rather give it to her alive—but please don't kill it!

**Woman 2:** Yes, go ahead and do as you say, Sir. Let the child be divided, since it isn't hers or mine.

**Solomon:** Give the child to the first woman. She is truly the mother, for she wants the child to live!

**Narrator:** When the people heard of Solomon's wisdom, they recognized the blessing of God. People came from all nations to hear him speak and to ask his judgment.

The Bible says that Solomon composed three thousand wise sayings, or **proverbs,** and many songs. He came to be regarded as the patron of all wisdom in Israel. For this reason he has been given credit for most of the wisdom books in the Hebrew Scriptures.

Solomon brought Israel great wealth and fame. He increased its trade and military power. He had two grand palaces built, one for him and one for his wife who was the Pharaoh's daughter. Solomon's reputation led to a visit from the Queen of Sheba. You can read about it in 1 Kings 10:1–10.

## The Wisdom of the Proverbs

Read the following proverbs. Write what you think each one means.

**1.** Go to the ant, O sluggard, study her ways and learn wisdom . . . (Proverbs 6:6)

_____

_____

**2.** He who refreshes others will himself be refreshed. (Proverbs 11:25)

_____

_____

**3.** He who oppresses the poor blasphemes his Maker, but he who is kind to the needy glorifies him. (Proverbs 14:31)

_____

_____

**4.** Listen to counsel and receive instruction, that you may eventually become wise. (Proverbs 19:20)

_____

_____

Look in the Book of Proverbs and write a proverb that you like.

_____

_____

### A Work of Wonder

God gave Solomon the honor of building a permanent dwelling place for the ark of the covenant. Solomon commanded that only the finest materials be used for the Temple of Jerusalem. After seven years the Temple was completed. The people of Israel gathered on the day of dedication to offer sacrifice and praise to God. The priests brought the ark of the covenant in a great procession and placed it in the Temple.

Solomon stood before the people and praised the Lord: "Is it possible for God to dwell among men? If the heavens cannot contain your greatness, how much less can this Temple which I have built contain you?"

Then Solomon blessed the whole community of Israel saying: "May the Lord be with us as he was with our fathers. May this prayer remain always before the Lord that he will defend Israel, and that all peoples of the earth may know that the Lord is God. May he draw our hearts to himself, so that we may faithfully serve him."

## The End of Solomon's Reign

Solomon ruled for many years. A clever plan led to his downfall. To keep peace with neighboring countries, Solomon married many foreigners. To please his pagan wives, Solomon built a temple for their idols. He, too, began to worship an idol. God was displeased. He told Solomon that most of the kingdom would not be ruled by his descendants. After Solomon's death, the kingdom was divided. Ten tribes in the north kept the name **Israel.** The two tribes in the south became known as **Judah.** A few kings ruled the various tribes of Israel for a short time. But never was there so great a king as David or so wise a king as Solomon.

What "idols" lead boys and girls your age away from God?

_____

_____

How will a wise person remain faithful to God?

_____

_____

_____

## Things to Do at Home

1. Read part of the Book of Proverbs. Ask family members to print their favorite proverb on a card that may be cut into a shape or symbol. String these on a hanger to form a "Wisdom Mobile." Your parents might be interested in the alphabetical poem on the perfect wife, Proverbs 31:10–31.

2. Nathan got a point across to David by telling a story. Jesus did the same thing when he told parables. Can you think of a story you could tell a friend who hurts others by teasing them too much?

3. Give examples of how David or Solomon showed or failed to show these qualities of a good leader:

   | | |
   |---|---|
   | obedience | service |
   | fairness | courage |
   | wisdom | self-control |

4. Do research on the psalms. Write a report about what you learn. Find a psalm verse or two that you like. Letter it neatly on paper rolled and colored brown along the edges to look like a scroll.

## We Remember

**How was David a great king?**
David united the kingdom, made Jerusalem the capital, and repented after he sinned.

**What is Solomon known for?**
Solomon is known for his wisdom and for building the Temple of Jerusalem.

### Words to Know
proverbs      Israel      Judah

## We Respond

Lord God, bless our leaders with wisdom and courage. Keep them faithful to your laws. In their weakness, be their strength.

# We Review

**Like Father, Like Son?** Complete this chart that compares King David to King Solomon.

**1.** David committed adultery and murder.

Solomon committed the sin of _____.

**2.** David repented.

Solomon _____.

**3.** David wrote psalms.

Solomon wrote _____.

**4.** David wanted to build a temple but had a royal family tree instead.

Solomon built _____.

**5.** David united the kingdom.

Solomon, because of his sins, _____ it.

**Relationships** Identify the relationship between the following pairs of people. This might be a family relationship or a general one, such as teacher and student.

**1.** David, Solomon

_____

**2.** Nathan, David

_____

**3.** Bathsheba, Uriah

_____

**4.** Uriah, David

_____

**5.** Bathsheba, Solomon

_____

**6.** Bathsheba, David

_____

**7.** Queen of Sheba, Solomon

_____

**Places**   What are two other names for Jerusalem? Explain why Jerusalem has these other names.

_____ because _____

_____ because _____

After the division, what was the northern kingdom called? _____

What was the southern kingdom called? _____

**Being Healed**   What remedies would you suggest for a person who has been wounded by sin? Write three things he or she should do as soon as possible.

**1.** _____

**2.** _____

**3.** _____

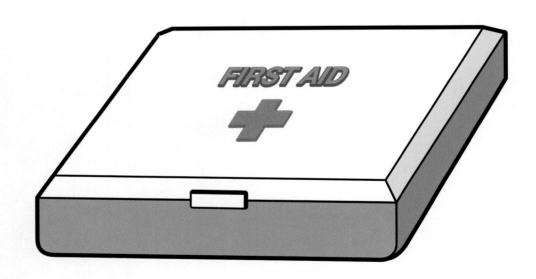

# 20 God Leads the Chosen People

## Word Hunt

Find and circle sixteen words from this unit.

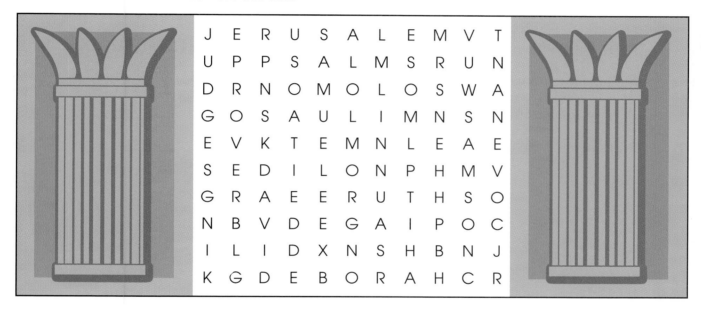

```
J E R U S A L E M V T
U P P S A L M S R U N
D R N O M O L O S W A
G O S A U L I M N S N
E V K T E M N L E A E
S E D I L O N P H M V
G R A E E R U T H S O
N B V D E G A I P O C
I L I D X N S H B N J
K G D E B O R A H C R
```

Using the words you circled, identify each person or thing described.

**1.** Leaders called by God to free the Israelites from their enemies _____

**2.** Anointed leaders of Israel _____

**3.** Substance used to anoint kings, priests, and prophets _____

**4.** Last and greatest judge of Israel _____

**5–7.** Three other famous judges of Israel _____

**8.** First king of Israel _____

**9.** The greatest king of Israel _____

**10.** King who asked for the gift of wisdom and who built the Temple _____

**11.** City where the Temple was built _____

**12.** Prophet who pointed out David's sin _____

**13.** A wise saying _____

**14.** Prayer-songs written to praise and worship God _____

**15.** The solemn agreement God made with the people chosen to be his own _____

**16.** A loyal Moabite who was an ancestor of Jesus _____

## Opening Lines

Suppose each of the following sentences is the opening line of a book.
What judge or king would the book most likely be about?

1. The giant fell to the ground with a thud. _____

2. "Put him in the front line to be killed," commanded the king. _____

3. Jealousy turned the handsome king's face an ugly purple. _____

4. The boy awoke with a start; someone had called his name. _____

5. "I want a temple built in honor of the goddess Astarte!" _____

6. Music rose from his harp like a prayer. _____

7. What would you ask for if you could have anything you wished? _____

8. His temple would not be of stone, but of flesh—his descendants. _____

## Hebrew Prayers

Read Psalm 21 in your Bible. Pick out your favorite verse and print it here.

_____

_____

Now, in the heart, write your own prayer-song praising God for the good things he has done for you.

Dear Lord, this psalm comes from my heart.

# Looking Back at Unit 4

In this unit you learned that even in the Promised Land the Israelites did not remain faithful to the Lord. Influenced by their neighbors, they often worshiped false gods. When they turned from God and trusted in themselves, the Israelites became weak. Their enemies overcame them, and in their suffering the Israelites recognized their sin. As a people of hope, they knew how to deal with their mistakes. They cried to God for help. God sent the judges to deliver them from their enemies.

But the people wanted a king. Samuel, the last judge, anointed Saul as the first king of the Israelites. Anointing is a sign of God's choice and gives the person special rights, powers, and duties. However, Saul did not use his rights and powers to fulfill God's will. He disobeyed God and followed his own will.

Samuel secretly anointed David, a young shepherd, as king of Israel. When Saul died, some of the leaders of the people asked David to be their king. David was a great leader and united the tribes of Israel as a nation. David loved God, and when he sinned, he was sorry and did penance. To show his love for God, he wrote psalms of praise and sorrow for sin.

David's son Solomon was the third king. God gave him wisdom and an understanding heart to help him rule. Solomon built the Temple where all Israelites came to worship God. After a time, however, Solomon forgot that he ruled in God's name. The kingdom became weaker and split into two kingdoms.

To summarize the characteristics of these three kings: Saul, the warrior, had physical strength. Solomon, the builder, had great intelligence. Both fell because of pride and selfishness. David, the poet and musician, had both physical strength and intelligence. Beyond this, David loved and forgave. He was a balanced human being. When he sinned, he learned from his mistake and grew. He became a fully human being, in the image and likeness of God—a man after God's own heart.

## Living the Message

Can you give yourself a check (✓) for each statement?

- ❏ **1.** I can tell some important facts about each of the first three kings of Israel.
- ❏ **2.** When I make a mistake, I stop to think what I should do so it will help me grow.
- ❏ **3.** I am aware that when I was anointed at Baptism I became a child of God with certain rights and powers.
- ❏ **4.** When I am a leader, I try to help others do what God wants.
- ❏ **5.** I plan to use my special gifts to serve God and others.

## Planning Ahead

We are all called to be leaders in some way. We can learn to be good leaders from Jesus. Ask him to send the Holy Spirit to teach you. Then read some things he tells us about leaders: Matthew 20:24–28, Mark 9:34–37, Luke 17:3–4.

Describe the kind of leader you will try to be.

_____

_____

_____

# Celebration: Leadership in God's Name

*(Distribute slips of paper to all.)*

**Song**

**Leader 1:** The Israelites had many different leaders after they reached the Promised Land. Each leader was chosen by God to help the people follow in his ways. David was the greatest of the leaders. He loved God and tried to serve him faithfully. When he sinned, he was sorry and did penance. He was kind and just. He taught his son Solomon to be a good leader and to depend on God for help.

**Reader 1:** Solomon asked for gifts to help him be a good leader. *(Read 2 Chronicles 1:7–12.)*

**Leader 2:** God gave Solomon these gifts to help him rule his people wisely. However, after a time, Solomon forgot that his gifts were from God. He forgot that he was to lead the people in God's name.

**Leader 3:** God has given us many leaders. Some of them we know. Others we see on TV or read about in the newspaper. Some leaders are good and seem to have received special gifts from God to lead his people.

**Activity** Tell about someone who is a good leader. Tell what special gift you think God has given that person.

**Leader 4:** God asks us to be leaders sometimes, too. Whether we are leaders in a game, in a family, or in our nation, we all need God's help. Let's think of the gift we need from God to be good leaders and write it on the paper we have received.

*(Take time to think and write. Place your papers on the plate near the Bible.)*

**Leader 4:** Let us ask God for the gifts we need.

**Prayer** Say a silent prayer.

**Reader 2:** Please respond: We thank you, God, for good leaders. *(Read Psalm 21:1–7, stopping at every period for the response.)*

**Song**

## A French Lent

The Gireau family observes the day before Ash Wednesday in the way their family has for generations along with other Western European families. Long ago because the use of meat and fats was limited during Lent and keeping fresh food cold was difficult, people had to use up what they had on hand by making special food. On Tuesday before Ash Wednesday they would eat fat cakes, or what we call pancakes. They would also hold a festival called a carnival (from the Latin *carne vale,* which means "farewell to meat"). The day before the forty days of Lent became known as Mardi Gras, which is French for "Fat Tuesday."

The children in the Gireau family enjoy two other special Lenten foods that originated in Western Europe: pretzels and hot-crossed buns. There is a legend that pretzels were invented by a priest who wanted people to remember to pray during Lent. The pretzel is in the shape of arms crossed in prayer.

Because Lent is a somber season, the word *alleluia* (which means "Praise the Lord") is not heard. During the Middle Ages the French began a custom to bid farewell to the word. Tuesday evening before Lent choirboys carried a small coffin out to the churchyard and buried it until Easter. The Gireaus have a small flag that says "alleluia" at their family prayer corner. On Ash Wednesday they hide the flag until Easter.

Using some of these customs would make your Lent more meaningful. The day before Lent your family might enjoy a breakfast of extra rich pancakes served with warmed applesauce, strawberries or cherries, fruit preserves, or syrup. You might make pretzels together using this recipe:

**Pretzels**

1 package of yeast
1 1/2 cups warm water
1/2 teaspoon sugar
4 1/2 cups flour

1 egg yolk
2 tablespoons water
Coarse salt

Dissolve yeast in the water and add sugar. Stir in flour and knead for 6 minutes. Cover dough in a greased bowl and let it rise until double in size. Divide the dough into 14 pieces and roll out into bread sticks. Whip the egg yolk and two tablespoons of water together and brush lightly over the sticks. Sprinkle the salt over them and bend them into a pretzel shape with the two arms crossed and resting at the top of the loop. Bake for 12 minutes at 450°F on a nonstick cookie sheet.

Unscramble the names and put them in the proper column.

| | **Judges** | **Kings** |
|---|---|---|
| MNOOOLS | _____ | _____ |
| OSSMAN | _____ | _____ |
| LASUEM | _____ | _____ |
| LASU | _____ | _____ |
| BDHEOAR | _____ | _____ |
| DONGEI | _____ | _____ |
| VADDI | _____ | _____ |

**Bible Smile**

When the teacher asked why David was able to kill Goliath, what did one little boy answer?

*He drank his milk.*

(Answers: Judges: Samson, Samuel, Deborah, Gideon; Kings: Solomon, Saul, David)

# Wisdom from Proverbs

Fill in the blanks using the words in the box.

| | |
|---|---|
| bones | poor |
| might | succeed |
| virtue | entrust |
| joyful | |

Happy is he who is kind to the _____!
> *Proverbs 14:21*

_____ your works to the LORD and your plans will _____.
> *Proverbs 16:3*

Better a little with _____, than a large income with injustice.
> *Proverbs 16:8*

A _____ heart is the health of the body,
but a depressed spirit dries up the _____.
> *Proverbs 17:22*

A wise man is more powerful than a strong man,
and a man of knowledge than a man of _____.
> *Proverbs 24:5*

(Answers: poor; Entrust, succeed; virtue; joyful, bones; might)

# Prophets Prepare
the Way of the Lord

## The Super Season

The basketball season was great! The sixth-grade team at St. Peter's Middle School was having a winning streak! The newspapers praised the team and the coaching staff. Each time the team won a game, the championship came closer.

Students who were not on the team wanted the school to win the championship, but things they didn't like began to happen. Basketball players and cheerleaders were often excused from homework. Other students received detentions if they missed an assignment. While team members practiced, those not on the teams had to cover classroom and school duties.

No one mentioned the band concert in which Brenda had played a beautiful flute solo. The letter Tom had written to the local newspaper was not even posted on the bulletin board. Mr. Gladdon, a teacher, stopped tutoring Lan and Sally after school. He had to take care of business so he could get to the evening games.

Then Mr. Gladdon was sick for a week, and Mrs. Philips, a substitute, took her place. It did not take her long to discover that basketball fever was throwing school life off balance.

Many basketball players came each day without their homework and did poorly on tests. Several parents asked Mrs. Philips not to give homework until the basketball season was over.

The main purpose of the Friday Mass seemed to be to ask for a successful game on the weekend. Little attention was given to praying for the people of the world. Desire to praise and thank God for his goodness and love did not seem present.

Since she would only be at the school for a few days, Mrs. Philips knew she could not really change things. But she did know that she must speak up and tell people what she saw. They did not see the bad things that were happening. They saw only the successes of the team. Mrs. Philips was sure things were not the way God wanted them to be. Basketball had become much too important!

Mrs. Philips had been looking for a permanent teaching job. She knew that if she spoke up about this situation she might never get one—at least not at St. Peter's—but she knew she must respond to God's call. She must speak out!

## Prophet—Called to Speak

**Prophets** are people God calls to speak his word to others. God gives prophets the special gift of seeing things as they truly are. They see good as good and evil as evil. They see the goodness and holiness of God, and they see sin pulling people away from God. The prophets' main roles are to criticize and to energize. They know sinners will not want to hear God's word and may ridicule and persecute them if they speak out. Still the prophets take the risk and deliver God's message to the people.

Prophets sometimes tell what will happen in the future, but we should not think of them as looking into a crystal ball. Rather, God gives them the grace to understand what will happen if people continue to act in a certain way. Prophets are sent not to foretell, but to tell forth, to call people to repent and to believe.

## Mrs. Philips Speaks Out

**1.** What does Mrs. Philips see as evil? Is it basketball? Success? Explain.

_____

_____

_____

_____

**2.** What "word" does Mrs. Philips know God wants her to speak?

_____

_____

_____

**3.** What risk does Mrs. Philips take if she speaks out about what she sees?

_____

_____

_____

**4.** What do you think Mrs. Philips could say about the future of the basketball fans?

_____

_____

_____

**5.** How could Mrs. Philips deliver her message?

_____

_____

_____

_____

_____

_____

## Old Testament Prophets

Can you tell something about each of the following men to show that they were prophets?

Moses _____

Samuel _____

Nathan _____

After Solomon's death, when the kingdom of Israel was split, the chosen people and most of their kings became unfaithful to the Lord. God called prophets to remind them of the covenant. The prophets encouraged them to turn from sin to God and to live as his people. They warned them that the kingdom would suffer and fall if they continued to live only for pleasure.

We have accounts of some of the prophets' lives and preachings in Sacred Scripture. Each prophetic book is named for a prophet. We call the prophets whose names are given to the four longest books the **major prophets.** The other prophets are **minor prophets.** They are Isaiah, Jeremiah, Ezekiel, and Daniel. All the prophets spoke God's word to Israel, and they speak his word to us today.

1. Color the northern kingdom, Israel, orange.

2. Color the southern kingdom, Judah, green.

3. Color Damascus, Ammon, and Moab yellow-orange. They were governed by Israel.

4. Color Edom and Philistia yellow-green. They were governed by Judah.

5. Place an **X** on the dots for Jerusalem and Samaria, the capitals of the two kingdoms.

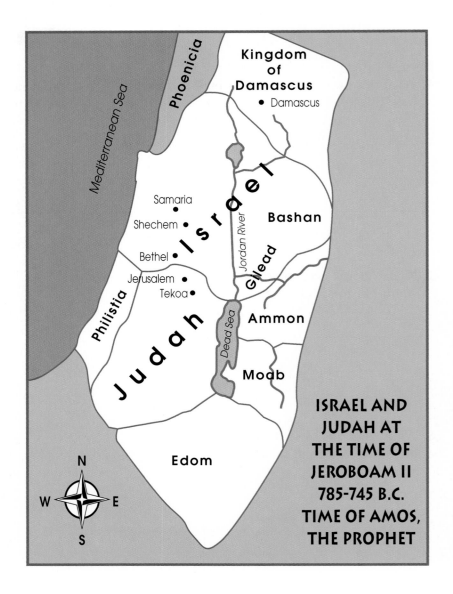

ISRAEL AND JUDAH AT THE TIME OF JEROBOAM II 785-745 B.C. TIME OF AMOS, THE PROPHET

## Elijah the Prophet

Elijah is one of the most famous prophets. He tried to call his people back to worship the one true God.

Read Matthew 17:1–3. When did Elijah appear in Christ's life?

_____

Read Luke 9:18–20. Who did some people think was Elijah?

_____

Early prophets were often advisors to kings, especially to those who led the people in worshiping idols. During Elijah's time the northern kingdom was ruled by wicked Ahab and his equally wicked queen, Jezebel. Ahab once desired the vineyard next to his property. Naboth, the owner, did not want to sell it. Jezebel arranged to have Naboth falsely accused of a crime. Naboth was stoned to death, and Ahab got his vineyard. But Elijah spoke to Ahab about his double-dealing and foretold his punishment. Ahab repented.

Jezebel worshiped **Baal.** One day Elijah held a secret contest between the God of Israel and Baal. When he proved that Baal was a fake, Jezebel vowed to kill Elijah. She did not succeed though. The Bible says that when Elijah's work was finished, he passed on his spirit to the prophet Elisha. Then a fiery chariot came down and carried Elijah away. Recall that during the seder meal the door is opened for Elijah's return.

## Amos the Prophet

Nearly 800 years before the coming of Jesus, Israel, the northern kingdom, was powerful and rich. However, it had serious problems. Worship was done with great ceremony, but it was offered from empty hearts. Rites used to worship pagan gods were introduced into the worship of the true God. Most of the people were poor and weak. According to the covenant, the few who enjoyed the wealth and power of Israel were to share with and care for the poor, but the wealthy and powerful ceased to take care of them. Instead, they took all they could from them. To remind his people of their responsibilities, Yahweh called Amos to be his prophet.

Amos raised sheep and took care of sycamore trees in Tekoa, a town in Judah. There God told him, "Go prophesy to my people Israel." So Amos went to the northern kingdom to speak God's Word. It was his mission to tell the people there that if they continued in their idol worship and injustices, they would meet with doom and destruction.

Like a lion, Amos attacked the rich city people. He even called the wealthy ladies fat, lazy cows. He caused so much trouble that the priest got King Jeroboam to banish Amos from the Temple. Amos was not recognized as a prophet until his prophecy of woe came true: Israel was conquered by Assyria.

Read Amos 5:14–15. What reasons does Amos give the people for seeking good rather than evil?

_____

_____

## Chosen by God

In his preaching, Amos reminded the people that Yahweh has a special love for them. This love brought with it great responsibilities. One of these was to make the true God known to other people. Yahweh was the God of all people, and he wanted to be known and loved by them. The Israelites were to spread the knowledge of the Lord by the way they lived, faithfully keeping the covenant.

Because God had shown such great love for his people, their sins were even more serious. Worst of all, they didn't even recognize their sins. Through Amos God told the people:

> You alone have I favored,
>    more than all the families of the
>       earth;
> Therefore, I will punish you
>    for all your crimes.
>
> Amos 3:2

The Israelites had been looking forward to the Day of the Lord. On that day God would come to conquer their enemies and make them the world's most powerful nation. Amos told them that the Day of the Lord would indeed come, but it would be a day of doom and destruction. On that day they would suffer for all their sins.

## The Justice of God

A key verse in the Book of Amos tells us:

> Let justice surge like water,
> and goodness like an unfailing
>    stream.
>
> Amos 5:24

Amos helped the people of Israel understand what God commanded by the second great law. When people think of justice, they are usually thinking of human justice. This justice gives to all people what they have earned or deserve.

The covenant, however, commands more. We are to model our lives on God's justice, which surges like an unfailing stream. All people are to share the goods of the earth. No one person or group of people is to live in luxury while others are in need.

When people live according to divine justice, they are concerned about others. They are willing to sacrifice and to practice mercy. God's justice asks that all people have what they need to live a truly human life.

What do people need to live a truly human life?

_____

_____

### Where Is God's Justice?

Here are some of the evils Amos condemned in Israel. Check (✓) those he would find if he were to prophesy in our country today.

- ❑ People were more concerned about themselves and their comfort than about justice.
- ❑ Rich people were trying to get richer and were not helping the poor.
- ❑ Some rich people looked down on the poor.
- ❑ Many people used sex simply for pleasure and amusement rather than as a gift from God.
- ❑ People sat in luxurious houses eating and drinking more than enough while the needy had little to eat.
- ❑ The poor were not able to protect themselves from the rich, even in the courts.
- ❑ Many people who were called to serve God were told to forget it and live like everyone else.

## Jesus and Justice

Jesus gave us an example of God's justice. His loving kindness was always so much more than we would ever think of. It was, indeed, like "an unfailing stream." He cured the sick, forgave sinners, gave food to the hungry and drink to the thirsty. He instructed the ignorant and comforted the sorrowful. He was patient with those who wronged him and gave his life for those who offended him.

Although we see much evil around us, we know that many people are trying to follow the example of Jesus. They show care and concern for every person. They try to find ways to help people in need. They live simply and share what they have. There are also rich people who use their money to help people who are in need.

## A Modern Prophet

For three years Archbishop Oscar Romero of El Salvador spoke out against injustice. His country was ruled and owned by only a few wealthy families. The rest of the people lived in extreme poverty. Priests and villagers who worked to improve this situation were beaten, killed, or they disappeared. The Archbishop condemned the government's violent tactics. He preached justice, love, and peace. He called for change. He broadcast the truth over the Church radio until a bomb destroyed the transmitter.

Romero's enemies started a campaign against him. Aware that he was on the list of those to be killed, Archbishop Romero pardoned those who would murder him. He offered his life for his people. While celebrating Mass on March 24, 1980, Archbishop Romero was shot to death. He was a martyr for the cause of human rights.

## Called to Social Justice

People who help others live truly human lives work for **social justice.** It is *social* justice because its goal is for all people to live together in love. People who work for social justice in a Christian manner follow Jesus' example. They practice the **works of mercy** listed on page 4 in this book under "Things Every Catholic Should Know." *Corporal* works of mercy are those that help meet the physical needs of people. *Spiritual* works of mercy help meet the needs of the spirit.

- After college, Angel Coleman, from Vermont, became a lay missionary. She lives and works with the poor in a slum in Brazil.
- In 1986, five million people joined hands to form a line stretching across America to raise money for the poor.
- Eighth graders from Julie Billiart School help at a soup kitchen on Sundays in downtown Cleveland.
- The U.S. bishops wrote a pastoral letter called "Economic Justice for All," which gives guidelines for action.
- Curtis and Lisa Sliwa began the Guardian Angels, a group trained to patrol inner-city streets and subways in order to prevent crime.

Whom do you know who has worked for social justice?

_____

_____

## What Can You Do?

Here are some ideas to help you practice social justice.

1. Invite new, lonely, or culturally different students to join you.
2. When you outgrow good clothes, ask that they be given to someone else.
3. Try to learn to appreciate the food and customs of other countries.
4. Do not ask for expensive gifts for your birthday or Christmas. Suggest that your family share handmade gifts and fun.
5. Do without things made by companies that are unfair to their workers.
6. Participate in activities for social justice like bike-a-thons or marches.
7. Write letters and encourage others to do the same to promote just laws that will protect the poor and oppressed.

## Change Your Heart

Worship is meaningful only if it is a sign of the people's desire to do what God asks. God asked for goodness and justice, but the people paid no attention. God did not want their worship unless they changed their hearts and loved one another. Amos told the people that love for God and love for others go together.

What does God see when he looks into our hearts? Are our prayers and worship signs of our willingness to do what he asks? Are we trying to make justice and goodness flow like an unfailing stream?

No matter how empty or sinful our lives have been, it is never too late to be reconciled with God and to begin again. The Book of Amos ends on a note of hope. The sinners would die, but a day would come when Yahweh would restore the fallen house of David.

## Thing to Do at Home

1. Share with your family the description of a prophet given on page 153. Discuss ways parents are to be prophets for their children. Are children sometimes called to be prophets to their families?
2. Read Psalm 72 and pick out the verses which tell about God's justice. Pray the psalm, keeping in mind the needs of the poor.
3. Think of more ways you can practice social justice. For ideas, look at the works of mercy listed on page 4 of your book. Illustrate one of these ways.
4. Collect magazine and newspaper articles about people working for social justice or giving Christlike service to others. Divide them into two groups: those working on their own and those working with an organization. Share stories of several people whom you think are most Christlike in their love of others.
5. Our bishops carry out a prophetic role. Find out what issues they have addressed recently in documents and letters to the members of the Church.

## We Remember

### What is a prophet?
A prophet is a person God calls to speak his Word to others.

### What is the goal of social justice?
The goal of social justice is having all people live together in love by ensuring that all live truly human lives.

## Words to Know

| | |
|---|---|
| major prophets | prophets |
| minor prophets | social justice |
| corporal works of mercy | Baal |
| spiritual works of mercy | |

## We Respond

Decide what you can do this week to help one person live a more human life.

# We Review

**Pick a Picture**  Write the letter of the picture that matches the description.

A.

B.

C.

D.

E.

F.

G.

_____ **1.** The one a prophet speaks for

_____ **2.** One who wanted to kill Elijah

_____ **3.** What Ahab killed Naboth for

_____ **4.** How Elijah was taken up into heaven

_____ **5.** What Amos was taking care of when God called him

_____ **6.** What Amos told people to worship with

_____ **7.** What Amos said justice should be like

**Men and Their Message**  Fill in the missing words in the prophets' messages to the people listed.

**Israelites:**  The __ __ (__) __ __ __ __ will fall if you continue to sin.

**Jezebel:**  Stop worshiping __ __ __ __.

**Ahab:**  Repent for your greed and the __ __ (__) __ __ __ of Naboth or you will be punished.

**Northern kingdom:**  Stop worshiping idols and practicing __ __ __ __ __ (__) __ __(__)or you will be doomed.

**Israelites:**  Because of your sins, the Day of the Lord will be a day of __ __ __ __.

**Israelites:**  Practice __ __ __ __ __ __(__)and share earth's goods with the(__)__ __ __ .

Unscramble the circled letters to find one way you can heed the words of Elijah and Amos. Write it.

__ __ __ __ __ __

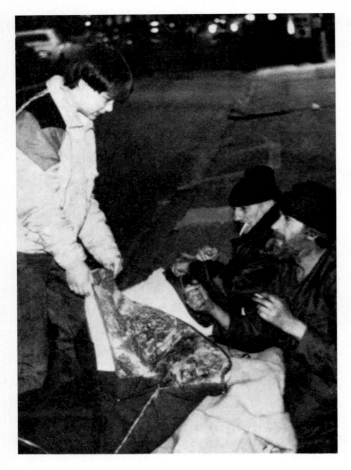

**A Young Prophet for Today**
After you have read the following story, answer the questions.

When Trevor Ferrell was eleven years old, he saw a program on television that changed his life and the lives of countless people. The program showed homeless men and women sleeping on the streets of Philadelphia. Trevor begged his mom and dad to take him there that night so he could give someone a blanket and one of his pillows. Finally they agreed and drove him downtown. There he found a man sleeping on a subway grate to keep warm. Trevor gave the man the blanket and pillow.

The Ferrells began going downtown every night, taking clothing and blankets that Trevor had gathered. Friends from their church and school began to help. Soon a food program was organized. Trevor's dad left his business so he could work full time for Trevor's Campaign. Now at a building called Trevor's Place, homeless people find shelter and are assisted in finding jobs and homes.

How did Trevor serve as a prophet to his family and country?

_____

_____

_____

_____

What is social justice?

_____

_____

_____

_____

How did Trevor practice it?

_____

_____

_____

_____

Did he practice the spiritual or corporal works of mercy?

_____

Which ones?

_____

_____

_____

_____

# Isaiah Proclaims the Promised Messiah

**22**

## A Prophet Touched by God

Our experience in life affects the way we see things. If you know how to swim, you may really enjoy a boat ride. If you almost drowned once and are afraid of the water, the same trip may be very unpleasant!

Isaiah had a special experience that changed his entire life. Isaiah was a prophet in Judah around 740 B.C. He was probably a nobleman, living in Jerusalem. From his book we know that he was an educated, skilled writer and a man of great faith. He was sensitive to God's presence in his life and the events around him. Like Amos, he defended the poor. Isaiah was active for a long time—possibly fifty years. During that time he advised several kings of Judah.

But what was the experience that changed Isaiah's life? It was his call.

When Isaiah saw the beauty and holiness of the Lord, he was filled with wonder. He saw clearly his own sinfulness and that of his people. He recognized how unfaithful they had been while Yahweh had always been loving and faithful to them. In Isaiah's vision an angel touched his lips with a burning coal to purify him.

Then Isaiah heard the Lord ask, "Whom shall I send? Who will be our messenger?"

Isaiah answered, loud and strong, "Here I am! Send me!"

In a vision, Isaiah saw the Lord surrounded by angels. Read Isaiah 6:3.

Write what the angels were saying.

_____

_____

When do we use these words?

_____

_____

Life for Isaiah was not the same after that. Once his heart was touched by God, he saw everything differently.

Think of a time when you felt close to God. When you think of God, what words come to your mind? Write them.

_____

_____

_____

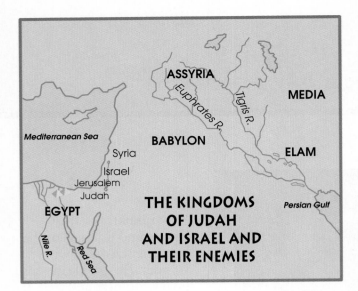

THE KINGDOMS
OF JUDAH
AND ISRAEL AND
THEIR ENEMIES

## The Book of Isaiah

The Book of Isaiah is a collection of some of the prophecies and warnings of Isaiah. Most of these are in chapters 1 through 39.

Chapters 40 through 55 were probably not written by Isaiah but by someone who studied him and was like him in thought and talent. The author of these chapters is called **Second Isaiah.** Chapters 56 through 66 may have been written by still another follower of Isaiah at a later time. He is called **Third Isaiah.**

## Trusting in God

Isaiah saw that God ruled the whole world, not just Judah and the chosen people. God worked through all events. He was in charge. Other people might trust in their power, their talents, or their armies, but Isaiah knew that only trust in God mattered.

When the Assyrians, Judah's enemies, threatened to attack, Isaiah saw the king become afraid. Isaiah explained that God used the Assyrians in his plan. Because the people had been so unfaithful, they would be conquered by their enemies. Only a few—a remnant—would be left, but God would continue his promises through this remnant.

The kings of Judah did not listen to Isaiah. The people trusted God when everything was fine, but when the future looked bad, they turned to their armies and war. They found it too hard to trust God.

Isaiah was calm and secure in his trust. He knew God would remain faithful because he had already shown his faithful love to them over and over. The people needed to believe in the covenant God made with them, but they also needed to act on what they believed.

Some of the most
beautiful lines
in Scripture are in Isaiah.
For instance:

I will never forget you.
See, upon the palms of my hands
    I have written your name.
            Isaiah 49:15–16

Say to those whose hearts are frightened:
    Be strong, fear not!
Here is your God . . .
    he comes to save you.
                    Isaiah 35:4

Comfort, give comfort to my people.
            Isaiah 40:1

Come now, let us set things right,
    says the LORD;
Though your sins be like scarlet,
    they may become white as snow;
Though they be crimson red,
    they may become white as wool.
            Isaiah 1:18

Isaiah's message of trust in God rather than in power and war is very important for people everywhere. What countries need his message today?

## The Suffering Servant and the Kingdom

The chosen people dreamed of the kingdom. They thought they had found it when they entered the Promised Land, but they were wrong. The people thought that they would have a perfect kingdom while the kings ruled and Jerusalem was powerful, but they did not.

The prophets tried to tell them that all kingdoms begin in the heart. All peace begins in the heart. All wars begin in the heart.

In Second Isaiah, the prophet speaks of a servant who will take upon himself all the sins and unfaithfulness of the people. This servant would suffer for many, but through his sufferings, the people would be saved. Love would save them. Then the true kingdom would come.

Jesus spoke of this kingdom often. And, like the servant spoken of by Second Isaiah, he suffered for the people in order to bring them the real kingdom. He showed them how to love, and that is their salvation.

Read the Scripture passages about the kingdom of God. Match them with the summaries.

_____ Matthew 5:19

_____ Luke 12:32

_____ John 3:5

_____ Luke 22:28–30

_____ Matthew 7:21

_____ Matthew 18:3

_____ John 18:33–37

**A.** The Father has given the kingdom to his flock.

**B.** The kingdom is not of this world.

**C.** Those who do God's will belong to the kingdom.

**D.** You must be born of water and the spirit.

**E.** You must become like children.

**F.** Those who remain faithful will enter the kingdom.

**G.** Those who keep the commandments will be great in the kingdom.

## Dreamers and Planners

One of our greatest gifts is our ability to dream, to see a better world. This desire to improve and grow has led to discoveries, new knowledge, and much more.

Some people dream but do nothing more. They want to be great or happy, but they do not plan or take steps to make their dreams come true. Other people dream and plan. They know that there will be sacrifice and pain in life as well as joy and peace. They take steps to make their dreams come true.

We all share the same dreams. We dream of being great. We dream of being loved. We want our family, friends, and others to look up to us. But if we want true greatness—the kind that is real and will last forever—then we need to be real people.

Real people love God and care about others. They know that God has called them for some very special purpose in life. They not only believe— they act on what they believe. Action is the difference between dreamers and planners.

# PLANNING FOR GROWTH

### 1 Know and Love God

Why did God make the world? What plan does he have for the world?

_____

_____

_____

Why did God make me? What plan does he have for me?

_____

_____

_____

### 2 Know and Love Myself

What are my strong points or my special qualities?

_____

_____

_____

What do I really need in life to help me overcome some of my weak points?

_____

_____

_____

How much am I willing to give of myself to God?

_____

_____

_____

How generous am I toward others with my gifts and my time?

_____

_____

_____

Have I thought about suffering and what it means? Am I willing to suffer with Christ in order to help save others and the world?

_____

_____

_____

### 3 | Reach Out to Others

When I make decisions every day, do I think of what God wants, what others want, or what I want?

_____

_____

_____

When I am with my friends, do I think about, talk about, and do things that will make them and myself better or selfish?

_____

_____

_____

What three things do I want in the future?

_____

_____

_____

Can I share these things with others? Will I still want these things when I grow old? Will they last or will they wear out with time?

_____

_____

_____

How am I working toward those things now?

_____

_____

_____

### 4 | Develop a Program for Growth

There are three steps to a good program for life:

*Pray.* Keep in touch with God. No happiness can be found without him.

*Make plans.* Think about what you will do today to be a better person.

*Evaluate your plans.* At the end of the day ask yourself "How did I make life a little bit better today? What can I do tomorrow?"

## Things to Do at Home

1. Ask two or three people to share with you a time they felt close to God. What advice do they give for staying close to him?
2. Listen to a recording of Handel's *Messiah*. Many of the lines are from Isaiah.
3. Bring in magazine or newspaper articles about people who seem to trust in God to protect them.
4. We use many readings from Isaiah during Advent. We use many readings from Second Isaiah during Lent. Ask to borrow a Lectionary. Read one or two selections from Isaiah from Advent and Lent. Try to figure out why these readings are appropriate.
5. Read chapter 53 of the Book of Isaiah and list phrases that seem to refer to Jesus.

### Words to Know
suffering servant

## We Remember

**Who was Isaiah?**
Isaiah was a great prophet who urged the people to trust in God. He foretold that God would save a remnant of his people and that a suffering servant would make up for the sins of the world.

## We Respond

Read Isaiah 41:9–10. Write what these words mean to you.

_____

_____

_____

## We Review

**Portrait of a Prophet**    Provide the missing information for a list of vital statistics about Isaiah.

1. Kingdom where he lived _____

2. Time he prophesied _____

3. People he advised _____

4. Aspect of God he saw in a vision _____

5. His words accepting his mission _____

6. People Isaiah foretold would conquer Judah _____

7. Type of person who would fulfill God's promises to the Israelites _____

8. Number of parts of the Book of Isaiah _____

**Jumbled Messages**   Write the letter of the alphabet that comes before each given letter to spell out the messages of Isaiah.

H P E   J T   I P M Z.

U S V T U   H P E',   O P U   X B S.

B   S F N O B O U   X J M M   Q B T T   P O

H P E T   Q S P N J T F T.

H P E T   L J O H E P N   X J M M   D P N F

U I S P V H I   B   T V G G F S J O H

T F S W B O U.

## The Times of Jeremiah

based on 2 Kings 22–25;
Jeremiah 1, 7, 18, 29–33, 38

Alfredo spent weeks practicing for the team. He was cut in the first tryouts. Maria studied all weekend for a test. When she got her paper back, there was a red D– at the top. Trying hard and then failing can happen to anyone. When it does happen, it is very frustrating.

The prophet Jeremiah was frustrated in his work with the Israelites. But today he is known as one of the greatest prophets.

Jeremiah lived in the southern kingdom of Judah. He was the son of a priest who lived in a small village near Jerusalem. When Jeremiah first heard God's call, he said, "I am too young." But God didn't think so. He told Jeremiah not to be afraid, but to do whatever he asked him. God promised to be with Jeremiah, giving him strength.

When God called Jeremiah, Josiah was king of Judah. He was a good king who wanted to serve God faithfully. During his reign a great discovery had been made in the Temple. A scroll of the Book of Deuteronomy had been found there. When it was read to King Josiah, he knew that changes must be made in the land. The people were not being faithful to the obligations of the covenant. They were worshiping the false gods of their neighbors. They were treating the one living God as if he were one god among many.

After listening to God's Word, King Josiah and the people renewed their promise to obey all that God asked of them. Josiah ordered his soldiers to destroy every shrine to a false god in the land. He declared that everyone was to worship Yahweh in the Temple of Jerusalem.

## Jeremiah's Warnings

The king passed laws to help everyone live as the covenant with God demanded. But the laws did not change the hearts of the people. After Josiah died, the people went back to their old ways. Jeremiah warned them that unless they stopped doing evil and worshiping other gods, the Temple would be destroyed and Jerusalem would be burned to the ground. His message is in the Book of Jeremiah and in the **Book of Lamentations.**

Jeremiah told the people that God was not pleased with their worship. They came to the Temple and prayed, but they did not treat others in the way he had shown them. They did not try to bring peace and justice to all. Jeremiah stood outside the Temple gates. He preached God's message fearlessly:

This is the temple of the LORD!
Only if you reform your ways,
if you treat each other fairly,
and not follow strange gods,
will I stay with you.
adapted from Jeremiah 7:4–7

But the people felt secure. They did not believe that God would let an enemy conquer the Holy City. They did not believe that God would let the Temple built to honor him be destroyed. So they continued to ignore the poor and needy. They continued to boast about their wealth. They even continued to adore false gods. They thought God would bless and protect them as long as they would go to the Temple to worship.

Of course, people did not like Jeremiah's message. They cursed him for pointing out their sins. They beat him, accused him of speaking against the king, and finally had him arrested.

After being released from prison, Jeremiah continued to preach that the Holy City would be destroyed. The people still refused to repent.

## At the Potter's House
One day God told Jeremiah to go to a potter's house. There Jeremiah watched the potter working at the wheel, fashioning a clay object with his hands.

Read Jeremiah 18:1–9.

What can a potter do if there is something wrong with the vessel he is making?

_____

_____

Who does the potter stand for? _____

Who is the clay? _____

What was God telling Jeremiah as he watched the potter?

_____

_____

_____

Write a prayer to God as your potter.

_____

_____

## The Fall of Jerusalem

The terrible things Jeremiah foretold came to be. Jerusalem was captured by the Babylonians from the East. All the treasures of the Temple and the palace were taken to Babylon. The soldiers and craftsmen were sent into exile there. Only the poor were left in the land.

The king of Babylon appointed a new king to rule the land he had conquered. The new king did not have the courage to do what was right. False prophets told the people to rise up against the Babylonians. But Jeremiah warned the king and the leaders that their situation would get worse if they rebelled. No one wanted to listen to Jeremiah. He was accused of working against his country and was thrown into a deep, muddy well. Jeremiah would have died there, but the king secretly gave permission for him to be pulled out. Jeremiah was kept in prison until Jerusalem was attacked a second time.

This time when the Babylonian army marched into the city the Temple was burned. More people were sent into exile. Jeremiah, however, was treated with respect. The Babylonian king had heard how he had told the people to surrender. Jeremiah was allowed to choose to stay in conquered Jerusalem or go to Babylon with the exiles. He chose to stay in Jerusalem. He loved his country and his people. Their failure to repent brought him great sorrow, but he would never desert them. Jeremiah knew that the exiles in Babylon needed to be comforted, too. He wrote them this message from God:

 When you seek me with all your heart, you will find me and I will help you.

adapted from Jeremiah 29:13

## The Promise of a New Covenant

Jeremiah also told the people that God intended to make a new covenant with them:

 The days are coming when I will make a new covenant with Israel. It will be different from the old covenant that I made with them after I led them out of Egypt. That one they broke, and I was forced to show them I was their master. But with this new covenant I will write my law upon their hearts. Then I will be their God and they will be my people. Everyone will know me, because I will forgive their evildoing and remember their sin no more.

adapted from Jeremiah 31:31–34

Jeremiah's whole life proclaimed God's everlasting love. He was faithful to God even when it meant suffering for him.

## Exile in Babylon

based on Ezekiel 1, 18, 34, 36, 37

The first people taken from Judah to Babylon did not believe Jeremiah, who said many years would pass before they would see Jerusalem again. After all, were they not God's chosen people? They believed that he would deliver them from the Babylonians and that the Temple treasures would be returned. They thought God would punish those who had taken the sacred articles from the Temple.

God was at work among his people in exile. He called Ezekiel, a young priest, to be his prophet in Babylon. In a famous vision, Ezekiel saw the glory of God. He was told to eat a scroll—the Word of God—which tasted like honey. Ezekiel started preaching to the first exiles. He helped them worship the only living God with all their hearts. Like Jeremiah, Ezekiel warned that Jerusalem would be destroyed. At first, the people did not accept his message and did not repent.

Ten years passed and the second group of exiles arrived in Babylon in 587 B.C. They brought with them the awful news of the destruction of both Jerusalem and the Temple. From that time on, Ezekiel no longer spoke of punishment for sin. Instead he told how God planned to bring the exiles back to their land and raise up a new Israel. His message was one of faith and love. Read Psalm 137:1–5 to see how the Israelites felt during their exile.

## More Visions

God granted Ezekiel several powerful visions. Picture this one: a plain is covered with hundreds of dry bones. At God's word, the bones come together again and form skeletons. Flesh covers them again. This vision conveys the message of hope: God's spirit will give his people new life and bring them back to their land. In another vision, God told Ezekiel that the people did not need to be in Jerusalem to worship God. God was with them just as much in Babylon as he had been in the Temple. Every city is his.

From still another vision the people learned that their experiences would help them grow. Ezekiel told the people that God wanted to use their exile in Babylon to teach them to look at things in a new way. God wanted them to repent. Through the exile, God would bring them closer to himself.

Many of the exiles felt sorry for themselves and blamed others for their misfortune. But Ezekiel pointed out that each individual shares in the responsibility for what the group does. He said it was not right to blame others when things went wrong. Instead, each one should look into his or her own heart and repent.

## What Is God's Message to Us?

God also speaks to us through the prophets. Their message is for all people everywhere. Read these passages from Ezekiel. Put a check (✓) in front of what God tells us in each passage. More than one sentence may be checked.

Ezekiel 34:11–16

_____ God loves us so much he won't let us suffer.

_____ God never neglects anyone, but takes special care of the weak and the wounded.

_____ If we turn to God when we have sinned, he will heal us.

Ezekiel 18:20, 25–28

_____ Each person is responsible for what he or she does or fails to do. No one can blame others for his or her sin.

_____ God can forgive our sin only when we admit our guilt and are sorry.

_____ God is always ready to forgive our sins no matter how great they are.

Ezekiel 37:12–14

_____ God can do anything, even bring the dead to life.

_____ The Holy Spirit calls us back to God and to life when we have sinned.

## Good from Evil

Many good things happened during the exile. The people came to realize their guilt and were ready to repent.

They studied what God had revealed about himself and wrote down the teachings of the prophets. Many books of the Bible were put together during the exile.

Since the people no longer had the Temple, they built places where they could gather to pray and read the Scriptures. These places were called **synagogues.** The Israelites did not offer sacrifice in the synagogues since this could be done only in the Temple. Every Sabbath they met in the synagogues to study God's Word and examine how faithful they were to it.

The people understood that their worship was not sincere unless they shared what they could with the weak and the suffering. They knew that they were responsible for their own deeds and the deeds of the group.

After forty years the Israelites were allowed to return home. Eventually the remnant rebuilt the Temple. Then Nehemiah, the governor, began political reforms. One of his projects was to rebuild the city walls. Ezra, a priest, guided the people in being faithful to the Law of Moses. During this time the children of Abraham became known as **Jews,** which means descendants of those who lived in Judah.

## Things to Do at Home

1. Ask your parents to share a time when good came from a disappointment or failure in their life.
2. Read about someone who courageously spoke out against an injustice. Pretend you are that person and write an entry for a diary. Tell one significant thing that happened. Then tell how you felt about it.
3. Find out how one of the following people was a prophet in his or her day. Be ready to tell one thing that person did to help those whose rights were not being respected.
   - Vincent de Paul
   - Catherine of Siena
   - Frances Cabrini
   - Martin de Porres
   - Damien of Molokai
   - Katherine Drexel
4. Who are some prophets active in the world today? Make a list with the help of your family and friends.

## We Remember

**What did the prophets Jeremiah and Ezekiel proclaim?**
Jeremiah and Ezekiel proclaimed that God's everlasting love would be shown through the exile.

> ### Words to Know
> Book of Lamentations
> synagogue
> Jews

## We Respond

Help us, God our savior,
   for the glory of your name.
Deliver us, pardon our sins
   for your name's sake.
             Psalm 79:9

## We Review

**Making Order**    Number these events in the order in which they occurred.

_____ Ezekiel's prophecy of a new Israel

_____ The finding of the Book of Deuteronomy in the Temple

_____ The exile to Babylon

_____ The destruction of Jerusalem and the Temple

_____ Josiah's laws that called the people back to the covenant

_____ The rebuilding of the Temple and the city walls

_____ Jeremiah's warnings not to rebel against Babylon

**5** **1** **2** **7** **3** **6** **4**

**Crime and Punishment**    Answer these questions.

1. For what sins were the Israelites conquered and exiled according to the prophets?

_____

2. To what country were the Israelites exiled?

_____

3. How long were they in exile?

_____

4. What is one good thing that came out of the exile?

_____

**Find the Match**   Write the letter of the term that matches the description.

**A.** Josiah

**B.** synagogues

**C.** Jeremiah

**D.** Ezra

**E.** exile

**F.** new covenant

**G.** Ezekiel

**H.** Jews

**I.** Nehemiah

**J.** Temple

_____ **1.** Only place where sacrifice was offered

_____ **2.** King who tried to reform his country

_____ **3.** Prophet who was attacked for his criticism

_____ **4.** Prophet who had a vision of bones that came back to life

_____ **5.** A good thing that Jeremiah promised for the people

_____ **6.** Term for the time the people of Judah were kept in Babylon

_____ **7.** Governor who worked for reform after the exile

_____ **8.** Places where the Israelites met to pray and read Scripture

_____ **9.** Descendants of those who lived in Judah

_____ **10.** Priest who guided the people in keeping the Law of Moses after the exile

# The Savior Is Jesus, the Son of God

**24**

## UPDATE

After the return of the exiles to Jerusalem, Palestine was governed by Persia, Greece, Egypt, and then Syria. In 167 B.C., the King of Syria forbade the practice of Judaism and persecuted the Jewish people. He had a statue of the Greek god Zeus erected in the Temple. Under the leadership of the **Maccabees,** a father and his five sons, the Jewish people rebelled. Finally the enemy was defeated, and the Temple rededicated. The feast of **Hanukkah** commemorates this event. Palestine was independent until the Romans conquered it in 63 B.C.

## The Last and Greatest Prophet

based on Luke 1:15–25, 57–80;
Matthew 3:1–7; 11:2–15; 14:3–12

Luke's Gospel gives the account of John's birth. Zechariah and his wife Elizabeth were called by God to be the parents of the greatest of prophets. He would be the one to prepare the people for the coming of the Messiah. Elizabeth and Zechariah were quite old at the time, and they had followed God's laws faithfully.

Read the announcement of this Good News as it is told by the gospel writer in Luke 1:5–25.

Luke tells us that God's promise to Zechariah was fulfilled when the time came for Elizabeth to have her child. A son was born, and that made Elizabeth and Zechariah very happy. Their neighbors and relatives thought the boy should be named after his father, but Elizabeth said his name would be John.

The people could not understand why the child's name would be John. No one in the family had that name. They asked the father, who still could not speak. He made signs for a writing tablet and wrote on it, "John is his name." At that moment Zechariah was able to speak again! He was filled with the Holy Spirit, and he spoke the following prophecy.

### Zechariah's Canticle

Blessed be the Lord, the God of Israel;
he has come to his people and set them free.

He has raised up for us a mighty savior,
born of the house of his servant David.

Through his holy prophets he promised of old
that he would save us from our enemies,
from the hands of all who hate us.

He promised to show mercy to our fathers
and to remember his holy covenant.

This was the oath he swore to our father
Abraham:
to set us free from the hands of our enemies,
free to worship him without fear,
holy and righteous in his sight
all the days of our life.

Then Zechariah looked upon his son, John, and continued:

> You, my child, shall be called the prophet of
>    the Most High;
> for you will go before the Lord to prepare
>    his way,
> to give his people knowledge of salvation
> by the forgiveness of their sins.
>
> In the tender compassion of our God
> the dawn from on high shall break upon us,
> to shine on those who dwell in darkness and
>    the shadow of death,
> and to guide our feet into the way of peace.
>        *Christian Prayer: The Liturgy of the Hours*

### John the Baptist's Preparation for the Messiah

It takes a lot of training to learn a profession. The more important or difficult the job, the longer and harder the preparation. An athlete must spend hours practicing to be tops in his field. A doctor must spend years studying and practicing medicine to become a good doctor. All of this takes **self-discipline,** which is planned control and training of oneself in order to improve.

John the Baptist had the most important work of all. His mission was to prepare the way for the Savior, the Messiah. Long ago the prophet Isaiah spoke of him, saying

A voice cries out:
In the desert prepare a way for the
    LORD.
Make straight a highway for our God.
        adapted from Isaiah 40:3

For the entire prophecy, read Isaiah 40:1–5.

John knew he had to prepare himself before he could help the people prepare for Christ's coming. He would go to the desert, a wilderness area, for his training. There he would discipline himself through prayer and penance.

Some Scripture scholars believe John may have joined the **Essenes,** who lived in the desert. They were a group of religious people who tried to live the covenant perfectly. They studied the scrolls of Scripture and hand-lettered copies of them. These people had many other strict rules and rites, including a bathing or purifying rite. That may be where John got the idea of using bathing, or baptism, as a sign of repentance. The Essene way of life was one of self-discipline—a good preparation for the hard life of a prophet!

### Preparing the People

The Gospel of Matthew tells how John prepared the people for the coming of the Messiah. It says the Spirit came to John to tell him it was time to leave the desert. John's first appearance in public must have been startling. He was bearded, long-haired, and dressed in camel skin. He was tanned and toughened by his life of self-discipline in the desert. In a powerful voice John spoke with authority his message to the people:

# Repent, for the kingdom of God is near!

John proclaimed a baptism of repentance for the forgiveness of sin. But he also told the people that the One who would come after him would baptize with fire and the Holy Spirit.

Many people listened to John and were baptized by him. They asked him how they should repent of their sins, and he gave them some good suggestions. Finally Jesus himself came to the Jordan to be baptized by John. At first John objected, saying that Jesus should baptize him, but he did what Jesus wished. John then told his disciples to follow Jesus, the Lamb of God.

As Jesus began his public life, John was heard from less and less. He got into trouble telling King Herod that the king was living in sin, and Herod had him arrested. From prison, John sent his followers to Jesus. Jesus, in turn, praised John the Baptist, calling him the greatest of all children born of women and greater than a prophet.

Because of a foolish promise made at his birthday party, Herod had John beheaded. Read the story in Matthew 14:1–12. John's mission was completed; he had done well!

## Called to Be a Voice

God calls each Christian to be a voice like John the Baptist and to lead others to Jesus. Do you know anyone who has been a voice leading you to Jesus? Write the name of the person and explain how he or she has done this.

_____

_____

We need courage to become a voice like John. We need to know and love Jesus more, to be willing to sacrifice for him, and to speak up for what we believe.

Think of what you are willing to do for Jesus and complete the following sentences.

For Jesus I would be willing to sacrifice

_____

For Jesus I would be willing to speak up when

_____

I will try to come closer to Jesus by

_____

## The Promise Fulfilled

God's chosen people longed for the coming of the Messiah, who had been promised by God again and again. The prophets had announced the signs by which he would be known. On the day planned by God from the beginning of time, an announcement was made to Mary that the promise was about to be fulfilled. Mary was asked to be the mother of the Messiah.

Read the story in Luke 1:26–38.

What were the words of the angel Gabriel when he greeted Mary? _____

_____

What was the message of the angel to Mary?

_____

_____

Through whose power would this happen?

_____

What did Mary say when she agreed to be the mother of the Messiah? _____

_____

_____

When Mary said these words, God the Son became **incarnate,** he became man. He loved us so much that he became like us in all things except sin. We call this mystery the **Incarnation.**

The angel also told Mary that her relative Elizabeth was to have a son, even though she was quite old. The angel assured Mary that nothing is impossible with God.

The Gospel of Luke tells us that Mary went to visit Elizabeth in a little town in Judah. It gives us a prayer in which Mary praises and thanks God for all he has done. Her prayer of praise is called the **Magnificat.** Read Luke 1:39–56 for the whole story.

## Mary's Canticle of Praise

My soul proclaims the greatness of the Lord,
my spirit rejoices in God my Savior;
for he has looked with favor on his lowly
    servant.

From this day all generations will call me
    blessed:
the Almighty has done great things for me,
and holy is his Name.

He has mercy on those who fear him
in every generation.

He has shown the strength of his arm,
he has scattered the proud in their conceit.

He has cast down the mighty from their
    thrones,
and has lifted up the lowly.

He has filled the hungry with good things,
and the rich he has sent away empty.

He has come to the help of his servant Israel
for he has remembered his promise of
    mercy,
the promise he made to our fathers,
to Abraham and his children for ever.
    *Christian Prayer: The Liturgy of the Hours*

## Jesus Christ—the Messiah

Joseph and Mary were both from the family of David. At the time of the census they had to go to Bethlehem, the city of David, to register. While they were there, Mary gave birth to her son. They named him Jesus, as the angel had directed. He was the long-awaited One, the Messiah, the Christ. In him God established a covenant with us forever. Jesus fulfilled what was written in the Scriptures.

One day in the synagogue at Nazareth, Jesus proclaimed that a passage in Isaiah was fulfilled in him.

The Spirit of the Lord is upon me,
because he has anointed me
    to bring glad tidings to the poor.
He has sent me to proclaim liberty to
    captives
    and recovery of sight to the blind,
        to let the oppressed go free,
and to proclaim a year acceptable to the Lord.
Luke 4:18–19

### . . . the Center of Mary's Life

Christ's coming marked the start of a new understanding of salvation history. Mary was the first to grasp that new understanding, for she was the first to make Jesus the center of her life.

Mary watched Jesus grow up. She heard him teach during his public life. She knew his friends and his enemies. She knew of his miracles, and she was at the foot of the cross when he was crucified. No one has ever loved Jesus as Mary did.

Mary was with the apostles as they waited for the coming of the Holy Spirit. She was with them when they received the Spirit and began to teach about Jesus.

Mary is with us now as she was with her people then. She prays for us that we allow the Holy Spirit to work freely in us, as he worked in her and still works in the Church today.

### . . . the Center of Our Lives

How much does Jesus mean to you? Is he the center of your life? The questions below can help you determine the part he plays in your everyday living. Answer *yes, no, not sure,* or *sometimes.*

1. Do you realize that Jesus loves you and wants you to be happy? _____

2. Do you try to think, speak, and act as Jesus would? _____

3. Do you believe in Jesus and trust in his power? _____

4. Do you appreciate all that Jesus has done for you and thank him? _____

5. Is Jesus becoming more important in your life every day? _____

Think what you can do to be able to answer yes to every one of these questions. Then Jesus will truly be the center of your life!

## Preparing the Way of the Lord

Through his saving plan of love, God revealed himself and prepared his people for the coming of the Messiah. The people and events were part of salvation history. This time line shows the order of historical events and how much time passed between them.

| | Years before Christ (B.C.) |
|---|---|
| **Time of the Patriarchs**<br>Abraham (1850?)<br>Isaac<br>Jacob | 1900<br>1800<br>1700 |
| **Time in Egypt**<br>Joseph | 1600<br>1500<br>1400 |
| **Time of the Exodus**<br>Moses<br>Joshua | 1300<br>1200 |
| **Time of the Judges**<br>Gideon<br>Deborah<br>Samson<br>Samuel | 1100 |
| **Time of the First Kings**<br>Saul (1020–1000)<br>David (1000–961)<br>Solomon (961–922)<br>Elijah | 1000<br>900 |
| **Time of the Prophets**<br>Amos<br>Isaiah<br>Jeremiah | 800<br>700<br>600 |
| **Time of the Exile in Babylon**<br>(587–537)<br>Ezekiel<br>Second Isaiah | 500 |
| **Time of Restoration**<br>Third Isaiah | 400<br>300<br>200 |
| **Revolt of the Maccabees** (167) | 100 |
| **Roman Rule** (63)<br>John the Baptist<br>Mary | Year of Our Lord (A.D.) |
| **Fullness of Time** | |

**JESUS**

## Things to Do at Home

1. Share the time line on page 180 with your family. Then invite them to make a family time line, beginning with the wedding of your parents. List important dates and events and illustrate them with drawings or photos. When it is completed, join together in thanking God for his loving care of your family.

2. John prepared for his mission in life by prayer, penance, and fasting. How can we prepare for our mission in life? You might want to ask your parents how they prepared for their married or professional life.

3. As a family, view one or two favorite TV programs. Note whether the characters show any evidence of practicing self-discipline. The following questions might act as guides in discussing the programs.
   ✤ How did the main character practice self-discipline? What was the result? Was it worth the effort?
   ✤ How did the main character fail to practice self-discipline? What was the result? What could he or she have done to change things?

4. Find out more about Mary, God's mother and yours, and write a report. Investigate her privileges, her feast days, her appearances, or her shrines.

## We Remember

**What was John the Baptist's place in salvation history?**
John the Baptist was the last and the greatest prophet. He prepared the people for the coming of the Messiah by calling them to repent.

**Why is Mary important?**
Mary is the Mother of God because she is the Mother of Jesus, who is God incarnate.

### Words to Know

| | |
|---|---|
| Maccabees | Magnificat |
| Hanukkah | Incarnation |
| self-discipline | incarnate |
| Essenes | |

## We Respond

Blessed be the Lord, the God of Israel;
he has come to his people and set them
   free.
He has raised up for us a mighty savior,
born of the house of his servant David.

Zechariah's Canticle

Fill in the Jesus crossword by using the clues.

**John Prepared the Way for**

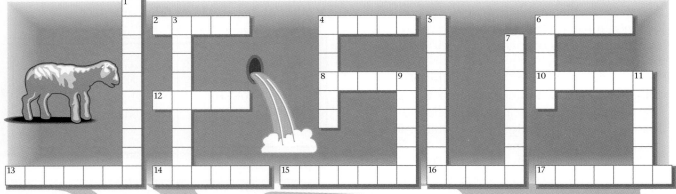

### Down

**1.** Jesus baptized with fire and the _____ _____.

**3.** The mother of John the Baptist

**4.** The river in which John baptized

**5.** The father of John the Baptist

**6.** How Zechariah and Elizabeth felt about the birth of John

**7.** John the Baptist _____ the way to the Lord.

**9.** The people asked Zechariah to _____ the name of his son.

**11.** Where the angel appeared to Zechariah

### Across

**2.** Jesus would bring light and _____.

**4.** John the Baptist told of his coming.

**6.** The angel told Zechariah that his prayer had been _____.

**8.** An ancestor of John's who had been king of Israel

**10.** Zechariah was a _____.

**12.** John baptized with _____.

**13.** John the Baptist was the last and greatest _____.

**14.** Christians are those who follow the teachings of _____.

**15.** John preached that Jesus would _____ sins.

**16.** The king who had John beheaded

**17.** The angel that appeared to Zechariah

**A Promise Passed On**   Complete this summary of salvation history. Use the time line on page 180.

- God called Abraham, the first patriarch, about (1) _____ B.C.

- Nearly (2) _____ hundred years later, Joseph, one of Jacob's sons, was sold into

  slavery in Egypt. Jacob and his family settled in Egypt during a great famine in Canaan.

  After living peacefully there for many years, the descendants of Israel were forced into slavery.

  The Israelites lived in Egypt about (3) _____ hundred years.

- Finally about 1280 B.C., (4) _____ led the Israelites out of Egypt. After forty years,

  the freed people entered the Promised Land under Joshua's leadership.

- The time of the judges lasted about (5) _____ hundred years. Two of the judges

  who led the Israelites to victory over their enemies were (6) _____

  and (7) _____ .

- The time of the kings began in 1020 B.C. when Samuel anointed (8) _____ as first

  king of Israel. The greatest king of Israel, King (9) _____ ruled from 1000 to

  (10) _____ B.C. David's son, King (11) _____ died in 922 B.C.

- After Solomon, the kingdom was divided. In 722 B.C. the northern kingdom of Israel fell to the

  Assyrians. In 587 B.C. the southern kingdom of Judah fell to the Babylonians. The people were exiled

  to (12) _____ . Forty years later, in 537 B.C., the Jews were permitted to return

  to their own land.

- The time of restoration and waiting for the Messiah lasted about four hundred more years.

  During this time the Syrians oppressed the Jewish people until the (13) _____

  overthrew them. Eventually the (14) _____ conquered Palestine in 63 B.C.

  *When Jesus was born, the fullness of time had arrived. God had become one of us to save us!*

## Song and Procession
(*Students carrying Bible and candles lead, followed by those bearing banners and the box of hearts.*)

## Introduction

**Rally Leader:** We are gathered here today not only to honor God's prophets from the past, but to encourage one another to accept the challenging role of being prophets today. This means being ready and willing to turn our life over to God completely by resisting evil and doing good. It means helping others return to him in mind and heart. It takes great courage and self-discipline, but we want to serve the Lord and proclaim his Word. Let's stand now and hear it for God!

**All:** (*Sing a spirited Amen, Alleluia, or another acclamation.*)

**Reader:** (*Read Ephesians 4:22–24.*)

**All:** Thanks be to God!

## Song

## Banner Presentations
(*One at a time, students with banners step to the front center and stand there while the rally leader reads the message of their prophet. After each message, all sing "We Do!" or a similar acclamation.*)

AMOS

**Rally Leader:** Elijah, prophet of the one true God, said, "It is wrong to worship false gods. The Lord is the one true God." Do you promise to love and worship our God?

**All:** "We Do!"

**Rally Leader:** Isaiah, the prophet of the Messiah, said, "Take courage. The Messiah will come to save you. He will be the Son of David, wise and powerful." Do you promise to prepare for the coming of the Messiah to all people by living in peace?

**All:** "We Do!"

With expression                                        Sister Mary Andrew Miller, S.N.D.

We do! Al - le - lu, Al - le- lu----------------ia, The Lord will lead us on!

## JEREMIAH

**Rally Leader:** Jeremiah, the prophet of the New Covenant, said, "Because of your sin the enemy will destroy Jerusalem and leave your land empty. But God will establish a new covenant with you." Do you promise to stay away from sin and draw closer to God?

**All:** "We Do!"

**Rally Leader:** Amos, the prophet of social justice, said, "You are cheating others and living dishonestly. See that justice is done, for justice must flow like water." Do you promise to be just and honest in dealing with God and others?

**All:** "We Do!"

**Rally Leader:** Ezekiel, the prophet of hope, said, "God will be a shepherd to you, leading you back to your own land." Do you promise to follow the Good Shepherd in loyalty, love, and peace?

**All:** "We Do!"

**Rally Leader:** John the Baptist, prophet of repentance, said, "You must have a change of heart to obtain forgiveness. Repent, for one greater and more powerful than I is coming, and he will save you from your sin." Do you promise to repent, and to put on the mind and heart of Jesus?

**All:** "We Do!"

**Rally Leader:** Now let's join in some cheers for God! (*Cheerleaders lead cheers.*)

### Prayer

**Rally Leader:** Let us bow our heads and take a few moments to pray to God in the quiet of our hearts. (*Pause*)

**Reader 2:** (*Read Jeremiah 32:38–41.*)

**All:** Thanks be to God.

### Acceptance of Mission

**Rally Leader:** At this time we ask those who are willing to accept the role of prophet to come forward, and, one at a time, take a heart from the box. Read the message you have chosen, and then pin on the heart.

### Song (*Sung while students process up for their hearts*)

### Prophet's Pledge

**All:** I praise and thank you, heavenly Father,
   for showing me the way to you through
      your Son.
   I promise I will do my best in the role of
      prophet today.
   I will obey your laws,
   I will work for peace and justice,
   I will fight evil and warn others of it, and
   I will do my best to lead others to you by
      showing them your love.
   Help me to do your will. Amen.

### Song

**EZEKIEL**

## Messages of the Prophets

Putt your way through the messages of the prophets by reading the Bible passages indicated beneath each prophet's flag.

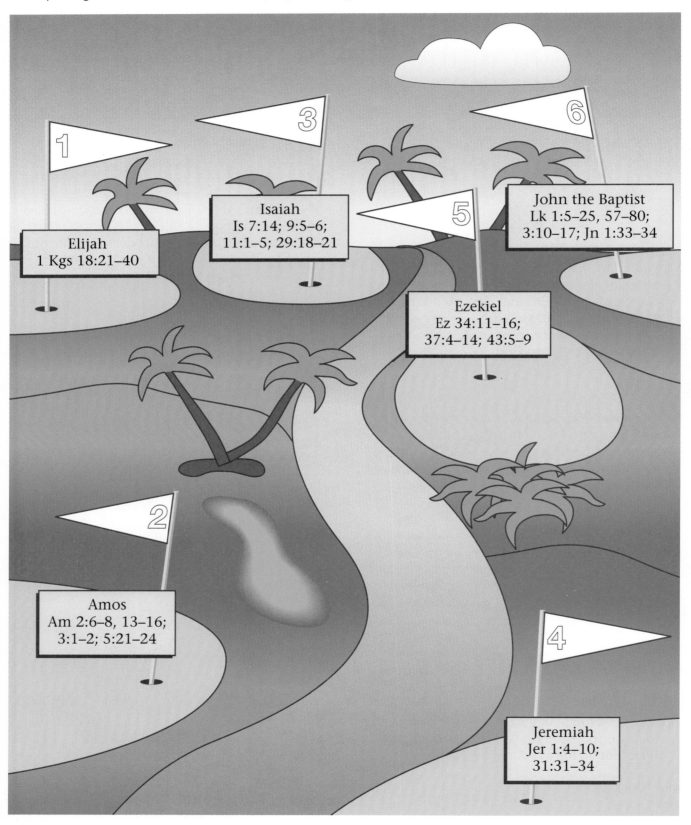

Elijah
1 Kgs 18:21–40

Isaiah
Is 7:14; 9:5–6;
11:1–5; 29:18–21

John the Baptist
Lk 1:5–25, 57–80;
3:10–17; Jn 1:33–34

Ezekiel
Ez 34:11–16;
37:4–14; 43:5–9

Amos
Am 2:6–8, 13–16;
3:1–2; 5:21–24

Jeremiah
Jer 1:4–10;
31:31–34

## Identifying Each Prophet

On the golf course of the previous activity, color each flag according to the code.

Prophet of social justice—green flag

Prophet of repentance—purple flag

Prophet of the one true God—red flag

Prophet of hope—orange flag

Prophet of the new covenant—blue flag

Prophet of the Messiah—yellow flag

## A Message to Remember

In Isaiah 48:17 there is a message from God that is good to remember when things go wrong or we can't understand what's happening around us. Read that verse. Then, in the space below, letter the words God says and decorate them.

# Looking Back at Unit 5

In this unit you have met several prophets whom God sent to speak his word to his people. They tried to convince the people to change their ways and live according to God's will. When the people did not listen, their sinful, selfish lives brought them sorrow and suffering.

Elijah was sent to call the king and the people to the worship of the one true God.

Amos is known as the prophet of social justice. He told the people that they must care for the poor and the needy. Amos was the first prophet whose teachings were written down.

Isaiah is the prophet of holiness because he had a vision of the holiness of God. Isaiah spent his life trying to convince the people that they, too, must be holy. He told them to trust the Lord and to serve him with their whole hearts.

Jeremiah was a young man when he was called to be a prophet. God promised to be with him and to help him. Jeremiah told the people how displeased God was when they came to worship him without repenting. Through Jeremiah, God promised a new covenant to his people.

Because of the sinful lives of the people, the kingdom of Judah became weak and was conquered. The people were taken to Babylon. God called Ezekiel to be his prophet there. Ezekiel's preaching helped the people realize that God was still with them in this foreign land, and he still loved them. During the exile, the people learned to worship God from their hearts.

John the Baptist was the last and greatest prophet. God called him to prepare the way for Jesus. His message was that the time for the Messiah to come was here. He told the people to repent and believe in God's love and forgiveness.

The message of the prophets is for us, too. God loves us and wants us to show our love for him by the way we live. He wants us to make his Son Jesus the center of our lives, just as Mary made him the center of her life. Only when we do this will we be able to come with loving hearts to worship God.

## Living the Message

Can you give yourself a check (✔) for each statement?

❏ **1.** I can explain why God sent prophets to his people and tell something about the messages of Elijah, Amos, Isaiah, Jeremiah, Ezekiel, and John the Baptist.

❏ **2.** I know that God has a special love for the poor and needy and wants me to love them and share what I have with them.

❏ **3.** I try in any way I can to help those who have less than I have.

❏ **4.** I am trying to make God "tops" in my life.

❏ **5.** When something bad happens, I believe God can use the situation to bring about good.

## Planning Ahead

Think about the messages of the prophets. Below, write the message that you think is most important for people to hear today. Write how you want to respond to this message. Write something you can do to spread the prophet's message.

Message _____

_____

Your response _____

_____

Spreading the message _____

_____

# FAMILY FEATURE

## Salt for the Earth

The Hillert family takes its call to be prophets in the world today seriously. They know that at Baptism they received a share in Christ's role of prophet. To begin a family meeting one night, they held a celebration of salt to remind them to be witnesses for Christ. Your family might wish to have a similar prayer service.

That night for supper the Hillerts had soup that was low in salt. (You might cook soup from scratch without using canned broth or salty soup base.) Then baked potatoes without seasoning or sauce were served. As the salt was passed, Mr. Hillert commented how salt makes everything taste better.

After supper Mrs. Hillert set a large salt shaker on the table with a lit candle. She read Matthew 5:13, Lisa read Mark 9:50, and Mr. Hillert read Luke 14:34–35. Then Mr. Hillert commented that our blood is mildly salty water with blood cells floating in it. Our tears and sweat are salty too. Although we are salty people, we must pray and work harder to be the salt of the Earth as Jesus meant. Then Mr. Hillert took the salt and made the sign of the cross over it in blessing. He prayed,

> "God, we thank you for the gift of salt that makes our food taste good and that preserves food and heals us. May we be like this salt in your creation, making everything in the world better because we came into contact with it. For we are the salt of the Earth." Everyone repeated, "We are the salt of the Earth."

The family passed the salt around, and each person took a few grains and tasted them. They discussed how they could be salt in a particular situation.

After the meeting, the Hillerts enjoyed snacks of buttered and salted popcorn, salted nuts, and pretzels.

# Prophet Puzzle

Find and circle the names of the prophets and words related to them.
They are horizontal, vertical, and diagonal.

```
D E J U S T I C E F L U O R
M A E X N O L L B B O D E M
E P N E X D P C O A M E J S
S B P I C M E S S A G E O I
E E C U E Q R T C L E A H T
R V O T P L B A B Y L O N E
V S V Z M O L E I D I C P X
A M E Z E K I E L S J O T I
N A N E F I D S O N A T U L
T S A J E R E M I A H I A E
C I N U O Q A B L A F S A K
N R T W M E S S I A H P N H
```

repent          Daniel
Elijah          Isaiah
Jeremiah        Ezekiel
Baal            Amos
covenant        servant
exile           John
Word            Babylon
Temple          Messiah
justice         message

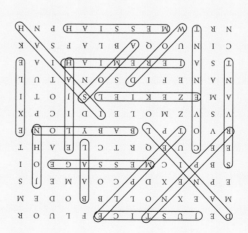

## Message for Today

In the box write advice a prophet might give people today.

_____

_____

_____

_____

_____

_____

_____

_____

_____

_____

_____

_____

_____

_____

_____

_____

_____

_____

# SUPPLEMENT

# November: The Month of All Souls

## Our Family of Faith

November is the month set aside by the Church for us to grow in awareness of our family of faith. We call this family the Communion of Saints. We are the members of the family still journeying on earth on our way to our heavenly homeland. There are family members who have completed the journey and are already in heaven with the Father—the saints. There are those who have completed their journey on earth but are not yet ready to enter the Father's glory. We call these people the souls in purgatory.

These souls are certain that they will spend eternity in heaven. Their experience of waiting, a final preparation for their entry into God's presence, is called **purgatory.** It is a time to be purified of every trace of sin. The desire to be with God is so great that it burns like a fire in the souls in purgatory. But they know they are not ready to be united with the all-holy God. They truly want to wait until they are.

## All Saints' Day

On November 1 we celebrate with all those who have responded to God's call and are now in heaven with God. The saints are always willing to pray for us if we ask them. The example of their lives helps us follow Jesus more closely.

Name a favorite saint and tell why you like him or her.

_____

_____

## All Souls' Day

November 2 is set aside to remember those who are in purgatory waiting for their entrance into heaven. We can help them by praying for them and asking God to take them into his presence soon.

The Church asks us to pray for the holy souls in purgatory during the entire month of November. They can also pray and intercede for us. We can ask them to help us when we are in need.

> ### Prayer for the Souls in Purgatory
>
> Eternal rest grant to them, O Lord,
> and let perpetual light
> shine upon them.
> May they rest in peace. Amen.

Are there some special people who have died that you will pray for during this month? List their names below.

_____

_____

_____

Pray for all those in purgatory, especially those who have no one else to pray for them.

# Advent: Seeking the Light of Christ
## (A Jesse Tree Celebration)

Use this celebration to make a Jesse Tree and review the story of the Messiah's coming.

**Leader 1:** We who have received the light and life of Jesus in Baptism recall in the season of Advent that darkness once covered the earth. It was God who dispelled the first darkness, which was the darkness of nothingness. God dismissed this darkness with the light of creation. The sun, the moon, and the stars gave light to the world. But a second darkness came, the darkness of sin, and it overshadowed all people. Once again God dismissed the darkness. He promised to send his only Son as Redeemer, to be the light and the life of all people.

**Leader 2:** The Jesse Tree, named for the father of David, tells the story of God's wonderful promise and its fulfillment. Each symbol recalls something about the Messiah or the people who helped prepare the way for him.

(*Students show and explain the symbols, then place them on the tree.*)

**Student:**  (*World: a circle with land/water forms drawn on it*) God created the world and everything in it for us. This is the beginning of the story of his love for humankind.

**Student:**  (*Adam and Eve: apple with two bites missing*) The sin of Adam and Eve, our first parents, changed the course of history. Their "happy fault" brought the promise of a Redeemer.

**Student:**  (*Noah: ark and/or rainbow*) God saved Noah and all who followed him into the ark. All who follow Christ faithfully will be saved. After the flood, God made a covenant never again to destroy the world by a flood. With Christ's death, a new covenant was formed that people would be saved from sin and eternal death.

**Student:**  (*Abraham and Isaac: ram in bush or an altar*) Abraham was willing to sacrifice his only son at God's word. Jesus, God's only Son, was willing to sacrifice himself to his Father's will.

**Student:**  (*Jacob: ladder going to heaven*) Jacob had a vision of a ladder reaching heaven, with angels going up and down on it. Christ would be the one to unite heaven and earth.

**Student:**  (*Joseph: coat of many colors*) Joseph's brothers, out of envy, sold him as a slave. Jesus was sold for thirty pieces of silver. In the end Joseph saved his family and the known world, just as Christ died to save us all.

**Student:**  (*Moses: tablets of stone*) God made a covenant with Moses and the chosen people. The people broke God's laws in many ways. God told them he would plant a new law in their hearts that would not pass away. Christ was to bring that law.

**Student:**  (*Ruth: bundle of wheat*) Ruth, an important member of the family of Jesus, was not an Israelite, but a Gentile. She was loyal to Naomi and worked in the fields to gather food. Ruth became the grandmother of King David.

**Student:**  (*Jesse: flower with stem and root*) Isaiah prophesied that the Messiah would be the flower springing from the root of Jesse, and that he would sit on the throne of David. Jesse was David's father.

**Student:**  (*David: harp, crown*) David was the greatest king of Israel and a man of God. The Messiah would be born from his family line. Christ the Messiah would be the new King, ruling over heaven and earth.

**Student:**  (*Solomon: Temple, crown*) Solomon, son of David, was known for his wisdom and for the great Temple he built for the worship of God. Christ came to show us how to worship the Father and to make our hearts a temple.

**Student:**  (*Judith: sword*) Judith was the deliverer of her nation because she defeated the enemy by killing their general with a sword. She is also a sign of Mary because she, like Mary, did God's will and was called "the glory of Jerusalem and the joy of Israel."

**Student:**  (*Prophets: scroll*) Prophets foretold things about the Messiah: where he would be born, who his parents would be, the kind of life he would live, how he would die and rise. Their prophecies are part of Scripture.

**Student:**  (*John the Baptist: baptismal shell*) John the Baptist, the last and greatest of all the prophets, prepared the way of the Lord and called the people to a baptism of repentance. He was privileged to baptize Jesus himself!

**Student:**  (*Bethlehem: loaf of bread*) Micah foretold that the Savior would be born in Bethlehem. The name means "house of bread." Jesus would give himself to be our Bread of Life.

**Student:**  (*House of David: six-pointed star*) This star has become the emblem of the House of David. Today it is used as a symbol of Judaism. Jesus Christ, born of the family of David, can truly claim it as his own.

**Student:**  (*Joseph: carpenter's tools*) Saint Joseph was the foster-father of Christ and the husband and protector of Mary. He worked as a carpenter and probably taught Jesus the trade.

**Student:**  (*Mary: fleur-de-lis, lily, or decorated M*) God chose Mary, a young Jewish woman, to be the mother of his Son. It was through her yes to God that the promise was fulfilled and God became man!

**Student:** (*Jesus: five-pointed star*) A new star appeared in the heavens on the night Jesus, our Redeemer, was born. He came as the Light of the World to banish the darkness of sin and ignorance forever!

### Song

**Leader 3:** The world which awaited the light did not know it when it came. But the light was real, and it still shines upon us.

**Reader:** Please stand for a reading from the Gospel of St. John.

In the beginning of all things was the Word. He was with God, he was in God, he was God. And everything that was made, was made through him. Everything that was made in him has life, life for the light of all. This light shines on in a darkness that cannot overcome it. John was a man sent by God to testify to the light, so that everyone would believe. He gave witness to the real light which gives light to everyone. Not everyone accepted the light. Those who did accept the light became the children of God.

adapted from John 1:1–12

**All:** Praise to you, Lord Jesus Christ.

**Leader 4:** Sometimes, instead of preparing for the light, we turn to darkness. During Advent we seek out the light which is Christ and ask him to take away that darkness. We ask him to brighten every part of our lives. We welcome him into our hearts. He comes to us, and he comes to others through us.

**Leader 5:** Let us pray that the light of Christ be upon us. Let us pray to be delivered from the darkness.

**Student 1:** Lord, when we are in the darkness of selfishness . . .

**All:** Let your light be upon us.

**Student 2:** Lord, when we are in the darkness of dishonesty or laziness . . .

**All:** Let your light be upon us.

**Student 3:** Lord, when we are in the darkness of ingratitude . . .

**All:** Let your light be upon us.

**Student 4:** Lord, when we are in the darkness of thoughtlessness . . .

**All:** Let your light be upon us.

**Student 5:** Lord, whenever we are in the darkness which is apart from you . . .

**All:** Let your light be upon us.

Song

**Leader 6:** As we recall the coming of Christ in history, and experience his comings in the mysteries of faith, let us prepare our hearts to know him and to accept him more eagerly each day.

**Silent Time**
Think of what you can do to prepare for the coming of Christ. How can you be more like Jesus? How can you be a light to others? You may want to write your thoughts in a prayer.

Dear Lord, during Advent I will prepare for your coming by

_____

_____

_____

_____

**Leader 7:** Let us pray.

**All:** Lord, help us to prepare
your way into our hearts.
Help us to bring down the
mountains of our pride and
selfish ways.
Help us to fill up the valleys in
our lives by doing the good
things we should.
Help us to smooth out our rough
ways by showing kindness and
gentleness to everyone.
We want to prepare a straight
path for you by sincerely
trying to live with you as our
Light and Life. Amen.

Song

# Our Lady of Guadalupe, Mother of the Americas

## Her Personal Appearance

Juan Diego was an Aztec Indian in Mexico and a convert to the faith. On Saturday, December 9, 1531, he was walking to church for Mass when a beautiful lady, surrounded by light, appeared to him. She told him she was the Immaculate Virgin Mary, the mother of the true God. She expressed her desire to have a shrine built there at Tepeyac Hill, so she could show her love for the people. She said,

> Ask for my help. Here I will listen to people's prayers, and I will help them.

Mary then asked Juan to tell the bishop of her desire. Juan did so, but the bishop didn't believe him. Juan returned to the lady and suggested she send to the bishop someone who could talk better. Mary told Juan he was the one she had chosen for this work, and she would bless him for helping her.

The second time Juan visited the bishop, he was told to ask "his Lady" for a sign that she was truly the Mother of God. When Juan did so, Mary told him to return the next day for the sign.

In the meantime, however, Juan's uncle became very ill, and Juan had to stay home to care for him. By Tuesday the uncle was dying, so Juan set off to get a priest. On the way he met the Holy Virgin. Embarrassed, he apologized for not meeting her the day before. Mary replied,

> Now listen to me. Do not let anything bother you, and do not be afraid of any illness, pain, or accident. Am I, your mother, not here? Are you not under my shadow and protection? What more could you want? Don't worry about your uncle. He is well already.

Mary then told Juan to go to the top of the hill and gather the flowers he would find growing there. Juan knew that nothing grew on that rock hill, let alone in the middle of winter! However, he did as the Virgin told him and climbed the hill. At the top he found gorgeous roses! He picked them and brought them to Mary, who arranged the roses in his *tilma,* or cloak. She told Juan to take them to the bishop.

## Her Miraculous Image

When the bishop saw Juan, he wanted to know what he had in his tilma. Juan opened it, letting the fragrant roses fall in a shower to the floor. You can imagine the bishop's surprise at seeing roses in winter! As he looked, however, the bishop saw an even greater miracle. There on Juan's tilma a beautifully painted image began to appear! Juan gasped! It was his Lady!

The bishop cried out, "The Immaculate!" Then he knelt and with tears asked the Blessed Mother's pardon for not believing Juan.

On that same day, Mary appeared to Juan's uncle and cured him. Uncle Bernadino went to the bishop and told how he had been cured. He also gave the bishop a message from the Virgin, saying that she would "crush the serpent's head." The bishop did not understand the Indian's language. He heard the Indian words for "crush the serpent" which sounded like "Guadalupe," the name of Mary's shrine in Spain. Thinking that the Virgin wanted the new shrine to have the same name, the bishop called her Our Lady of Guadalupe.

The picture of Our Lady of Guadalupe has meaningful symbols. Its main message is that Mary loves us and wants to help us. The cloak itself is made from the rough fibers of a cactus plant. If this type of material is painted on, it will not last more than twenty years. Yet the picture remains fresh and beautiful on the cloak after 450 years! It can be seen above the main altar in the Shrine of Our Lady of Guadalupe in Mexico.

The feast of Our Lady of Guadalupe is celebrated by the Church on December 12. Do you know why that date was chosen?

| December | | | | | | |
|---|---|---|---|---|---|---|
| Sunday | Monday | Tuesday | Wednesday | Thursday | Friday | Saturday |
| 1 | 2 | 3 | 4 | 5 | 6 | 7 |
| 8 | 9 | 10 | 11 | (12) | 13 | 14 |
| 15 | 16 | 17 | 18 | 19 | 20 | 21 |
| 22 | 23 | 24 | 25 | 26 | 27 | 28 |
| 29 | 30 | 31 | | | | |

## Prayer to Our Lady of Guadalupe

Mother of mercy,
Teacher of hidden and silent sacrifice,
to you, who come to meet us sinners,
we dedicate on this day all our being and our love.
We also dedicate to you our life, our work,
our joys, our weaknesses, and our sorrows.
We wish to be entirely yours
and to walk with you
along the way of complete faithfulness
to Jesus Christ and his Church;
hold us always with your loving hand.

**1.** How can we dedicate—give ourselves wholeheartedly—to Mary?
**2.** What hidden and silent sacrifice can we perform?
**3.** How can we walk the way of complete faithfulness to Jesus and the Church?

# January: The Month of the Holy Family

## Families—Jesus' and Mine

When a man and a woman seal their love in marriage, their union creates a family, the Church in a home. A family is a special gift from God. Most people are born into a family with whom they live. Others are adopted or chosen as family members. Still others, because of death or some other tragedy, are not with their own family now but with people who are called to act as their family. What makes a happy family?

When God the Son became a man, he was born into a unique family called the Holy Family. All families can learn from the Holy Family, but none can be just like it. Each family is unique.

Think about the Holy Family and your family. List two ways these families are alike.

1. _____

2. _____

Now list two ways these families are different.

1. _____

2. _____

Think of one thing that makes it easy for your family to love and serve God.

_____

Think of one thing that makes it hard.

_____

## My Family and I

Each family has different gifts, different strong points. That is good! People should look for the strong points of their families and try to make them grow even stronger. Every member of the family is responsible for helping the family grow in happiness.

Rate yourself from 1 (once in a while) to 5 (almost always) on the following checklist.

**1.** I praise the members of my family when they do something well. _____

**2.** I thank members of my family when they do things for me. _____

**3.** I do my share of the work at home. _____

**4.** I speak respectfully to the members of my family and do not use put-downs. _____

**5.** I pray that the members of my family will love God and each other and help spread God's love to others. _____

Total _____

Try to remember these five points every day. At the end of January, the month dedicated to the Holy Family, rate yourself again. If your total is higher, you have probably helped make your family happier.

Think of at least one good thing that makes your family special. Thank God for that gift. Pray to the Holy Family, asking Jesus, Mary, and Joseph to help your family grow in love and service of God and one another.

# March: The Month of St. Joseph

Joseph, descendant of the royal house of David, is honored as the husband of Mary on March 19. In addition, the whole month of March is dedicated to him.

In the first chapter of St. Matthew, we read that an angel came to Joseph in a dream to tell him to take Mary as his wife, for her child was of the Holy Spirit. That child, whom he was to name Jesus, would save the people from their sins. So Joseph became Mary's husband. The marriage bond also made him the legal father of Jesus, Son of God. For these reasons he is honored as the Guardian of the Holy Family, next in holiness and dignity to Mary, Mother of God.

Though Scripture tells us very little about Joseph directly, we can learn much from what we read there. We recognize the virtues he practiced in the events of his life.

**Faith** He accepted God's word through an angel to take Mary as his wife.
**Obedience to Civil Law** He went to Bethlehem to register for the census.
**Obedience to Religious Law** He and Mary took Jesus to the Temple forty days after his birth to present him to God and to offer sacrifice.
**Obedience to God's Word** He took Mary and Jesus on a hurried journey to Egypt in the middle of the night to save Jesus' life.
**Faithfulness to Duty** He worked hard as a carpenter to support Jesus and Mary.
**Love** He provided love, comfort, and security for his family at Nazareth.
**Trust** He trusted in God in all the events of his life.

As we think about Joseph, we see how he became a saint by pleasing God in the little things of everyday life. He teaches us, as Mary does, to live for Jesus.

St. Joseph probably died some time before Jesus began his public life of teaching. What a beautiful death he must have had, with Jesus and Mary at his side! Can you see why we honor Joseph as patron of a happy death?

Just as St. Joseph took care of the Holy Family, so he cares for the Church, the family of God. In 1870 Pope Pius IX named him Patron and Protector of the Universal Church.

Because St. Joseph sanctified labor by doing it for Jesus and Mary, Pope Pius XII proclaimed him Patron of Workers. May 1 is celebrated as the feast of St. Joseph the Worker to emphasize the dignity of the worker and the value of honest work.

One thing Joseph has in common with his wife, Mary—he can't refuse a favor! He is willing to help us in any way he can. All we have to do is ask!

During March, we should honor St. Joseph in a special way. We can show our love for him especially by praying to him and by imitating his holy life. What are your plans for celebrating St. Joseph's month?

# Lent: The Springtime of the Church Year

Every year we wait for spring. The chirping birds, the fresh shoots of green grass, the gentle and steady rains, and the warm sunshine tell us that new life is coming. We look forward to seeing it in all its beauty. But new life comes in spring only because other things have died. Their death was a necessary step in the birth of new life.

Lent is the springtime of the Church year. It is a time of preparation. During Lent, Christians devote themselves to prayer, fasting, and almsgiving to prepare themselves for the joy of Easter. Easter celebrates the Paschal Mystery,

the mystery of our dying to sin and rising with Christ to the new life of grace. Jesus loves us so much that he was willing to suffer and die for us. Through his sacrifice he saved us from sin, and through the sacraments he shares his life with us.

When we truly love God and others as Jesus has taught us, we are living the life of grace. During Lent we look closely at how we are taking care of the life of God within us. We follow the Church law to fast and abstain. We try in a special way to die to sin and to live in love. The Church gives us six weeks of Lent to

prepare for Easter. Each of us will experience Easter joy if we use this time to become the best person we can be. The life of grace, like all life, is meant to grow. But like other kinds of life, grace needs certain conditions for growth. Our Lenten practices provide the conditions. The more we live in the spirit of Lent, the better we will be able to enjoy the new life Jesus has given us. Are there some bad habits you need to correct or some good ones you want to form? What kind of preparations do you want to make?

How much do you know about Lent? Fill in the missing words below and complete the crossword puzzle.

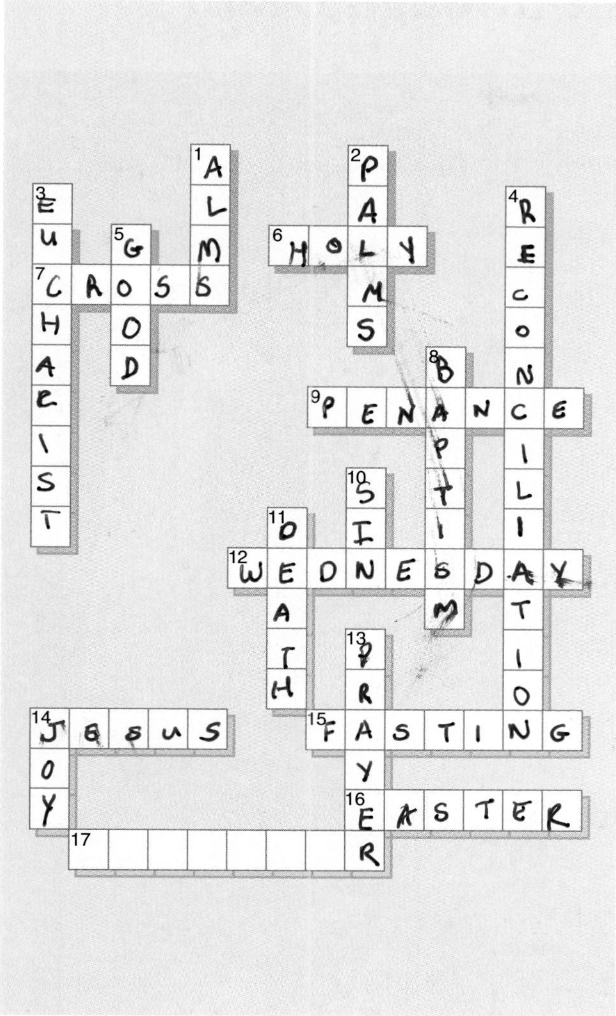

The crossword grid (with handwritten answers):

1. A L M
2. P A L M S
3. E U C H A R I S T
4. R E C O N C I L I A T I O N
5. G O O D
6. H O L Y
7. C R O S S
8. B A P T I S M
9. P E N A N C E
10. S I N
11. D E A T H
12. W E D N E S D A Y
13. P R A Y E R S
14. J E S U S / J O Y
15. F A S T I N G
16. E A S T E R
17. P A S S O V E R

Lent begins on Ash __Wednesday__ .
(12 across)

On this day the priest or other minister makes the

sign of the __Cross__ on our forehead
(7 across)

with ashes made from burning blessed

__Palms__ . The words of the minister
(2 down)

and the ashes remind us that Lent is a time of

__Penance__ . Lenten practices help us
(9 across)

live the life we receive at __Baptism__ .
(8 down)

We open our hearts to God's love by the Lenten

practices of __Prayers__ , __Fasting__ ,
(13 down)        (15 across)

and giving __Alms__ to those in need.
(1 down)

We think about how __Jesus__ was willing
(14 across)

to sacrifice his life for us and we celebrate his

__Death__ and resurrection.
(11 down)

We participate in his Paschal Mystery by turning

from __Sin__ and by celebrating the
(10 down)

Sacrament of __Reconciliation__ .
(4 down)

The last Sunday of Lent begins __Holy__ Week. It is a week when
(6 across)

everyone who loves Jesus tries to participate in the liturgies. The Holy

Thursday liturgy celebrates Christ's gift of the priesthood and the Holy

__Eucharist__ . No Mass is celebrated on __Good__ Friday.
(3 down)                                    (5 down)

During the liturgy of that day, the Passion is read and we ask God that the

sufferings of Jesus may free all people from sin. During the solemn

__Easter__ Vigil we remember that most holy night when our
(16 across)

Lord Jesus Christ passes from death to life. We celebrate our own

__passover__ from sin and praise God for sending us Jesus.
(17 across)

Celebrating Lent prepares us for true Easter __Joy__ .
(14 down)

JOY IN NEW LIFE

# The Easter Triduum: Life through Death

We take many mysteries in our life for granted. But there is one mystery that is so important to us as Christians that we spend special days renewing and celebrating it. That mystery is the death and rising of Jesus.

Each Sunday is a celebration of the Resurrection. But each year we set aside days to recall Christ's passing through suffering and death to resurrection. Holy Thursday, Good Friday, Holy Saturday, and Easter Sunday are the celebration of the one act of redemption.

The Easter (or Paschal) Triduum is the high point of the Church year, just as the death and resurrection of Jesus is the high point of all salvation history. But what we celebrate during these days is a puzzle, a contradiction. How can death bring life? How does pain lead to joy? Part of the answer is mystery and will remain mystery. It is the Paschal Mystery, the passion, death, and resurrection of the Lord.

We share in this mystery by our baptism. By water and the Spirit, marked by the sign of the cross, we, too, have died and have been given new life. Through Baptism we are called to die to sin and to live in Christ. We become part of the whole Christian family, the Body of Christ.

Our life is one of dying and rising every day. We die to our pride and selfishness in order to bring life to others through our service and love. When people look at us, they should see the death and rising of Jesus in our lives.

## Holy Thursday
Lent ends on Holy Thursday. The Easter Triduum begins with the Evening Mass of the Lord's Supper. At that Mass we recall Jesus giving himself to us under the appearance of bread and wine. We also see Jesus serving others as he washed the feet of his disciples.

In every service during the Easter Triduum symbols remind us of life through death. Bread and wine are powerful symbols. Wheat must be ground and purified to become bread. Grapes must be crushed to become wine.

## Good Friday
On Good Friday we recall the passion and death of Jesus, knowing at all times that he freely gave his life for us. The cross is his sign of victory. Love and forgiveness triumph over hatred. Through his death the Church is born and the hopes of all the ages are fulfilled.

The wood of the cross was a sign of defeat and shame. But Jesus turned it into a sign of victory and hope. Good Friday invites us to die with Christ to all that is not life-giving in our hearts. It is a time to appreciate the overwhelming love Jesus has for us.

## Holy Saturday

Holy Saturday begins as a quiet day of waiting. It is a day of forgetting self and living for others, preparing for the night of all nights.

## Easter Vigil and the Resurrection

The Easter Vigil service begins after sundown with the lighting and blessing of the new Easter fire. The large Paschal Candle, the symbol of Christ our light, is lit from this fire. The people present share in this new light and new fire that fills the darkness with light. The baptismal waters, sign of our birth and life in Christ, are blessed. The readings during the liturgy recall all of salvation history and the saving acts of God. The resurrection of Christ is proclaimed. Our new life in him is proclaimed, too, as we celebrate and receive Jesus in the Eucharist.

The Easter Vigil is a special time for those who have been waiting to be received into the faith. On this night they will be baptized into Christ and the community of believers. New Catholics are baptized, confirmed, and share in the Eucharist for the first time.

The Easter Triduum is a celebration of life, of dying and rising. It is the celebration of our passing from death to life in Jesus. It is a sign that death is not the final answer. It is a reminder that God the Father loves us so much that he gave his only Son so that we may find our way home to him.

## Acrostic

Use the clues to complete the acrostic.

| | | |
|---|---|---|
| **R** | We recall Christ's passion and death on Good _____. | F R I D A Y |
| **E** | Jesus freely gave his _____ for us. | L I F E |
| **S** | _____ is the sacrament of our dying and rising. | B A P T I S M |
| **U** | The Easter Triduum begins with the Evening Mass of the Lord's Supper on Holy _____. | T H U R S D A Y |
| **R** | The Paschal _____ is the passion, death, and resurrection of Jesus. | M Y S T E R Y |
| **R** | The Easter _____ is lit at the beginning of the Easter Vigil service. | F I R E |
| **E** | The high point of the Church year is the _____ Triduum. | E A S T E R |
| **C** | The Paschal _____ is the symbol of Christ our light. | C A N D L E |
| **T** | _____ means three days. | T R I D U U M |
| **I** | _____ is the evening before a great feast. | V I G I L |
| **O** | The _____ is our sign of victory. | C R O S S |
| **N** | The Easter Triduum is a celebration of dying and _____. | R I S I N G |

Read the explanations of the Easter symbols below. Add your own thoughts and drawings. Then design your own symbol of life and write an explanation of it.

# Symbols of Life

### Water
Without water we could not survive. Plants need it, animals need it, and we need it. It is life-giving in more than one way. Through the waters of Baptism we die to sin and rise to new life.

### Candles, Fire, Light
The Easter Vigil begins with the lighting and blessing of the Easter fire. Light and fire are powerful symbols. The Paschal Candle is lowered into the water three times during the Easter Vigil service.

### Butterfly
A butterfly reminds us of spring. It is also a symbol of the resurrection. The butterfly begins life as the caterpillar, makes a chrysalis, and later emerges from it as a beautiful butterfly.

### Decorated Eggs
An egg is a sign of new life. The chick breaks its shell and comes forth to a new life. At Easter we celebrate Jesus' breaking of the bonds of death and his bursting forth from the tomb with new life.

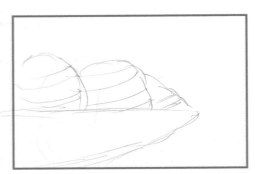

### Your Symbol

# Pentecost: The Spirit Forms the People of God

You are learning how God began shaping a people thousands of years ago. With the coming of Jesus, God built on what was begun with Abraham and the chosen people and continued it. Then on Pentecost the Spirit of God came to Mary and the disciples of Jesus and filled them with power to be the people of God.

Jesus had promised that the Father would send the Spirit to be a helper. At the Last Supper he said, "He will teach you everything and remind you of all that I told you." Forty days after Jesus rose from the dead, he returned to the Father. We call this the Ascension. Before Jesus left, he again promised his followers the gift of the Spirit.

At Jesus' directions his followers prayed and waited in Jerusalem. Nine days after the Ascension, a noise like a strong, driving wind filled the house where they were. They saw what was like tongues of fire resting on each one of them. They began to speak in different languages.

Because it was the Jewish feast of Pentecost, a harvest feast, people from all nations were gathered in Jerusalem. When the disciples came out and proclaimed the good news, everyone could understand them. In the story of Babel, sin had caused people to speak many languages, so they were divided. Now in Jerusalem the Spirit used the gift of languages to unite people in the knowledge of God's love.

The people were used to associating God with fire. In Hebrew Scriptures God first spoke to Moses in the form of a burning bush. Later, God guided the chosen people to the Promised Land as a column of fire at night. At Pentecost, God again used the symbol of fire as he gifted us with his loving presence.

Where else in the Bible is God associated with wind or breath?

Every year fifty days after Easter we celebrate the presence of the Spirit with us in the Church. On this feast of Pentecost we recall that the Spirit of God dwells within us and works in us to spread the good news to the world and bring about the kingdom of God.

During the Eucharist on Pentecost we pray a special prayer before the Gospel called a **Sequence.** Here are three of the verses we address to the Holy Spirit:

> Come, Holy Spirit, come!
> And from your celestial home
>   Shed a ray of light divine.
>
> Heal our wounds, our strength renew;
> On our dryness pour your dew;
>   Wash the stains of guilt away:
>
> Bend the stubborn heart and will;
> Melt the frozen, warm the chill:
>   Guide the steps that go astray.

Circle all the verbs that highlight what we are asking the Spirit to do.

You can turn to the Holy Spirit, our counselor and our comforter, for help in difficult situations. What problem can you pray to the Spirit about right now?

# May: The Month of Mary

We honor Mary with many titles, but the greatest title of all is Mother of God. Mary is truly the mother of God for she gave birth to Jesus, the Son of God. We honor Mary for giving us Jesus our Savior, and we ask her to help us follow her Son faithfully.

Although Mary was always a virgin, she is a mother to all of us. She loves and cares for us. If we listen to her when we pray, we will learn how we can be better followers of Jesus.

One beautiful title of Mary is Mother of Perpetual Help. Mary is called Mother of Perpetual Help because she is always interceding for us, asking her Son to grant us all that we need to be holy and happy. Mary will always help us when we call on her.

Pictures of Our Lady have different titles. The picture on this page is called Mother of Perpetual Help. Whenever we look at it we can pray,

MARY
Mother of Perpetual Help
PRAY FOR US

The Memorare

Remember, O most gracious Virgin Mary, that never was it known that anyone who fled to your protection, implored your help, or sought your intercession was left unaided. Inspired with this confidence I fly unto you, O Virgin of Virgins, my mother. To you I come, before you I stand, sinful and sorrowful. O Mother of the Word Incarnate, despise not my petitions, but in your mercy hear and answer me.

Amen.

# Jonah: A Fish Story

Read the Book of Jonah, which is only two pages long. Then fill in the blanks in this summary.

The Lord sent Jonah to preach against the enemy

city of _____. Frightened, Jonah boarded a ship and sailed in another direction. A terrible storm came up. The captain woke Jonah and told him to rise up. The sailors cast

_____ to find out whose fault the storm was. They discovered that Jonah was to blame, for he was fleeing from his God.

Jonah said, "Throw me into the

_____." The men finally did as he asked and then prayed to Jonah's God. The storm stopped.

The Lord sent a large _____ that

swallowed Jonah. _____ days later Jonah was spewed out on the shore. Then Jonah went to Nineveh as God had directed. He predicted that the city would be destroyed in

_____ days for its wickedness.

As a result, all the people, along with the

_____ and the animals, fasted and did penance. So God did not punish them.

Jonah, however, was disappointed that God did not destroy the city. He complained to God and then sat outside the city to watch.

God had a _____ _____
grow up over Jonah's head to shade him. The next

morning a _____ killed it and Jonah suffered from the heat. He wanted to die. God said to Jonah, "You are concerned about a plant. Should I not be concerned over 120,000 persons who can't tell their right hand from their left, not to mention the many

_____?"

What lessons do you think God is teaching us through this story?

_____

_____

_____

# Judith: A Brave Woman with Beauty and Brains

Read the following imaginary letters of Judith's maid to her friend Sarah and learn the story contained in the Book of Judith.

### 1

Dear Sarah,

I have just begun a new job as maid to the widow Judith. Ever since her husband died three years ago, this beautiful woman has lived a life of prayer and fasting. Everyone respects her for her goodness and wisdom. Looks like my life will be pretty easy from now on.

Anna

### 2

Dear Sarah,

Everyone knows that Nebuchadnezzar, king of Assyria, plans to destroy the whole world with his armies. His general, Holofernes, has conquered city after city. He is forcing all people to worship his king as a god. Today everyone here in Bethulia is preparing for an attack. We are fasting and praying to God.

Anna

### 3

Dear Sarah,

Holofernes has reached us. His men discovered our water sources and seized them. We have been without water for several days. People are fainting in the streets. Some are begging our leaders to surrender. Uzziah declared that if God doesn't help us within five days, we will surrender.

Anna

### 4

Dear Sarah,

I can't believe my lady Judith. She actually scolded Uzziah for putting time limits on God. Then she said to our leaders, "Let me pass through the gate tonight with my maid. The Lord will rescue Israel by my hand." The rulers agreed. Judith prayed. Then she dressed in beautiful garments and jewelry and packed some food. She and I then walked out of the city toward the Assyrians. I handed this letter to someone at the gate. It might be the last you hear from me.

Anna

# 5

Dear Sarah,

What an amazing woman Judith is. As soon as we left Bethulia, the Assyrians arrested us. Judith explained that we were fleeing from the town because we knew it was going to be destroyed. She offered to show Holofernes a route to capture the city easily.

You could tell the soldiers were impressed by Judith's beauty. They took us straight to Holofernes. Judith told him that the Israelites were to die because they had sinned against God. We stayed in camp for three days. Each night we went out to pray. On the fourth night Holofernes called for Judith to dine with him. I could tell he was wild about Judith from the way he looked at her.

At that meal Holofernes drank so much that he lay on his bed in a drunken stupor. Judith took his sword, grasped his hair, and cut off his head! She gave it to me to carry in our food pouch. We went out as we usually did to pray, but instead we returned to Bethulia. The town rejoiced, praising God and Judith.

Anna

Dear Sarah,

It is the day after our safe return. This morning our men pretended to attack. The Assyrians ran to awake Holofernes and found his headless body. Because of their confusion, we overwhelmed them. Judith led everyone in a song of thanksgiving to God. Beware of serving good widows!

Anna

# Job: A Man of Suffering

The Book of Job makes us think about the mystery of suffering. Read this play about Job's story.

## Cast

**Narrator   Job   Job's Wife   Messengers 1, 2, 3, 4**

**God   Satan   Young Man   Friends 1, 2, 3**

**Narrator:** Job was a good man and wealthy. He had seven sons and three daughters. He owned more livestock than any other man in the East. One day Satan and God had a conversation about Job.

**God:** Where have you come from?

**Satan:** From roaming the earth.

**God:** Have you noticed my servant Job? There is no one as good as he is on earth.

**Satan:** No wonder Job respects you. You have protected him and his family. You have made him wealthy. Take these things away and he will turn from you.

**God:** Behold, all that he has is in your power.

**Narrator:** Job's luck turned.

**Messenger 1:** (*to Job*) Your oxen and donkeys were grazing and the Sabeans carried them off and killed your herdsmen. I alone escaped to tell you.

**Messenger 2:** Lightning struck and killed your sheep and their shepherds. I alone have escaped to tell you.

**Messenger 3:** The Chaldeans seized your camels and killed their keepers. I alone have escaped to tell you.

**Messenger 4:** Your sons and daughters were eating and drinking at the house of your oldest son. A great wind shook the house and it collapsed, killing all the young people. I alone have escaped to tell you.

**Job:** (*wailing and falling to the ground*) Naked I came forth from my mother's womb, and naked shall I go back again. The Lord gave and the Lord has taken away; blessed be the name of the Lord.

**Narrator:** God and Satan discussed what happened.

**God:** Have you noticed Job is still good and God-fearing, although evil fell on him without cause?

**Satan:** Threaten his life and he will surely turn against you.

**God:** He is in your power.

**Narrator:** Job became covered with boils from head to toe.

**Job's Wife:** Why don't you just curse God and die?

**Job:** We accept good things from God. Should we not accept evil?

**Narrator:** Three friends of Job heard of his suffering and came to comfort him.

**Job:** Why was I ever born?

**Friend 1:** You must have done something wrong to deserve this.

**Job:** God, why are you attacking me?

**Friend 2:** Pray. God might help you.

**Job:** I will complain to God.

**Friend 3:** Confess your sin to the Lord.

**Job:** What are my sins?

**Young Man:** Job, God is just. We should not challenge him.

**God:** Job, stand up like a man. I will question you, and you tell me the answers. Where were you when I founded the earth? Who determined its size? And who shut within doors the sea and said, "Thus far shall you come but no farther?"

Have you ever commanded the morning? Have you entered the storehouse of the snow? Do you give the horse his strength? Let you who argues with me answer.

**Job:** I have dealt with great things I do not understand. I take back what I said and repent.

**Narrator:** The Lord gave to Job twice as much as he had before. He again had seven sons and three daughters, and he lived to be one hundred and forty. Suffering remains a mystery, but we trust Divine Providence to direct everything for good.

# Esther
## Queen of Courage and Faith

Ahasuerus, king of Persia, gave a six-month feast to display his country's riches. All went well until the seventh day. A banquet was held at the capital city, Susa.

 Esther

 Ahasuerus

 Mordecai

Haman

Go tell Queen Vashti to come, so everyone can see her beauty.

**The servant returns.**

My Lord, the queen will not come.

How dare she refuse!

Divorce her and find someone more worthy.

So be it.

Hear ye. Hear ye. Vashti is no longer queen. Let all lovely girls be brought to the palace. She who most pleases the king will be queen.

Mordecai, a Jewish man in Susa, had adopted his beautiful cousin, Esther. She, too, had to go before the king. Mordecai warned her not to reveal that she was Jewish.

I choose Esther for my wife. She is beautiful and I love her more than all the others.

210

**Not long after . . .**

Haman, for your loyalty I make you the highest official in the land.

Good. Everyone must bow to me.

Look, every day that Jew Mordecai refuses to bow to you.

I bow to God alone.

Your majesty, there is a people who do not obey your laws. Let's destroy them.

Do as you please. Here is my official seal.

Hear ye. Hear ye. The king orders all Jews put to the sword on the fourteenth day of the twelfth month, Adar.

Your highness, Mordecai is in sackcloth and ashes, and he is crying loudly.

Find out why.

What's wrong?

Haman convinced the king that all Jews were dangerous. We are to be killed. Tell Esther to plead with the king for us.

How can I do that? Anyone who goes to the king without being summoned is killed unless the king extends his scepter. Tell Mordecai that.

Mordecai says that you will be killed with the rest. Maybe you are queen just for this crisis.

Tell Mordecai to have the Jews fast for three days. Then I will go to the king.

Esther and the Jews prayed and fasted. Then Esther put on her beautiful robes and went to the king. The king looked angrily at Esther. She started to faint.

What is it, Esther? You can have anything you want, up to half my kingdom.

Please come to a banquet at my house with Haman.

**At Haman's house.**

The queen invites me to dinner, but Mordecai spoils my joy. He still refuses to bow to me.

Why not build a gallows 75 feet high and have him hanged?

Good idea.

**That night the king couldn't sleep. He went over some old records.**

Look at this. A man named Mordecai once saved my life, and I never rewarded him.

**The next morning . . .**

Haman, what should be done for a man the king wishes to reward?

He must mean me.

He should wear the king's robe and crown and ride the king's horse. The noblest officials should clothe him and go before him crying his praise.

You are my noblest official. Do this for the Jew Mordecai.

As you wish.

# God's Saving

B.C.    1900    1850?    1800    1700    1650?    1600

## STORIES OF THE BEGINNING

CREATION, SIN AND THE PROMISE, CAIN AND ABEL, THE FLOOD, THE TOWER OF BABEL

ABRAHAM
OUR FATHER IN FAITH

**PATRIARCHS**
ISAAC
JACOB

JOSEPH
SOLD INTO SLAVERY

1100    1000    961    900    800

SAUL

DAVID
GREATEST KING OF ISRAEL

**KINGS**

SOLOMON
BUILDER OF THE TEMPLE

**PROPHETS**
ELIJAH  ISAIAH
AMOS

# Plan of Love

1500    1400    1300    1280?    1200

**THE EXODUS**

**THE COVENANT**

**JUDGES**
GIDEON  SAMSON
DEBORAH  SAMUEL

721    700    600    587    500

**JEREMIAH**
**FALL OF THE NORTHERN KINGDOM**

**EZEKIEL**
**FALL OF THE SOUTHERN KINGDOM**
**AND EXILE TO BABYLON**

RETURN TO
JUDAH,
MACCABEES,
AND
REDEDICATION
OF
THE TEMPLE

**JESUS**
**CHRIST**
THE
**FULFILLMENT**
OF
**GOD'S PLAN**
**A.D.**

# GLOSSARY

## Pronunciation Key

| | | | | | | | | |
|---|---|---|---|---|---|---|---|
| **a** | h*a*llow | **ie** | l*ie*, sk*y* | **uh** | r*u*t, hom*i*ly | **s** | *s*tart, pre*ss*, *c*ent |
| **ah** | f*a*ther | **o** | l*o*t | **oo** | s*oo*n, allel*u*ia | **sh** | ten*si*on, sta*ti*on |
| **aw** | str*aw*, bef*o*re | **oh** | *ow*n, l*oa*n, l*o*ne | **yoo** | m*u*sic, b*eau*ty | **th** | *th*is, for*th* |
| **ay** | m*ay*, tr*a*de | **ow** | c*ow*, h*ou*se | **g** | *g*et | **z** | *z*oo, i*s* |
| **e** | p*e*t, f*ai*r, f*e*rret | **oy** | b*oy*, b*oi*l | **j** | *j*uice, e*dg*e | **zh** | mea*s*ure, vi*si*on |
| **ee** | s*ee*n, sc*e*ne | **u** | f*u*ll, g*oo*d | **k** | *k*itten, *c*at | | |
| **i** | h*i*t | | | **kw** | *qu*it, *qu*arrel | | |

**Aaron** (ER uhn): The brother of Moses who acted as his spokesman. Aaron was also the first high priest of the Hebrews.

**Abraham** (AY bruh ham): Father of the chosen people. Abraham came from Ur. God changed his name from Abram to Abraham, made a covenant with him, and called him to move to Canaan.

**Abstinence** (AB stuh nuhns): The practice of denying oneself food, drink, or other pleasures. Days of abstinence are days on which we do not eat meat. For Catholics over the age of fourteen, Ash Wednesday and all Fridays of Lent are days of abstinence.

**Advent** (AD vent): The four-week season of the liturgical year spent in preparation for Christmas.

**Anointing** (uh NOYNT ing): Putting oil on things or people to dedicate them to the service of God. The anointing of the kings of Israel was a sign that they were chosen to rule God's people.

**Ark of the covenant** (KUHV uh nuhnt): The chest that contained the laws of the covenant, the tablets with the Ten Commandments written on them. The ark was carried with the Israelites during their journey in the desert. It was captured by the Philistines but later returned. King David brought it to the Temple in Jerusalem, where it remained until the Temple was destroyed in 587 B.C.

**Astrology** (uh STROL uh jee): A false science that claims to foretell the future by studying the influence of the sun, moon, and stars on human life; the belief that the stars and planets control life.

**Authority** (uh THOR uh tee): The right to command, to require obedience, to take action, to make decisions.

**Baal** (BAYL): False god or gods worshiped by the people of Canaan and other ancient peoples. The prophets of Baal offered human sacrifices to win favors from their gods.

**Babylon** (BAB uh luhn): An ancient city on the Euphrates River, the capital of Babylonia, famous for wealth, luxury, and evil. The people of Jerusalem were exiled to Babylon when the Babylonians destroyed their city in 587 B.C.

**Benjamin** (BEN juh men): The youngest son of Jacob; Joseph's youngest brother. He became his father's favorite son after Joseph was sold into slavery in Egypt.

**Bible** (BIE buhl): A collection, or library, of sacred books. The Bible contains the Hebrew Scriptures (Old Testament) and Christian Scriptures (New Testament). Seventy-three books are in the Bible. The books of the Bible were written over a period of nine hundred years and tell of God's love and revelation to his people.

**Birthright** (BUHRTH riet): The privileges that belong to the first male child born in a family, including the right to inheritance and authority over his brothers and sisters. Esau sold his birthright to Jacob.

**Blasphemy** (BLAS fuh mee): Mocking or hateful speech concerning God. Blasphemy may include insulting or making fun of sacred persons or things.

**Blessing** (BLES ing): A wish or prayer for happiness, good fortune, and God's favor for a person or thing.

**Bronze** (BRONZ) **serpent** (SUR puhnt): The object that God had Moses make and lift up on a pole in order to heal people who had been bitten by a snake. It prefigured Jesus' being lifted up on the cross to save all people.

**Canaan** (KAY nuhn): The land located between Syria and Egypt that God promised to the descendants of Abraham. This was the Promised Land to which the Israelites journeyed through the desert. It is the old name for Palestine.

**Charism** (KAR iz uhm): A special gift or grace given by God to a person for the good of others.

**Chrism** (KRIZ uhm): A blessed mixture of olive or plant oil and balsam or perfume used during Baptism, Confirmation, and the ordination of priests and bishops.

**Christ** (KRIEST): The title of Jesus, from the Greek word *Christos* meaning "anointed one" or "the anointed of God." (The Hebrew word is *Messiah*.)

**Conscience** (KON shuhns): The power within a person to judge whether an act is good or bad right here and now.

**Consecration** (kon suh KRAY shuhn): The act of setting apart as holy or for the service of God. The dedication of a person or thing to God in a special way.

**Consequences** (KON suh kwen suhz): The results or effects of choices.

**Covenant** (KUV uh nuhnt): A sacred agreement between individual persons, or groups, and God. In the Old Testament, God promised to protect and deliver his people in return for their loyalty. In the New Testament, the covenant is the bond we have with God through Christ. Marriage is a covenant made between two people in the presence of God.

**Cursing** (KUHR sing): Calling down evil or injury on some person or thing. Asking God to harm a person or thing.

**David** (DAY vuhd): The second and greatest king of Israel. Under David the tribes of Israel were united into one great nation. He made Jerusalem capital of his newly united kingdom.

**Dead Sea Scrolls:** A collection of scriptural and other manuscripts discovered in 1947 near the Dead Sea, Palestine, site of the Qumran community of Essenes. The scrolls were preserved in clay jars hidden in the caves.

**Descendants** (di SEN duhnts): Those who are born of a certain family or group. People who are offspring of a certain ancestor.

**Elijah** (i LIE juh): The prophet called by God to proclaim him as the only God. Elijah called for faithfulness to the covenant and commandments.

**Encyclical** (in SIK li kuhl): A letter, written by the Pope, containing the Church's teaching and guidance.

**Evolution** (ev uh LOO shuhn): The theory that there was a slow, continual change from a lower form of life to a higher, more complicated form. Catholics may hold this theory up to a certain point. Catholic belief holds that God creates each human soul directly and separately.

**Exile** (EG ziel): A forced or voluntary removal from one's country or home. It was also the period of the chosen people's captivity in Babylon.

**Exodus** (EK suh duhs): A Greek word meaning "a way out" or "departure." The name of the second book of the Bible. The Exodus of the Israelites includes their departure from Egypt, their wanderings through the desert, and their journey to the Promised Land.

**Ezekiel** (i ZEE kee uhl): The prophet who spoke to the Israelites while they were exiled in Babylon. Ezekiel brought a message of hope to his exiled people.

**Ezra** (EZ ruh): The priest who guided the Jewish people in being faithful to the Law when they returned to the Promised Land after the Exile.

**Faith** (FAYTH): The God-given power and habit by which we believe in God and all that he has revealed. We receive this power at Baptism.

**Free will:** The ability to choose.

**Grace:** God's love shared with human beings. Grace is a gift of God, a sharing in his life. Actual grace is a temporary help from God that enables us to know and do what is right at a certain moment.

**Hanukkah** (HAHN uh kuh): The Jewish feast that commemorates the Maccabees' overthrow of the Syrians and the rededication of the Temple.

**Hebrew** (HEE broo) **Scriptures** (SKRIP chuhrs): Another name for the Old Testament.

**Hebrews** (HEE broos): The name of the Israelite people. The people descended from Abraham. (Also called Jews, from the name Judah, after the Babylonian Exile.)

**Holiness** (HOH lee nis): Closeness to God shown through love, goodness, and kindness. A holy person tries to grow and develop all the gifts God has given him or her.

**Holy days of obligation** (ob luh GAY shuhn): Special days in which we honor Jesus, Mary, or the saints by required participation in the Eucharist.

I

**Idol** (IE duhl): An image of a false god. The pagans worshiped many idols.

**Idolatry** (ie DOL uh tree): The worship of false gods—a sin against the first commandment.

**Incarnate** (in KAR nuht): Made flesh. Having received a bodily form.

**Incarnation** (in kar NAY shuhn): The mystery of Jesus Christ's taking on a human nature. The Incarnation took place when Mary agreed to become Jesus' mother.

**Inspiration** (in spuh RAY shuhn): God's action in directing the human authors and editors of the Bible. God guided their thoughts and desires to pass on to others those truths that he wanted to teach.

**Intellect** (IN tuh lekt): The power of the soul that enables us to learn, to reason, to think, and to judge.

**Intercession** (in tuhr SESH uhn): Prayer or petition on behalf of another or others. Asking a favor for another.

**Isaac** (IE zik): One of the patriarchs. The son of Abraham and Sarah. The father of Jacob and Esau.

**Isaiah** (ie ZAY uh): A great prophet of Judah. He urged the people to trust God completely. He also foretold the signs and characteristics of the promised Messiah. He warned that Israel would be conquered but that God would preserve a remnant of the people.

**Israel** (IZ ree uhl): The name God gave to Jacob. The descendants of Jacob and the land on which they lived. Israel is also the name given to the northern kingdom during the time of the kings. Its capital was Samaria. Later, the name Israel was applied to all the chosen people, including those of the southern kingdom, Judah.

**Jacob** (JAY kuhb): The son of Isaac and Rebekah. He was renamed Israel by God. He had twelve sons who eventually became heads of the tribes of Israel.

**Jeremiah** (jer uh MIE uh): The prophet called to warn the people in Judah because they were unfaithful to the covenant with God. Jeremiah is called the "prophet of the new covenant."

**Jericho** (JER uh koh): The first city in the Promised Land conquered by Joshua.

**Jerusalem** (juh ROO suh luhm): The City of David, also known as Zion. It was the capital of the southern kingdom of Judah and was the home of the ark of the covenant at that time.

**Jesus** (JEE zuhs): A name meaning "God saves" or "God is salvation."

**Jews** (JOOZ): Members of the tribe or kingdom of Judah. The name given to the chosen people after the Babylonian Exile. It means descendants of those who lived in Judah or whose ancestor was Jacob.

**John the Baptist** (BAP tist): The great prophet who preached a baptism of penance to prepare the way for the Messiah; son of Zechariah and Elizabeth and relative of Jesus.

**Joseph** (JO zuhf): The young, favored son of Jacob who was sold by his brothers into slavery in Egypt but became a high official there. Joseph saved his family from the famine by bringing them from Canaan to the land of Goshen in Egypt.

**Joshua** (JOSH oo uh): The leader of the Israelites after the death of Moses. Joshua led the Israelites into Canaan and conquered the land.

**Judah** (JOO duh): One of the twelve sons of Jacob (Israel); he received the special blessing that he would rule his brothers and that the Messiah would come from his tribe. The name given to the tribe or descendants of Judah. Later, Judah was the land of the southern kingdom. Its capital was Jerusalem.

**Judges** (JUHJ uhz): The temporary leaders of Israel after the death of Joshua until the beginning of the rule by the kings. There were twelve judges during this time. The judges were sent by God to save his people. They often led the Israelites in battle and encouraged them to be faithful to Yahweh.

**Judgment** (JUHJ muhnt): A decision. A process of forming an opinion or evaluation.

**Justice** (JUHS tuhs): The virtue that obliges us to give every person his or her rightful due. Fair treatment of everyone.

# L

**Law, Books of:** The Pentateuch. The first part of the Old Testament. The Hebrew word for "law" is Torah.

**Lectionary** (LEK shuhn er ee): A book containing the Scripture readings used at Mass for Sundays, weekdays, feast days, and other occasions. It also contains the responsorial psalms and Gospel (Alleluia) verses.

**Lent:** The six-week season of the liturgical year spent in preparation for Easter.

**Levites** (LEE viets): The descendants of Levi. These were the priests of the Israelite people. In place of land, they received a city in the land of the other tribes.

**Liturgical** (li TUR ji kuhl) **year:** The yearly cycle during which we celebrate the mystery of the life, death, and resurrection of Jesus. Celebrations in honor of Mary, the saints, and angels are also included in the liturgical year. The liturgical year begins with the first Sunday of Advent and ends with the feast of Christ the King.

**Liturgy** (LIT uhr jee) **of the Eucharist** (YOO kuh rist): The second main part of the Mass in which Jesus becomes present, offers himself in sacrifice again, and comes to his people in Holy Communion. During the Liturgy of the Eucharist, bread and wine become the Body and Blood of Jesus.

**Liturgy of the Word:** The first main part of the Mass, in which God's Word is proclaimed. God speaks to us during the Liturgy of the Word.

# M

**Maccabees** (MAK uh beez): A family of five sons that led the Jewish rebellion, in 167 B.C., against the Syrians who ruled Palestine and persecuted the Jews. The Maccabees won independence for Palestine that lasted until 63 B.C.

**Magnificat** (mahg NIF i kaht): Mary's prayer or song of praise when she visited Elizabeth after the Annunciation (see Luke 1:46–55).

**Manna** (MAN uh): The bread that God sent to the Israelites throughout their journey in the desert. Manna appeared on the ground and was gathered every day except the Sabbath.

**Matzoh** (MOT suh): Flat, thin pieces of unleavened bread eaten by Jews during the Passover.

**Messiah** (me SIE uh): The Hebrew word for "anointed one." (The Greek word is *Christos*.) The Messiah is the one promised by God to deliver all people from sin. The Messiah would bring peace, salvation, and happiness. Jesus is the Messiah promised in the Old Testament.

**Mezuzah** (muh ZOO zuh): A case attached to the doorposts of some Jewish homes as a reminder of their faith. It contains a small scroll on which is inscribed Deuteronomy 6:4–9, 11:13–21, and the name of God (Shaddai).

**Midian** (MID ee uhn): The land north of Arabia and east of Egypt. Moses fled to Midian from Egypt.

**Midianites** (MID ee uhn iets): Members of the tribe or people from the land of Midian. Gideon led attacks on them when they invaded Israelite land.

**Mortal** (MAWR tuhl) **sin:** A deliberate turning away from God that separates us from sanctifying grace and causes the supernatural death of the soul; a serious offense.

**Moses** (MOH zuhz): The prophet and leader chosen by God to lead the Israelites from slavery in Egypt to freedom in the Promised Land.

# N

**Nehemiah** (NEE [h]uh mie uh): The governor who began political reforms and rebuilt the city wall when the Jewish people returned after the Exile.

**New Testament** (TEST uh muhnt): The second part of the Bible which tells about the life and teachings of Jesus Christ and the beginnings of the early Church. There are twenty-seven books in the New Testament. It is also called the Christian Scriptures.

# O

**Oath** (OHTH): A solemn statement that one is speaking the truth, calling God himself to witness that what one says is true.

**Obligations** (ob li GAY shuhns): Duties or commitments we have because we have agreed to them and accepted certain rights and privileges. That to which one is bound.

**Old Testament** (TEST uh muhnt): The first part of the Bible that tells of God's revelation of himself and his will up to the time of Christ. Also called the Hebrew Scriptures. There are forty-six books in the Old Testament.

**Ordinary Time:** In the liturgical year, the time between the seasons of Christmas and Lent, Easter and Advent.

**Original sin:** 1. The first sin committed by Adam, who as the head of the human race disobeyed God and lost the right to heaven for himself and his descendants; 2. the absence of sanctifying grace and the tendency toward evil with which human beings are born.

**Ouija** (WEE juh) **board:** A board with the alphabet and other signs on it through which messages from the spirit world are supposedly communicated.

# P

**Palestine** (PAL uhs tien): The land of Canaan; the Holy Land; the Promised Land. The land given to Abraham's descendants by God.

**Passover** (PAS oh vuhr): The feast at which the Israelites celebrate their deliverance from Egypt and their covenant with God. The feast of Passover commemorates the angel of death's passing over the homes of the Israelites. This feast is also called the Pasch.

**Patriarch** (PAY tree ark): The father and ruler of a family, tribe, or race. Abraham, Isaac, Jacob, and Jacob's sons were patriarchs.

**Pentateuch** (PEN tuh t[y]ook): Meaning "five scrolls" and referring to the first five books of the Bible: Genesis, Exodus, Leviticus, Numbers, Deuteronomy. The Pentateuch tells of the beginnings of God's special people, creation, and the covenant. It is sometimes called the Torah.

**Perjury** (PUHR juhr ee): The telling of a lie after swearing before God to tell only the truth. Telling a lie under oath. Calling on God to witness to a falsehood.

**Pharaoh** (FER oh): The title given to the Egyptian kings or rulers.

**Plague** (PLAYG): A disastrous evil that destroys or seriously harms. In the Old Testament, it refers to a series of disasters in Egypt after which Pharaoh let the Israelites leave.

**Potiphar** (POT i fahr): An officer in the court of the Pharoah who bought Joseph as a slave and afterward had him put in prison.

**Prayer:** The loving awareness or thought of God in one's life. Speaking and listening to God with mind, heart, and voice.

**Prefigure** (pree FIG yuhr): To show or to suggest beforehand.

**Principles** (PRIN suh puhls): Rules of conduct or truths that we believe in strongly enough to act on.

**Profanity** (proh FAN uh tee): Mistreating in speech or action a sacred person, place, or thing. In speech, profanity refers to using God's name carelessly.

**Prophet** (PROF uht): A person called on by God to speak or write his word to others.

**Proverb** (PROV uhrb): A wise saying. A short statement expressing a deep truth. King Solomon is thought to have spoken thousands of proverbs.

**Providence** (PROV uh duhns): God's watching over us with loving care. His loving guidance and awareness of all that happens.

**Psalms** (SAHMZ): Prayer-songs written to praise and worship God. King David wrote many psalms. The Book of Psalms contains a collection of 150 psalms.

**Pure spirits:** Beings that have no physical body. Angels are pure spirits.

**Purgatory** (PUHR guh tohr ee): A place where, or condition through which, holy souls are purified after death if necessary before they can enter heaven.

**Qumran** (KUM rahn): An area close to the Dead Sea in Palestine. It is believed the Essenes lived near Qumran because a collection of their scrolls was found there.

**Reconciliation** (rek uhn sil ee AY shuhn): The healing of the separation between self and God or between self and others. The return to a happy and holy relationship with God and others after it has been weakened or destroyed by sin.

**Remnant** (REM nuhnt): A small remaining part. A surviving group. Isaiah foretold that the chosen people would be conquered by their enemies and that a faithful remnant would be left through whom God would continue his promises.

**Reparation** (rep uh RAY shuhn): Making up for a wrong or injury. The attempt to restore things to their normal condition.

**Repentance** (ri PEN tuhns): Sorrow for doing something wrong coupled with determination to make up for what was done and to avoid repeating the act.

**Reuben** (ROO buhn): The oldest son of Jacob.

**Revelation** (rev uh LAY shuhn): All that God has taught us about himself and his will for his people. Scripture and tradition are the sources of revelation.

**Rite** (RIET): The form of a ceremony, including the actions and words to be used.

**Sacred** (SAY kruhd) **Scripture** (SKRIP chur): The Bible.

**Salvation** (sal VAY shuhn) **history:** The story of God's love, which shows how God entered into history and carried out a plan to save all people.

**Sanctifying** (SANK tuh fie ing) **grace:** God's divine life within us. Sanctifying grace is a free gift of God that makes us holy and enables us to share his life and friendship on earth and to enjoy him forever in heaven.

**Sanctuary** (SANK choo wer ee): A holy place. In a church, the area around the altar.

**Saul** (SAWL): The first king of Israel. Saul was anointed by Samuel.

**Savior** (SAYV yuhr): The title given to Jesus Christ because he gained salvation for all.

**Seance** (SAY ons): A meeting at which the group tries to make contact with the spirits of the dead.

**Seder** (SAY duhr): The Hebrew word meaning "order of service." In a seder celebration a ceremonial dinner is held and God is praised as the story of his saving love, the delivering of the Israelites out of Egypt, is told.

**Self-discipline:** The planned control and training of oneself in order to improve.

**Shiloh** (SHIE loh): The city where the ark of the covenant was placed after the Israelites entered the Promised Land.

**Simhat** (sim HAHT) **Torah** (TOH ruh): A Jewish feast that expresses gratitude for the Torah and the Word of God.

**Sin:** A turning away from God. A deliberate rejection of the law of God. The Greek word for sin is translated as "miss the mark."

**Social justice:** The effort to help others live truly human lives. This can be done by trying to make groups in society better serve the good of all.

**Statutes** (STACH oots): Laws or regulations.

**Sukkot** (sook OHT): The Feast of Tabernacles or Feast of Booths. A Jewish festival in which the tents and temporary shelters used during the Israelites' journey through the desert are recalled.

**Supplication** (suhp luh KAY shuhn): A humble prayer to God in which one asks for things.

**Swearing:** Taking an oath.

**Synagogue** (SIN uh gog): A Jewish center for prayer and the study of Scripture. Synagogues came into being during the Exile when the Israelites could not go to the Temple, the place of sacrifice.

**T**

**Temple** (TEM puhl): The center of Jewish religion in Jerusalem where sacrifices were offered. The original Temple was built by Solomon.

**Tent of Meeting:** The sanctuary or tabernacle God instructed Moses to build to house the ark of the covenant. The Tent of Meeting was a sign of God's presence from which God spoke to the people.

**Torah** (TOH ruh): The general Hebrew word meaning "law." It is sometimes used to refer to the first five books of the Bible. It can also refer to all of the Jewish law revealed by Yahweh in the Old Testament.

**Tradition:** Christian beliefs that have been passed down by spoken word, teachings, customs, and example. Together with Scripture, tradition is the source of revelation.

## U

**Uncreated** (uhn cree AY tuhd) **spirit:** A purely spiritual being that has no beginning and will have no end. God is the only uncreated pure spirit.

**Unleavened** (uhn LEV uhnd): Containing no yeast. Unleavened bread is eaten at the Passover meal.

**Ur** (UHR): The city located in Chaldea from which Abraham moved early in his life. Abraham moved to Haran from Ur.

## V

**Values:** Goals, ideals, or ideas we believe in or hold as important and worthwhile. Whatever we consider of great worth or importance.

**Virtue** (VUHR choo): A habit of doing good.

**Votive** (VOH tiv) **Masses** (MAS uhz): Eucharistic liturgies that celebrate the mysteries of the Lord or honor Mary and the saints.

## W

**Wisdom:** The power of judging rightly. A love for what has to do with God.

**Works of mercy:** Good deeds done for others out of love for God and for people according to Christ's word (see Matthew 5:3–10). Those works that meet the physical needs of people are called corporal. Those that meet their spiritual needs are called spiritual.

## Y

**Yahweh** (YAH way): The word used to express the name by which God identified himself to the chosen people. Yahweh means "I am who am." Out of respect the Israelites never said this name but replaced it with other names.

## Z

**Ziggurat** (ZIG uh raht): A temple tower, similar in shape to a pyramid, built by the pagans to honor their gods.

# INDEX

Good Friday, 200
Grace, 29, 107, 109

## H

Habakkuk, 17
Habits, 107–109
Haggai, 17
Hannah, 131
Hanukkah, 175
Happiness, 29, 39, 86, 94, 106
Haran, 43, 46, 52
Heaven, 114–15
Hebrew Scriptures. *See* Old
    Testament
Herod, 177
Holiness, 135
Holy Communion. *See* Sacraments,
    Eucharist
Holy days of obligation, 4, 90
Holy Family, 196, 197
Holy Father, the. *See* Pope
Holy Saturday, 201
Holy Spirit, 172, 177, 179, 197, 203
Holy Thursday, 199, 200
Holy Week, 199
Hosea, 17
Human beings
    creation of, 22, 39
    destiny of, 24, 26
    dignity of, 22, 24
    freedom of, 29, 80, 86

## I

Idolatry, 82, 168
    Baal, 124, 155
    golden calf, 82, 85
    Israelites fall into, 124, 168–69
Incarnation, 178, 181
Inspiration, 14, 19
Intellect, 25, 29, 37
Isaac, 66–69, 180
    Abraham's sacrifice of, 46–48
    birth of, 44
    blesses Jacob, 51, 54, 56
    prefigures Jesus' sacrifice, 191
Isaiah, 154, 161–63, 166–67. *See also*
    Prophets of Israel
    Book of, 162
    Messianic prophecies of, 162–63,
        166–67, 176, 179, 184, 186
    vision of God's holiness of, 161, 188
Israel. *See* Jacob
Israel, kingdom of, 144, 149, 154, 155
Israelites, 96–97, 103, 130, 156, 159
    entry into Promised Land by, 111–13,
        124
    first kings of, 131–33, 144, 149–50
    God's covenant with, 82, 86, 121, 168
    origin of, 53
    pattern in lives of, 121, 125

## J

Jacob, 51–54, 56–58, 180
    chosen to lead Israelites, 53
    plots to receive Isaac's blessing, 51–52
    settles Israelites in Egypt, 61, 64
    visited by God, 53, 70
    vision of, foretells Christ's coming, 191

Jael, 126
Jeremiah, 154, 168–71, 173–74, 180, 184,
    186, 188. *See also* Prophets of Israel
    Book of, 168
Jericho, 113
Jerusalem, 154, 175, 203
    David buried in, 141
    destruction foretold and fall of,
        168–71, 173, 184
    home of prophets, 161, 168
    made capital of Israel, 138, 144
    Temple built in, 143, 147
Jesse, 137, 191
Jesus, 81, 175–83, 196, 203
    ancestry of, 128, 140, 147, 191–92
    Annunciation and birth of, 178–79,
        192
    closeness of Mary to, 179
    crucifixion of, prefigured, 103–104
    death and resurrection of, 104,
        198–99, 200–201
    as leader to our promised land, 114,
        116, 203
    as Light of the World, 191–93
    Messianic prophecies foretelling, 166,
        175–77, 184–88, 191–92
    as new Adam, 30
    as our Reconciliator, 104–106, 109
    and social justice, 157
Jews, origin of name, 172
Jezebel, 155
Job, 208–209
Joel, 17
John the Baptist, 175–78, 181, 182,
    185–86, 188, 192. *See also* Prophets
    of Israel
Jonah, 205
Jonathan, 132, 136, 137
Jordan River, 112–13, 177
Joseph, father of Jesus, 179, 192, 196, 197
Joseph, son of Jacob, 59–65, 66–68, 180,
    183, 191
Joshua, 96, 111–14, 121, 130, 180
Josiah, 168
Judah, son of Jacob, 60, 62, 96
Judah, southern kingdom, 144, 154,
    161–62, 172, 178, 188
Judges, 124–30, 149
    Book of, 124–28, 129
Judith, 206–207

## K

Kingdom of God, 163, 176
Kings of Israel, 131–33, 138–46, 149

## L

Laban, 52, 53
Lady of Guadalupe, 194–95
Lamentations, Book of, 168
Law. *See* Commandments
Law, books of, 16–17
Law, natural, 86
Leadership, 112, 115, 134, 138, 150, 175
Leah, 53
Lectionary, 77, 166
Lent, 90, 95, 166, 198–99
Levi, 113
Levites, 113

Liturgical year, 90, 95
Liturgy of the Eucharist, 77. *See also* Mass
Liturgy of the Hours, 175–76, 178
Liturgy of the Word, 77. *See also* Mass

## M

Maccabees, 175, 180
Malachi, 17
Manna and quail, 80–81, 84
Marah, 80
Marriage, 196
Martin de Porres, St., 173
Mary, Mother of Jesus, 178–79, 203
    Canticle of Praise (Magnificat) of, 178
    closeness to Jesus of, 179, 188
    and the Incarnation, 178, 181, 192, 204
    and Joseph, 179, 197
    Mother of Perpetual Help, 196, 204
    as new Eve, 30
Mass, 19, 77, 90, 106
Meribah, 97
Messiah
    birth of, 176, 191–93
    divinity of, 179
    expectations concerning, 163
    meaning of, 135, 179
    promise of, 62, 67, 161–62
    suffering of, 163
Micah, 192
Midian, 72–73
Midianites, 126
Miriam, 72, 76, 118
Missionary activities, 55, 156
Moab, 111, 114, 154
Moabites, 127, 147
Moriah, 47
Moses, 72–76, 134, 135, 180. *See also*
    Prophets of Israel
    and bronze serpent, 103
    called by God from the burning bush,
        73, 203
    dies before reaching Promised Land,
        111
    God's covenant with, 82, 191
    guides Israelites through
        wilderness, 80–82, 85, 96–97, 103
    leads Exodus, 75–76, 78, 121
    receives Ten Commandments, 82
    warns Pharoah of plagues, 74
Mother Teresa of Calcutta, 120
Mt. Nebo, 111
Mt. Sinai, 73, 80, 82, 85, 86, 96

## N

Naboth, 155
Nahum, 17
Naomi, 127–28
Nathan, 139, 140, 147
Nehemiah, 172
New covenant, 77
New Testament, 15, 18
Nile River, 72, 74
Noah, 31, 191
Numbers, Book of, 17, 96, 103

## O

Oaths, 89
Obadiah, 17

With Christ We Die and Rise

**Preparing for Easter**

Christ's saving death was completed and made perfect in his resurrection. Through Baptism, Jesus calls each of us to share in the mystery of his cross. Each year during the six weeks of Lent we recall Christ's saving love and we accept the cross in our life. We pray and we fast to prepare ourselves to enter into the fullness of resurrected life with Jesus. We give alms and do kind deeds, sharing the good things God has given to us.

**Directions for your Mosaic**

1.  Spend time in prayer each day. Every day that you do, color a triangle (▲) piece of the mosaic red or orange.

2.  Give up something; fast from doing it. Every day you are faithful to your fast and offer it in love to God, color irregular (⬡) pieces of the mosaic green.

3.  Each day you have quietly given alms amd shared God's love with others, color a rectangular (▬) piece of the mosaic yellow.

# Celebrating the Passover

### Introduction

**Leader 1:** We have gathered to celebrate the Passover, our feast of freedom and of God's saving love for his people. When the Israelites were slaves in Egypt, the Lord God sent Moses to deliver his people from that slavery. The Israelites never forgot the night they left Egypt. For more than three thousand years they have celebrated the Passover, thanking God for listening to their prayers and freeing them from slavery.

### The Lighting of the Candles

**Hostess:** *(Light the candles.)* Blessed are you, Lord God, King of the universe. You have blessed us by your commandments. Bless our homes, O Lord our God, and keep your light shining upon us.

*(All be seated.)*

### Proclamation of the Holiness of the Day

**Leader 1:** The blessing of the fruit of the vine proclaims the holiness of the day.

**Leader 2:** *(Hold the cup for all to see.)* Blessed are you, Lord God, for you have given us this special feast of Passover. It reminds us that you have freed us from slavery.

**All:** *(Lift up cups.)* Praise to you, O Lord our God, for bringing us to this feast. You created the fruit of the vine to gladden the hearts of your people. Continue to show us your love. *(All drink from the cups.)*

### The Washing

**Leader 1:** When we worship God we must have clean hearts freed from sin. *(Leader 1 pours water over Leader 2's hands.)*

**Leader 2:** Blessed are you, O Lord our God, King of the universe. You have blessed us by your commandments and have told us to worship you with pure hearts.

### The Greens

**Leader 1:** Green is a sign of the new life that renews the earth each spring. We dip greens like parsley, endive, or lettuce in salt water as a reminder that the years of slavery in Egypt were bitter years. But God heard the cries of our fathers and brought them to a new life.

**All:** (*Dip greens in salt water and put them back on the plate.*) Blessed are you, O Lord our God, King of the universe, Creator of all the fruits of the earth.

### Breaking of Bread

**Leader 2:** (*Pick up a matzoh wrapped in a napkin and unwrap it.*) This is the bread of the poor that our fathers were made to eat when they were slaves in Egypt. Let all who are hungry come and eat. Let all who are in distress come and celebrate Passover with us.

**Song Leader:** Let us welcome the feast of freedom with a song.

### Song

### The Story of the Deliverance from Egypt

**Leader 1:** In the celebration of the Passover meal, the youngest son asks questions of the father. The answers to these questions recall the meaning of the night.

**Son:** Why is this night of Passover so different from every other night?

**Father:** On this night we recall our freedom from slavery in Egypt.

**Son:** On all other nights we have rolls and all kinds of vegetables. Tonight we eat only bread without yeast in it. Why on this evening do we eat unleavened bread? Why do we eat bitter herbs?

**Father:** Our fathers left Egypt in a hurry and could not wait for the bread to rise so they made bread without yeast. We call it the bread of sadness. The bitter herbs remind us of the bitter times in Egypt before God freed our fathers.

**Son:** On all other nights we eat without any special festivities. Why on this night do we celebrate Passover?

**Father:** This is to remind us that God saw his people's sufferings and distress. Working signs and wonders, he brought them out of Egypt. In every generation enemies may arise against us, but God saves us.

**Reader:** A reading from the book of Exodus. (*Read Exodus 12:21–28.*)

### Explanation of Symbolic Foods
(*The leader holds up each food when asking about its meaning.*)

**Leader 1:** How did this holy day receive the name of Passover?

**Student:** The angel of death passed over the house of the families of Israel.

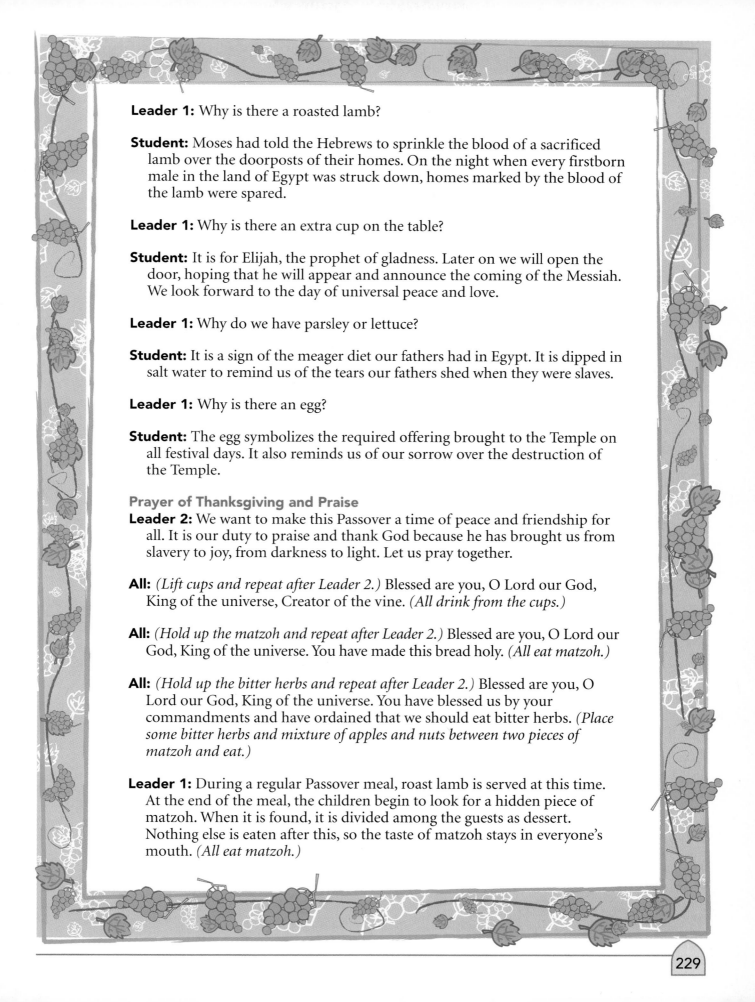

**Leader 1:** Why is there a roasted lamb?

**Student:** Moses had told the Hebrews to sprinkle the blood of a sacrificed lamb over the doorposts of their homes. On the night when every firstborn male in the land of Egypt was struck down, homes marked by the blood of the lamb were spared.

**Leader 1:** Why is there an extra cup on the table?

**Student:** It is for Elijah, the prophet of gladness. Later on we will open the door, hoping that he will appear and announce the coming of the Messiah. We look forward to the day of universal peace and love.

**Leader 1:** Why do we have parsley or lettuce?

**Student:** It is a sign of the meager diet our fathers had in Egypt. It is dipped in salt water to remind us of the tears our fathers shed when they were slaves.

**Leader 1:** Why is there an egg?

**Student:** The egg symbolizes the required offering brought to the Temple on all festival days. It also reminds us of our sorrow over the destruction of the Temple.

### Prayer of Thanksgiving and Praise

**Leader 2:** We want to make this Passover a time of peace and friendship for all. It is our duty to praise and thank God because he has brought us from slavery to joy, from darkness to light. Let us pray together.

**All:** *(Lift cups and repeat after Leader 2.)* Blessed are you, O Lord our God, King of the universe, Creator of the vine. *(All drink from the cups.)*

**All:** *(Hold up the matzoh and repeat after Leader 2.)* Blessed are you, O Lord our God, King of the universe. You have made this bread holy. *(All eat matzoh.)*

**All:** *(Hold up the bitter herbs and repeat after Leader 2.)* Blessed are you, O Lord our God, King of the universe. You have blessed us by your commandments and have ordained that we should eat bitter herbs. *(Place some bitter herbs and mixture of apples and nuts between two pieces of matzoh and eat.)*

**Leader 1:** During a regular Passover meal, roast lamb is served at this time. At the end of the meal, the children begin to look for a hidden piece of matzoh. When it is found, it is divided among the guests as dessert. Nothing else is eaten after this, so the taste of matzoh stays in everyone's mouth. *(All eat matzoh.)*

**Father:** Let us open the door now for Elijah. Stories tell us he returns to the earth to do good. Elijah will come as a simple poor man.

*(Student opens the door.)*

**All:** We hope Elijah is on his way.

**Leader:** We do not see him. He cannot be seen. He comes as the goodness that is in the hearts of the people. God grant that next year all people may live together in freedom as sisters and brothers.

### Grace after the Meal

**Leader 2:** Give thanks to the LORD, for he is good.

**All:** for his mercy endures forever.

**Leader 2:** Let the house of Israel say:

**All:** "God's love endures forever."

**Girls:** I was hard-pressed and falling, but the LORD came to my help.

**Boys:** The LORD, my strength and might, came to me as savior.

**Leader 2:** Give thanks to the LORD, who is good;

**All:** whose love endures forever.

Psalm 118:1–2, 13–14, 29

### Final Blessing

**Leader 1:** May the Lord bless us and keep us.

**All:** Amen.

**Leader 1:** May his face shine upon us and have mercy on us.

**All:** Amen.

### Song

- Have I taken anything that is not mine? Have I returned things that I borrowed? Have I damaged anything that belongs to someone else? Did I pay for or repair the damage?
- Have I always spoken the truth? Have I been kind in talking about other people? Have I guarded the good reputation of others as I would want them to guard mine? Have I kept secrets and promises?
- Do I choose good friends—those who will help me to be the person God calls me to be? Am I willing to be friendly to everyone or do I belong to a closed group of friends?
- Do I do what I can to help those who are poorer than I am?
- Have I avoided doing good things when I could and should have done them?
- Is something else I did bothering me because it was unloving?
- Is there something I want to talk about to the priest in confession?

6

## I Read God's Holy Word

Let us rid ourselves of every burden and sin that clings to us and persevere in running the race that lies before us while keeping our eyes fixed on Jesus, the leader and perfecter of faith. For the sake of the joy that lay before him he endured the cross, despising its shame, and has taken his seat at the right of the throne of God. Consider how he endured such opposition from sinners, in order that you may not grow weary and lose heart. In your struggle against sin you have not yet resisted to the point of shedding blood.

Hebrews 12:1–4

### Some Other Readings:

Mark 2:17  
Luke 15:1–10  
Matthew 5:13–16  
Luke 18:9–14  
John 15:9–14  
James 2:14–26

3

---

## I Confess My Sins to the Priest
- The priest welcomes me and I greet him.
- I make the Sign of the Cross.
- The priest says a prayer to remind me of God's forgiving love. I say, "Amen."
- The priest or I may read about God's forgiving love from the Bible.
- I make my confession. I may begin by saying: "Forgive me, Father, I have sinned. My last confession was (number of weeks or months) ago."
- I tell the priest my sins. When I finish I may say, "I am sorry for all my sins."
- The priest talks to me and gives me a penance.
- I pray an act of contrition.
- The priest prays over me and says the words of absolution. I say, "Amen."

## I Thank God for His Forgiving Love
The priest prays, "Give thanks to the Lord, for he is good." I answer, "His mercy endures forever."

## I Do My Penance

# Reconciliation Booklet

Jesus says, "Take my yoke upon you and learn from me, for I am meek and humble of heart; and you will find rest for yourselves. For my yoke is easy, and my burden light."

Matthew 11:29–30

Name: _____

## I Examine My Conscience

**Have I loved God?**

* Have I spent time praying to God each day? Did I try to give God my full attention when I prayed?
* Have I always used God's name with love and respect?
* Have I celebrated every Sunday and holy day by participating in the Eucharist? If I missed Mass, was it for an important reason? Have I really tried to pray and sing at Mass, or was I a distraction to myself and others?
* Have I thanked God for his goodness to me? Have I often told God I was sorry when I sinned? Have I often asked God to help me?

**Have I loved myself and others?**

* Have I been obedient and respectful to my parents and others who care for me? Have I loved and prayed for them? When I was a leader, did I try to do what I thought was best for everyone?

* Have I taken care of the gift of life? My life and the lives of others? Have I hurt myself by the use of drugs or alcohol? Have I hurt anyone else by fighting? By playing jokes? By calling people names? By mocking and taunting? By any unkind words? If I became angry or jealous, did I try to handle my feelings in a positive way?
* Have I asked forgiveness when I have hurt someone?
* Have I used the gifts of mind, spirit, and body that God has given me to bring happiness to others?
* Have I shown respect for my body? For others' bodies? Have I told stories, used obscene language, or looked at pictures that make fun of the human body? Have I touched my body or another's in a way that I shouldn't?
* Have I tried to take care of my things? Things that belong to others? Things in public places? Have I been careful not to waste God's gifts so that others can enjoy them too? Am I satisfied with what I have, or would I like to take what belongs to others? Do I share with others?

---

God loves us and asks us to love him, ourselves, and others. When we turn from him and fail in love, Jesus invites us to return to him so that he can forgive us. He has given us his Holy Spirit to help us. Let us now prepare to meet Jesus in the Sacrament of Reconciliation.

### I Pray to the Holy Spirit

Come, Holy Spirit, and help me to know how much God loves me and wants to forgive me. Help me to see and to love the goodness God has placed in me and in others. Show me how I have failed to love, and help me to be sorry for my sins.

Come, Holy Spirit,
   fill the hearts of your faithful
and kindle in them
   the fire of your love.

### I Pray an Act of Contrition
My God,
I am sorry for my sins with all my heart.
In choosing to do wrong
and failing to do good,
I have sinned against you
whom I should love above all things.
I firmly intend, with your help,
to do penance,
to sin no more,
and to avoid whatever leads me to sin.
Our Savior Jesus Christ suffered and died for us.
In his name, my God, have mercy.
                    Rite of Reconciliation

### I Plan for the Future
I think about how I should change to follow
   Jesus more closely.
I make a resolution and promise Jesus I will try
   not to sin again.

Teach us, good Lord,
to serve you as you deserve;
to give and not count the cost;
to fight and not heed the wounds;
to toil and not seek for rest;
to labor and not ask for reward
save that of knowing we do your will
through Jesus Christ our Lord.

**Act of Spiritual Communion**
My Jesus, I long for you in my soul. Since I cannot receive you sacramentally, come at least spiritually into my soul. As though you have already come, I embrace you. Never permit me to be separated from you.

4

## Morning Prayer
As soon as you wake up, make the Sign of the Cross and pray:

> O Jesus, through the Immaculate Heart of Mary, I offer you my prayers, works, joys, and suffering of this day in union with the holy sacrifice of the Mass throughout the world. I offer them for all the intentions of your Sacred Heart: the salvation of souls, reparation for sin, the reunion of all Christians. I offer them for the intentions of our bishops and of all members of the Apostleship of Prayer, and in particular for those recommended by our Holy Father this month.

---

Lord, we beg you to visit this house and banish from it all the deadly power of the enemy. May your holy angels dwell here to keep us in peace, and may your blessing be upon us always. We ask this through Christ our Lord.
> Liturgy of the Hours: Night Prayer

Holy God, holy strong One, holy immortal One, have mercy on us.
> Byzantine tradition

**Salve, Regina**
Hail, holy Queen, Mother of mercy,
hail, our life, our sweetness, and our hope.
To you we cry, the children of Eve;
to you we send up our sighs,
mourning and weeping in this land of exile.
Turn, then, most gracious advocate,
your eyes of mercy toward us;
lead us home at last
and show us the blessed fruit of your womb,
    Jesus:
O clement, O loving, O sweet Virgin Mary.

## Evening Prayer
Talk to God about what happened during the day. Tell God how you feel about it and thank him for being with you. Pray an act of contrition and any of the following prayers.

My God,
I am sorry for my sins with all my heart.
In choosing to do wrong
and failing to do good,
I have sinned against you
whom I should love above all things.
I firmly intend, with your help
to do penance,
to sin no more,
and to avoid whatever leads me to sin.
Our Savior Jesus Christ
suffered and died for us.
In his name, my God, have mercy.

Talk to God about the things you plan to do today. Ask God to help you do them well and for his glory. Pray any of the following prayers.

## The Shema

"Hear, O Israel! The LORD is our God, the LORD alone. Therefore, you shall love the LORD, your God, with all your heart, and with all your soul, and with all your strength."

Deuteronomy 6:4–5

O Lord, I give myself to you, I trust you wholly. You are wiser than I, more loving to me than I am to myself. Fulfill your high purpose in me whatever that be: work in me and through me. I am born to serve you, to be yours, to be your instrument. Let me turn my will over to you. I ask not to see, I ask not to know, I ask simply to be one with you in love.

John Henry Cardinal Newman

## Psalm 95

Come, let us sing joyfully to the LORD;
    cry out to the rock of our salvation.
Let us greet him with a song of praise,
    joyfully sing out our psalms.
For the LORD is the great God,
    the great king over all gods,
Whose hand holds the depths of the earth;
    who owns the tops of the mountains.
The sea and the dry land belong to God.
    who made them, formed them by hand.

Enter, let us bow down in worship;
    let us kneel before the LORD who made us.
For this is our God,
    whose people we are,
        God's well-tended flock.

## Psalm 23

The LORD is my shepherd; there is nothing I shall
    want.
    Fresh and green are the pastures where he
        gives me repose.
Near restful waters he leads me,
    to revive my drooping spirit.
He guides me along the right path;
    he is true to his name.
If I should walk in the valley of darkness
    no evil would I fear.
You are there with your crook and your staff;
    with these things you give me comfort.

You have prepared a banquet for me
    in the sight of my foes.
My head you have anointed with oil;
    my cup is overflowing.
Surely goodness and kindness shall follow me
    all the days of my life.
In the LORD's own house shall I dwell
    forever and ever.

Grail Translation

My Father, I abandon myself to you. Do with me as you will. Whatever you may do with me I thank you. I am prepared for anything. I accept everything, provided your will is fulfilled in me and in all creatures. I ask for nothing more, my God. I place my soul in your hands. I give it to you, my God, with all the love of my heart because I love you. And for me, it is a necessity of love, this gift of myself, this placing of myself in your hands without reserve in boundless confidence, because you are my Father.

Charles de Foucauld

Take and receive, O Lord, all my liberty, my memory, my understanding, all my will. All that I have and possess, you have given to me. I restore it all to you. I surrender it in order that you may dispose of it according to your will. Only give me your love and your grace and I shall be rich enough and shall seek nothing more.

St. Ignatius of Loyola

**My Page**

For favorite Scripture quotations, personal prayers, and reflections . . .

# God's Word

# Is Alive in

Name _____

God has gifted us with his Holy Word in Sacred Scripture. This Word will guide us wisely through all the events of our lives. We pray that we will really listen and be open as God speaks to us.

Father, we praise and thank you for your Holy Word.

We ask you to open our hearts and enlighten our minds as we come to know you better through the inspiration of your Word.

We ask you to give us strength to follow the plan you have for our lives. This plan will bring us closer to you. May we be led by your Son Jesus and guided by the truth of your Spirit.

Amen

Read 1 Timothy 4:12. Listen to the message Jesus gives you through the reading. Write your thoughts below.

_____

_____

_____

_____

_____

_____

_____

_____

Read Psalm 34:1–9. In the musical notes write words that describe how you felt after reading the psalm.

## Psalm 34

I will bless the LORD at all times;
  praise shall always be in my mouth.
My soul will glory in the LORD;
  that the poor may hear and be glad.
Magnify the LORD with me;
  let us exalt his name together.

I sought the LORD, who answered me,
  delivered me from all my fears.
Look to God that you may be radiant with joy
  and your faces may not blush for shame.
In my misfortune I called,
  the LORD heard and saved me from all distress.
The angel of the LORD, who encamps with them,
  delivers all who fear God.
Learn to savor how good the LORD is;
  happy are those who take refuge in him.

God loves you! And he is always near you.

List below the things you want to talk to God about.

_____

_____

_____

## Let Your Love Shine!

In each candle print the name of someone for whom you want to pray. Then on that day make a special effort to keep that person in your thought and prayers.

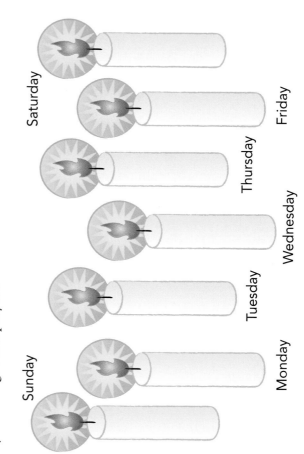

Sunday

Monday

Tuesday

Wednesday

Thursday

Friday

Saturday

## God's Word Leads to Victory

Read 1 Samuel 17:38–51 to discover how God led David the shepherd boy to triumph.

What special things did David use to help him?

_____

_____

In the crown below—*your crown*—are listed Scripture passages that suggest special things or actions that will help you to triumph and lead a happy life. Read the passages and then write key words or phrases on the crown that will help you remember.

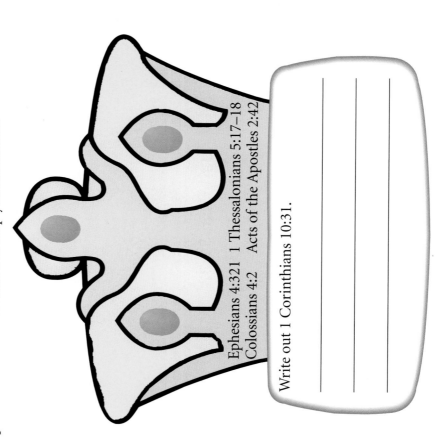

Ephesians 4:321   1 Thessalonians 5:17–18
Colossians 4:2        Acts of the Apostles 2:42

Write out 1 Corinthians 10:31.

## How to Pray God's Holy Word

1. Set aside some time every day to be with God.

2. Choose a place to pray—your room, church, outdoors.

3. Ask the Holy Spirit to help you understand. Speak to the Holy Spirit in your own words, very simply. For instance:

   > Please open my heart, Holy Spirit.
   > Help me to hear your words to me.

4. Read a short section from Scripture.

5. Think quietly about what you have read.

6. Speak to God from your heart.

## How to Remember God's Holy Word

1. Choose only one or two lines from Scripture at first. Read the verses slowly and carefully.

2. Pause and think about the passage prayerfully.

3. Say it in your own words.

4. Read it aloud several times.

5. Write it and say it by heart.

6. Check—repeat—check again!

---

Jeremiah was the first prophet chosen to tell the people about the new covenant God would make with them.

Read prayerfully the two readings from Jeremiah. Write your own prayer response to God in the heart.

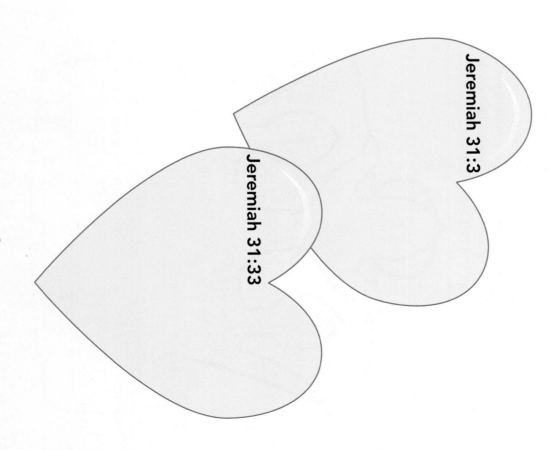

Jeremiah 31:3

Jeremiah 31:33

## Where and When to Pray God's Holy Word

Jesus gave us an example for prayer. Find the passages to discover more about where and when to pray.

| Where to pray . . . | When to pray . . . |
| --- | --- |
| Luke 6:12 | |
| Mark 1:35 | |
| Matthew 6:6 | |
| Luke 4:16 | |
| Luke 23:39–42 | |

St. Paul gave the Ephesians this advice (Read Ephesians 5:19–20):

_____

_____

_____

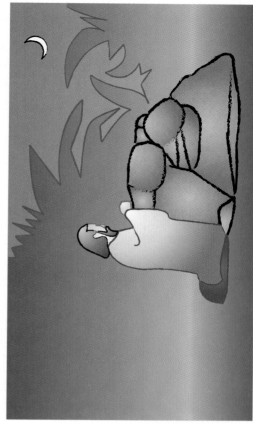

---

## R U A Grudge-Carrier or a Person-Forgiver

We all want friendship—to be a friend and to have friends. One of the easiest ways to lose a friend is to carry a grudge. It is much better to forgive and forget, because forgiveness helps build friendships. What does Scripture tell us about forgiveness? Fill in the chart and answer the questions.

| Scripture | Lesson Taught |
| --- | --- |
| Matthew 5:43–48 | |
| Romans 12:17–21 | |
| 2 Corinthians 5:17–20 | |
| Matthew 18:21–22 | |
| Colossians 3:12–14 | |
| 1 John 4:19–21 | |

What must you do to become a forgiving friend? How will you

carry out your plan?

_____

# Treasure Hunt

Choose a reading from Scripture. In the box write a word or phrase or draw a symbol to help you remember God's message to you.

When you are **thankful** read
Psalm 138    Luke 17:11–19

When you are **frightened** read
Luke 12:32    John 14:1–4

When you need **prayer** read
John 14:13–14    Matthew 7:7–11 or 18:19–20

When you need **love** read
John 15:15    Philippians 1:7–9

When you are **hopeful** read
Matthew 5:1–10    Matthew 28:20

When you are **discouraged** read
John 16:22, 33    Matthew 6:28–34

When you are **happy** read
Philippians 4:4–7    Psalm 23

When you need **forgiveness** read
Matthew 9:6–13    Mark 11:24–25

When you want to **follow Jesus** read
Luke 9:23–26    Mark 6:7–13

When you need **healing** read
James 5:13–16    Mark 5:35–43

a